I0795023

Postcard History Series

South Central Kentucky

Adair, Barren, Green, Hart, and Taylor Counties

Souvenir Postal.

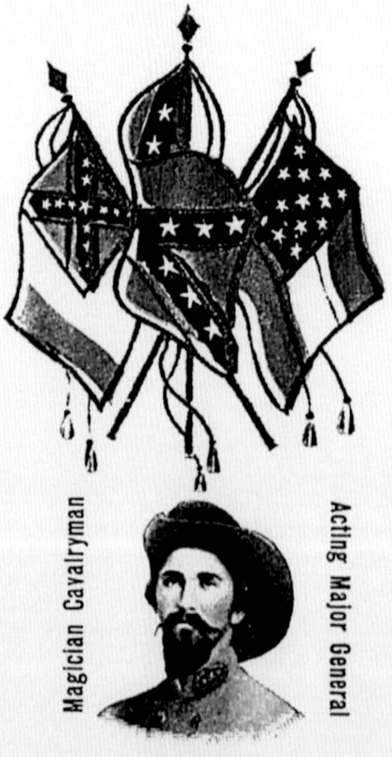

BRIG. GEN. JOHN HUNT MORGAN.
Born at Huntsville, June 1, 1825,
Killed September 4, 1864.

THE KENTUCKY PARTISAN.

Hath the wily Swamp Fox
  Come again to earth?
Hath the soul of Sumter
  Owned a second birth?
Down the western hill-slopes
  Starts a hero-form,
Stalwart, like the oak tree,
  Tameless, like the storm!
His an eye of lightning,
  His a heart of steel,
Flashing deadly vengeance,
  Thrilled with fiery zeal;
Hound him down, ye minions,
  Seize him if ye can;
But woe betide the hireling knave
  That meets him man to man!

'Tis no time for pleasure!
  Doff the silken vest!
Up, my men, and follow
  Marion of the West!
Strike with him for freedom;
  Strike with main and might,
'Neath the noon of splendor,
  'Neath the gloom of night.
Strike by rock and roadside,
  Strike in wold and wood,
By the shadowy valley,
  By the purpling flood,
Oh! when Morgan's war-horse
  Thunders in the van,
God! who would not gladly die
  Beside that glorious man!

—[Paul Hamilton Hayne.

CONFEDERATE GENERAL JOHN HUNT MORGAN. This is a rare 1905 undivided back postcard of controversial Confederate general John Hunt Morgan. He and his men, collectively known and referred to as "Morgan's Raiders," were in Adair County twice during the Civil War. In their Christmas Raid on January 1, 1863, they stole supplies, damaged the Union's supply line, and destroyed property. Six months later, they passed through Adair County on the way to Taylor County and the Battle of Tebbs Bend. There were both Confederate and Union victories in Barren County during the Civil War. Morgan's Raiders camped south of Glasgow in 1862 to celebrate Christmas. A skirmish occurred on Christmas Eve when Union scouts and a cavalry patrol were confronted. A Green Countian, Gen. Edward Henry Hobson left Greensburg with the Union soldiers under his command on July 5, 1863, in an attempt to locate Morgan's Raiders. Hobson and his men tracked Morgan from Lebanon through other Kentucky towns and into Indiana. In Hart County, the railroad bridge at Bonnieville was destroyed twice by Morgan's Raiders. The first time was in 1861 but the Union army was successful in rebuilding it. A year later, however, Morgan's Raiders burned it again and took 97 prisoners. While in Hart County in 1861, they also burned the Rio Bridge. On July 4, 1863, about nine miles south of Campbellsville in Taylor County, a cavalry unit led by Morgan encountered Union infantrymen under the command of Col. O.H. Moore. After a three-hour battle with Moore's troops, Morgan and his men withdrew with heavy losses. The place where it occurred is now known as Tebbs Bend Battleground.

POSTCARD HISTORY SERIES

South Central Kentucky

ADAIR, BARREN, GREEN, HART, AND TAYLOR COUNTIES

Carl Howell and Dixie Hibbs

Foreword by Byron Crawford

ARCADIA
PUBLISHING

ISBN 978-0-7385-1393-5

Published by Arcadia Publishing
Charleston, South Carolina

Printed in the United States of America

Library of Congress Catalog Card Number: 2001093048

For all general information contact Arcadia Publishing at:
Telephone 843-853-2070
Fax 843-853-0044
E-mail sales@arcadiapublishing.com
For customer service and orders:
Toll-Free 1-888-313-2665

Visit us on the Internet at www.arcadiapublishing.com

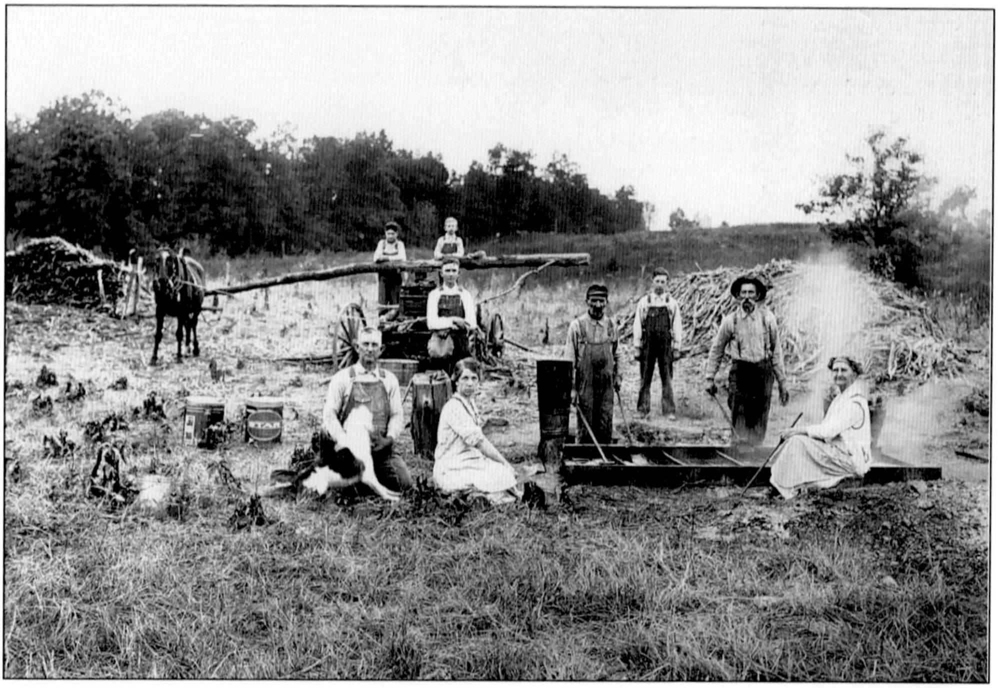

MAKING MOLASSES, *c.* 1929. This image depicts a stir-off near the edge of a cane field on the farm of Mr. and Mrs. William Henry Waters of the Canmer community. From left to right are (seated) Mr. H.H. Waters, Mrs. Essie (Short) Waters, and Mrs. Mary Frances (Phillips) Waters; (standing behind molasses pan) Mr. Will Poynter and Mr. William H. Waters; (young men standing) William Buckner and Archie Dean Waters; (standing behind pole) Carl Forbis and William O. Waters. The family horse's name was Flossie and the family dog was named Watch.

Contents

FOREWORD

Once again Carl Howell and Dixie Hibbs have opened a window upon a panorama of fascinating images of old Kentucky.

Many of us who have always imagined how interesting it would be to revisit the places, faces, and early 20th-century events of rural and small town Kentucky must reserve a special place for this book in our libraries.

The following pages are filled with moments when time stopped for only an instant and looked over its shoulder as the camera clicked. Those of us who love this state would not realize until nearly a century later the debt of gratitude that we owe to the many postcard photographers with cumbersome cameras who saved for us hundreds, perhaps thousands, of pages of Kentucky history that, but for their efforts, would have passed away on the swift wings of time to be remembered no more.

Carl Howell, a Kentucky and Lincoln historian and writer whose splendid collection of Kentucky postcards is without equal, and Dixie Hibbs, a widely respected research historian and writer, have already shared with us other volumes of early 20th-century scenes from Bullitt, LaRue, Hardin, Marion, Nelson, Spencer, and Washington Counties. And in this volume we are drawn again to a series of extraordinary photographs that illuminate those special moments when time stopped for a fleeting instant in Adair, Barren, Green, Hart, and Taylor Counties.

Within these pages, we will visit a 1914 Columbia mail run in Adair County; a famous cave explorer, Floyd Collins, examining bones and artifacts in Barren County in 1922; a "Cow Day" celebration in Green County around 1930; a river baptism in Hart County in 1929; and two tollgate houses in Taylor County in the early 1900s.

Such moments as these have been placed by fate into the hands of those who are most able to share them with fellow Kentuckians and others who appreciate their nostalgic and historic worth.

Thank you, Carl Howell and Dixie Hibbs, for *South Central Kentucky Postcards.*

Byron Crawford
Kentucky Columnist
Courier Journal

INTRODUCTION

Combining a wide range of vintage images with informative text, this volume examines the history of Adair, Barren, Green, Hart, and Taylor Counties through specially selected postcards created between 1900 and 1930.

Often the best if not the only sources of photographic images of our country's history are picture postcards, which were literally made by the thousands during the early 1900s. Although the great majority of these "little pieces of history" were soon destroyed or discarded after they were received in the mail, many have survived to reveal people, activities, lifestyles, architecture, landmarks, and history-making events that would otherwise be forever lost to future generations. Because they portray practically every type of subject and category, certain old picture postcards have become documents of social and historical significance.

Public gathering places such as courthouses, mills, railroad depots, and country stores long ago destroyed have been discovered on printed and real photo postcard images and included here. There are rare glimpses of churches, schools, colleges, hotels, resorts, and businesses that no longer stand. Interesting lifestyles and occupations now nonexistent and long forgotten are also presented. The reader will become familiar with people who were leaders of the small-town communities in which they lived as well as hardworking farmers, merchants, and other ordinary people who made lasting contributions by their works and deeds. From cave exploring to making molasses, from cutting timber to wheat threshing and numerous other activities—even moonshining—the array of subjects and scenes places a premium on variety and visual content.

The evolution of transportation in Kentucky, from horses, wagons, stagecoaches, buggies, and carriages to the advent of the automobile is portrayed in vivid detail. From ferry boat travel to the creation of the first bridges, from tollgate houses to the first crushed-rock roads, the remarkable changes in travel are chronicled in such a way that the reader can uniquely experience the atmosphere of a bygone era.

Although there was no rail travel in Adair County, the Louisville and Nashville (L&N) Railroad was an important and integral part of the economy of Barren, Green, Hart, and Taylor Counties during the early 1900s. Many businesses in the towns and communities within these counties depended greatly on the arrival of L&N passenger and freight trains to local depots. Consequently, we have attempted to include both images and historical data that will serve to highlight scenes from this area's railroad history when such travel was commonplace.

It is the opinion of the authors that the postcards included in this volume are among the rarest and best of existing images currently available to highlight the rich history of these counties during the first 30 years of the 20th century. In many instances, a postcard view is the only pictorial record that exists by which we can learn of a subject or area. As there was no television during this time, the picture postcard provided the best and most popular way to both illustrate and provide information about the special places, people, and events that were most meaningful to an area's residents. In some instances, messages written long ago by the senders now serve to provide important historical information that identifies the time, people, place, and event portrayed on the front side of a postcard.

From 1905 to 1920, postcard collecting became a fad throughout the United States. The highest quality picture postcards were actually printed in Germany until about 1914 and the onset of World War I. Many of the early postcard publishers took great pride in maintaining high standards of excellence. Their painstaking devotion to detail and timing is reflected in the content, clarity, and detail of their images.

In addition to printed postcards, certain black-and-white images now known and classified by collectors as "real photo" postcards provide some of the rarest and most historically accurate views available. These postcards are actual photographs with a postcard back. They were developed from negatives directly onto photo printing paper with "postcard" printed on the back of the card. Local photographers made many of the real photo postcards included in this book.

We have devoted much thought and deliberation in the painstaking selection of pictures to be included in this volume and only wish we could have presented more for the benefit and enjoyment of our readers. For numerous reasons, including historical content, subject matter, and rarity, we have included some real photo images, which may never have been made or printed with postcard backs. It is truly impossible to determine in every case whether certain early photographs were or were not previously or subsequently produced as real photo postcards.

Many of the postcards in this book have only recently been discovered and reveal scenes and individuals heretofore known only to a few people. Some were simply put away in drawers and forgotten. Others were placed in family albums long ago with little thought ever given to their content or possible historical relevance. While to many individuals these images have no value whatsoever, to others they are valued as prized collectibles that have been selectively handed down by a prior generation.

We have tried to be both inclusive and imaginative in our selection of images and to be accurate and informative in the accompanying text. For some of the scenes, we recommend use of a magnifying glass as many of them contain a wealth of details and data that will reward the reader upon closer examination and study. Ultimately, it is our wish that this book will assist in preserving some of the area's fascinating history and provide future generations with a lasting visual record of people, places, and events—but mostly, simply what life was really like—during those times.

One

Adair County

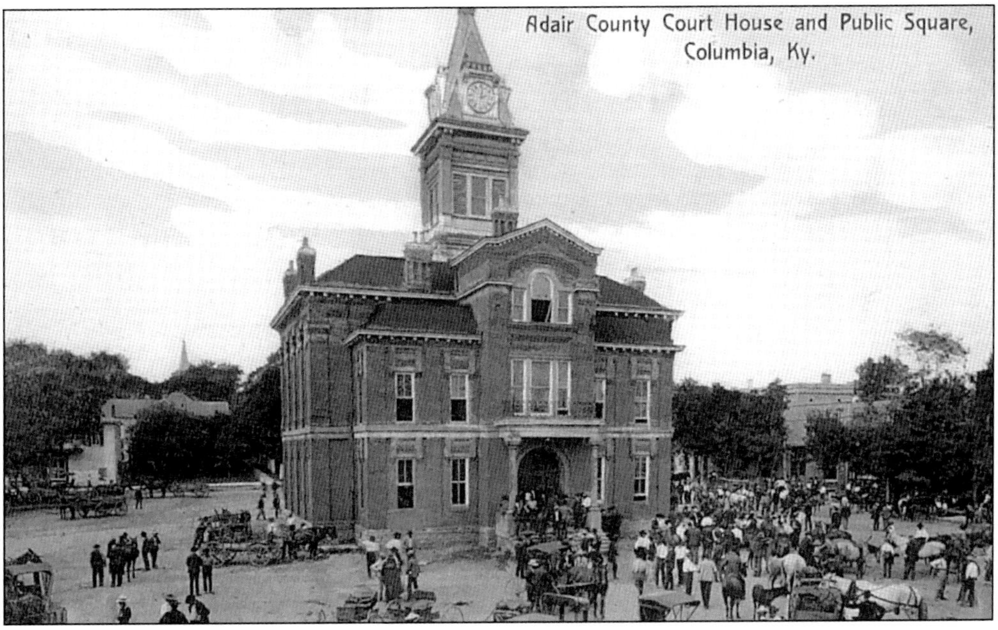

Adair County Court House and Public Square, *c.* 1909. Kentucky's 44th county was created in 1801 and is named for Revolutionary War general John Adair. Columbia was chosen as the county seat in 1802. The second courthouse, above, was designed by McDonald Brothers of Louisville and erected in 1885 by W.H. Hudson of Columbia for the bid of $17,486. Columbus Stone of Burkesville, Kentucky supplied the stone. When the court accepted the building, the cost was $31,230.37, clock not included. This view is from the east with the front door facing Jamestown Street. The building at right is the Conover Hotel, built in 1898. Note the stagecoach at the corner of the building. Hidden in the trees at left is a house built on the site where Jane Lampton, mother of Samuel Clemens, better known as author Mark Twain, formerly resided.

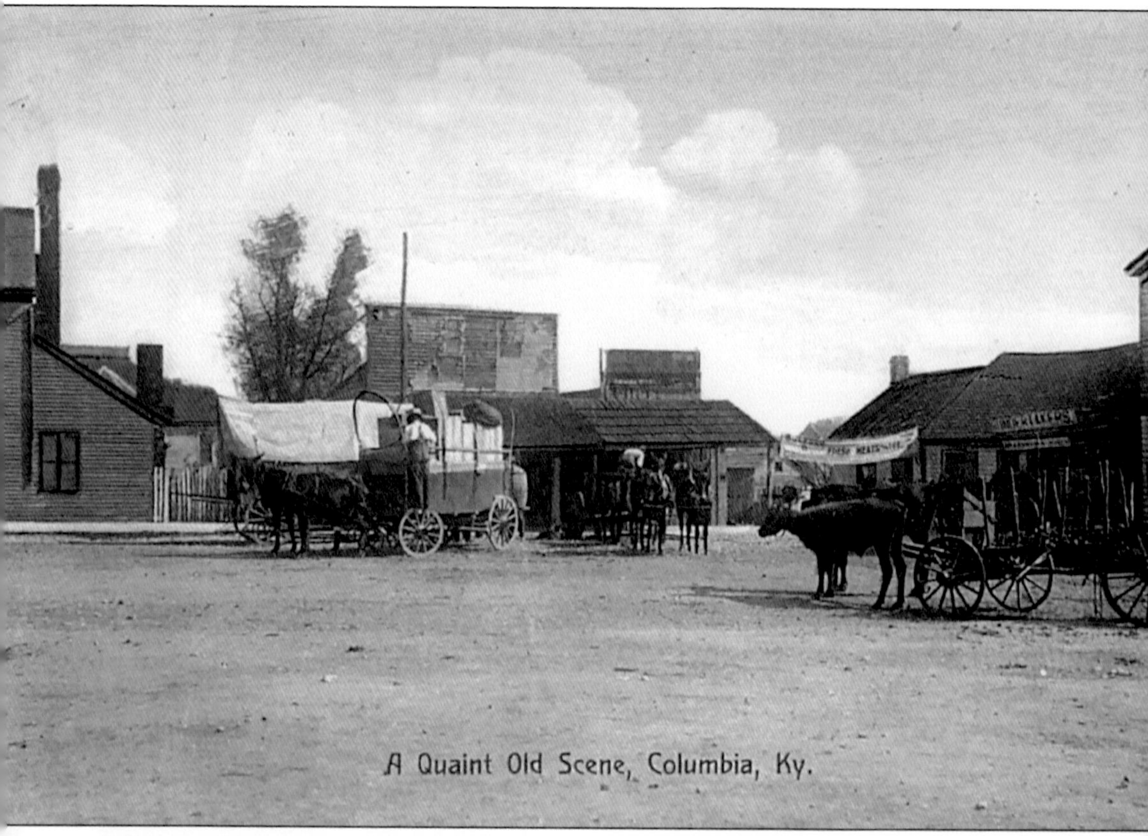

A Quaint Old Scene, c. 1909. Hadis Harvey hauled his produce of chickens, eggs, wool, etc. to Lewis Produce on the northeast corner of the public square. The frame house on the left is Smith Boarding House, next to Sam Lewis's produce house. Wolford & Co.'s building, promoting "fresh meats and ice" appears next. The small brick building partly hidden by a banner advertising "IGA-Fresh Meat" was originally built as a law office by Benjamin Shelby. Next is a smaller frame structure that was occupied as an undertaker's shop by Butler Jones. The two-story frame building was erected in 1807 and replaced by the Russell Building in 1909.

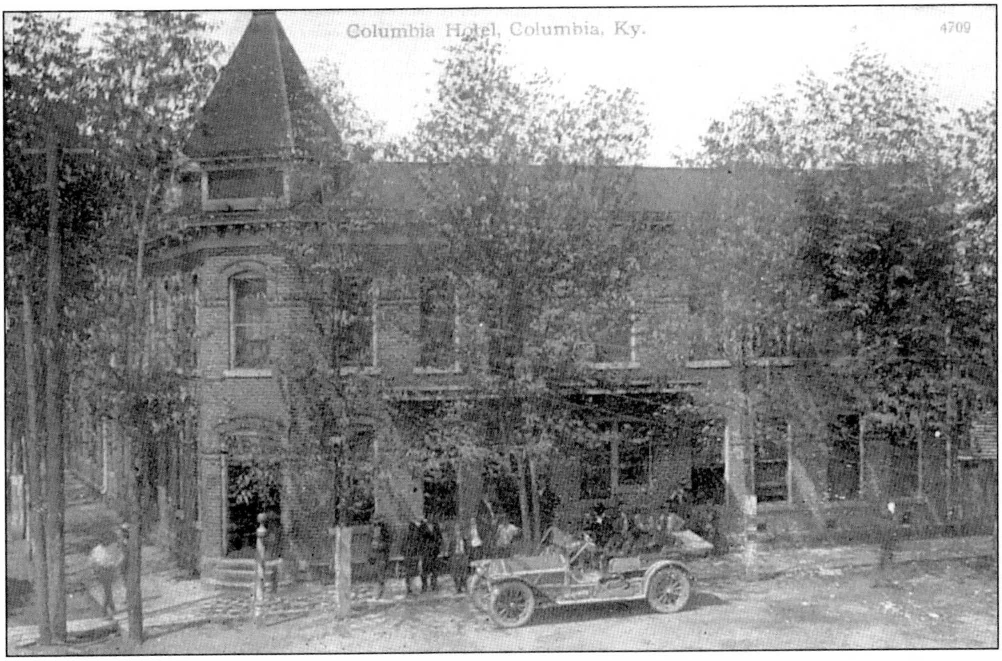

Columbia Hotel, c. 1915. Located on the corner of the public square and Greensburg Street, this hotel was built in 1898 by John N. Conover and called Conover Hotel. It opened with a formal banquet organized by the 20th Century Club, composed "of the cream of young gentlemen in Columbia." The hotel boasted 30 rooms and was built at a cost of $6,000. It replaced the Page House Hotel that burned in 1890. This building was destroyed by fire in 1977. Note the Maxwell automobile parked in the front.

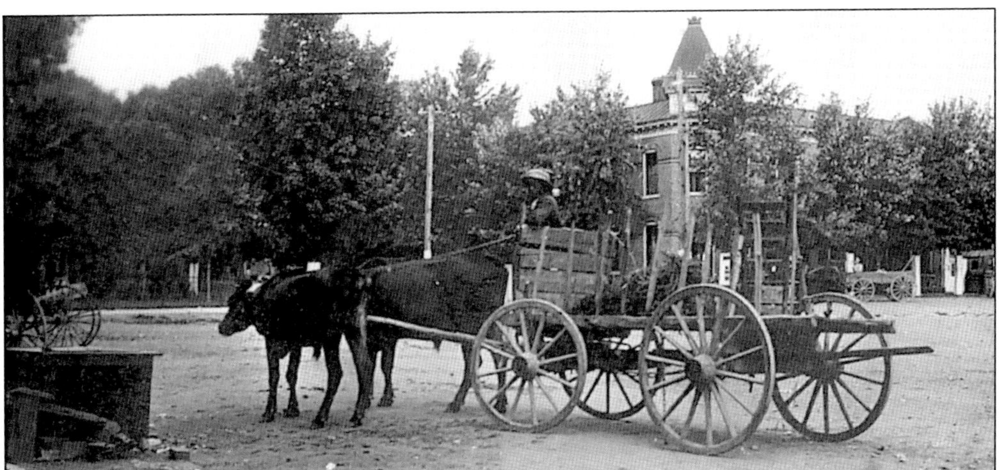

Columbia Square, c. 1904. This ox-drawn wagon on the southwest side of the square appears to be designed to haul logs. In the background one can see the Columbia Hotel. Confederate general John Hunt Morgan came through Columbia on July 3, 1863. Hand-to-hand fighting on the square and in the streets drove the Union soldiers out. Morgan threatened to burn the courthouse, as he did whenever he thought Union soldiers had used a public building. Mrs. Smith who ran a boarding house on the square thwarted this plan. After serving him a meal there, she told him that if he burned the courthouse, the fire would blow onto her home and destroy her only means of support. After testing the wind, he decided not to set it afire. This saved the courthouse, part of the square, and all of the Adair County records.

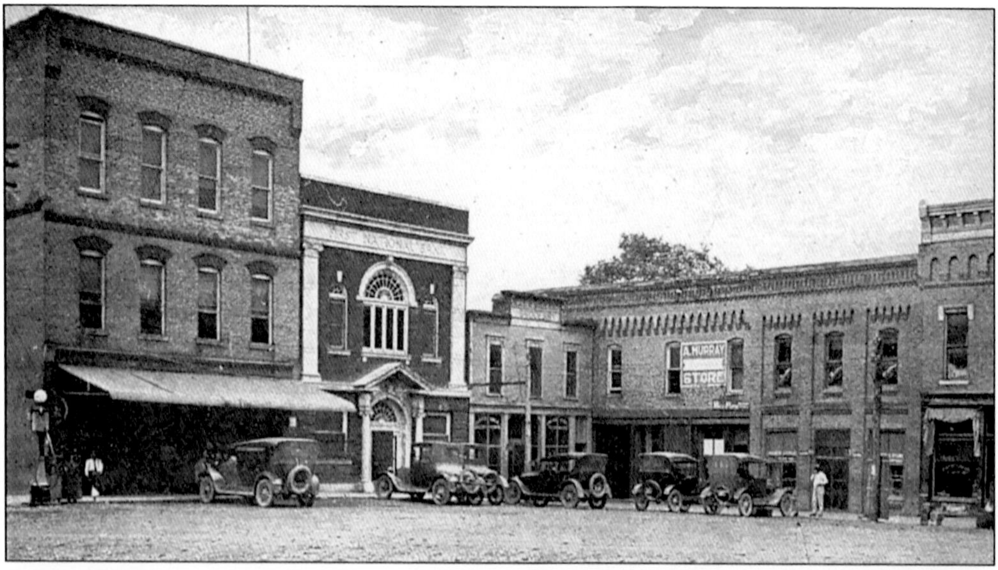

South Corner of Public Square, c. 1925. The Jefferies Building at left was erected in 1896 at the corner of Jamestown Street and the square. Dr. O.S. Dunbar rented a space for his dental office upstairs in 1909. Buggies, hardware, and farm equipment could be purchased downstairs. Note the gas pump in this view. Next door is the First National Bank, which was organized in 1903, then Barger Bros. Hardware and Murray's General Store.

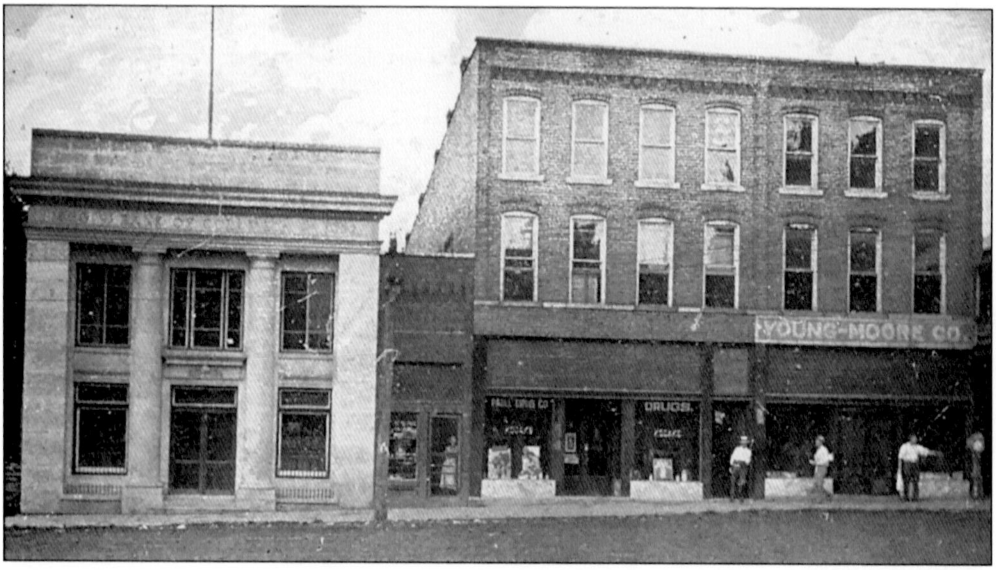

West Corner of Public Square, c. 1930. The buildings, from left to right, are Bank of Columbia, Mont Maupin's Barber Shop, Paull Drug Co. (established in 1885), and Young & Moore Confectionary. Bank of Columbia was organized in 1866 with T.T. Alexander as president. It was housed in a frame building on Burkesville Street and Jefferson Alley directly behind this one pictured. Chief of Detectives, Capt. Yankee Bligh of Louisville claimed that Frank and Jesse James, Cole and John Younger, and John Jarrett, a brother-in-law of the Youngers, were responsible for the robbery and murder of the cashier on April 29, 1872. They were never caught nor was the claim proven. These buildings were rebuilt after the fire of 1921 destroyed this block.

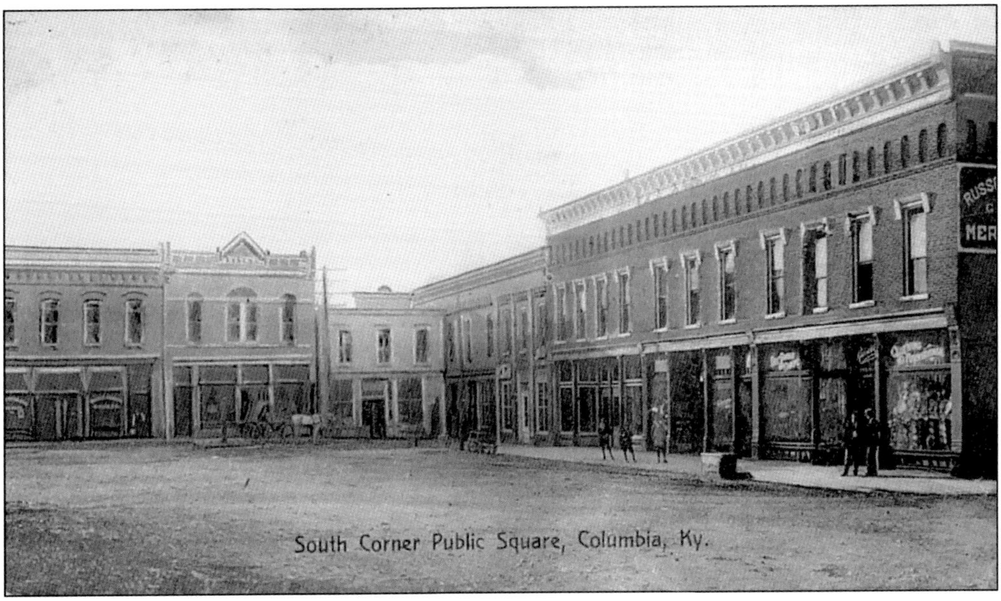

South Corner of Public Square, c. 1909. The first two buildings on the left were greatly changed by 1925. The buildings on the right are still standing and in use. The Russell & Murrell General Store at the corner of Burkesville Street boasts a mounting block for the convenience of its customers getting in and out of buggies.

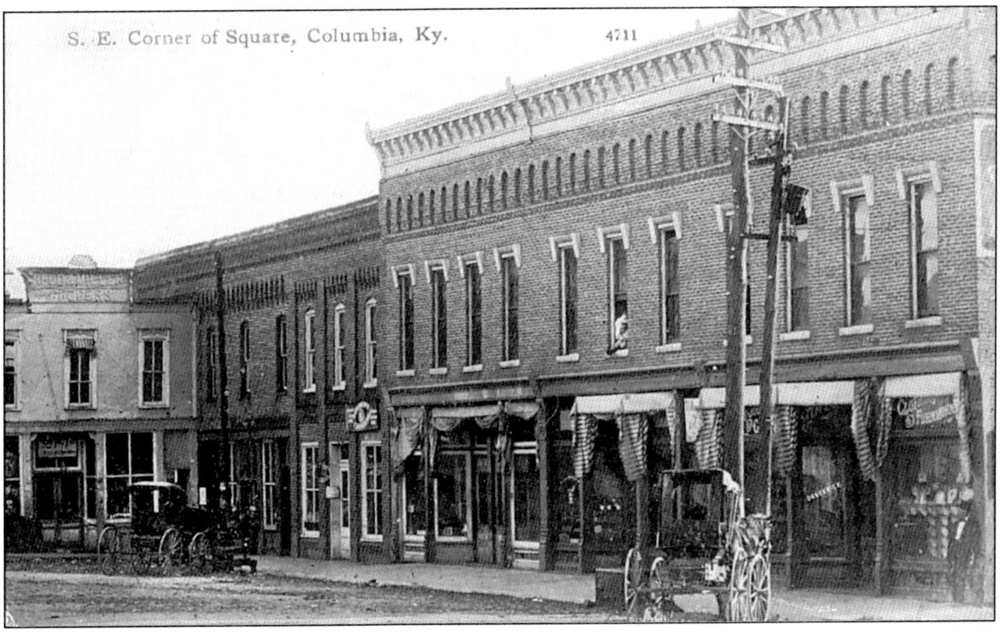

Southeast Corner of Square, c. 1910. On the left is the Miller-Reed Grocery, later Barger Bros. Grocery, where Henry Miller and his brother-in-law E.W. Reed started Columbia's first phone service with offices on the second floor. A passageway between the next buildings leads to the office of the *Adair County News* located in the building behind. A coal-oil engine powered the press, and it was said that everyone on the square could tell when the paper was being printed. The building at right was the Russell & Murrell General Store.

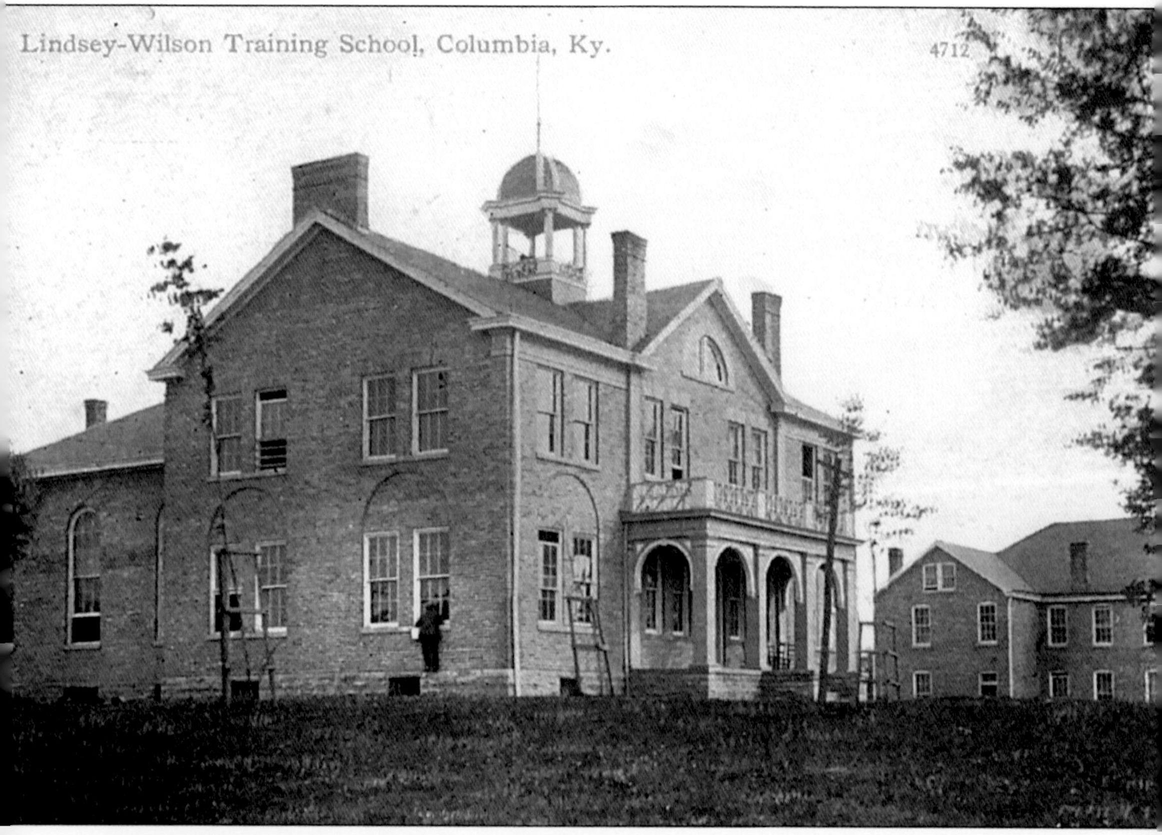

LINDSEY WILSON TRAINING SCHOOL, c. 1910. The Methodist Church raised an endowment of $10,000, due in large part to a gift of $6,000 from Mrs. Catharine Wilson of Louisville. She requested that the school be named in honor of her stepson and nephew and given the name Lindsey Wilson Academy. A nine-acre lot was purchased for $1,500, and the administration building was constructed in 1903. Architect Val P. Collins designed the building. Contractor George Fletcher agreed in 1903 to construct the building for $8,081. Before the carpenters and painters finished their work, the school opened in January 1904 with 222 students. The main building was a two-story, brick, steam-heated structure that contained a chapel, recitation rooms, commercial department, library, and laboratory. The chapel and all rooms were well lighted and had convenient means of ventilation. The 2,800-book library was on the second floor. The Chemistry and Physics Labs were in the basement. Phillips Hall, the girls' dormitory, is on the right. Before the boys' dormitory was erected, the boys lived on the second floor and the girls lived on the first floor of Phillips Hall. In 1909 it was enlarged with a new dining hall and additional boarding rooms. New furnaces were installed. In 1914 the boys' dormitory, with space for 80 boys, was built. In 1909 the school's name was changed to Lindsey Wilson Training School. Lindsey Wilson Junior College was established in 1923 as a church and preparatory school to be correlated with Vanderbilt University in Nashville. Fred Rainwater, a Cherokee long-distance runner from Pulaski County, planted the oak tree in front of the building in 1907. To celebrate Arbor Day, he dug up a white oak sapling in the woods nearby and planted it in front of the administration building. The sapling can be seen in the photo. Surrounded by a protective framework, the Rainwater Oak still stands on the campus in 2001.

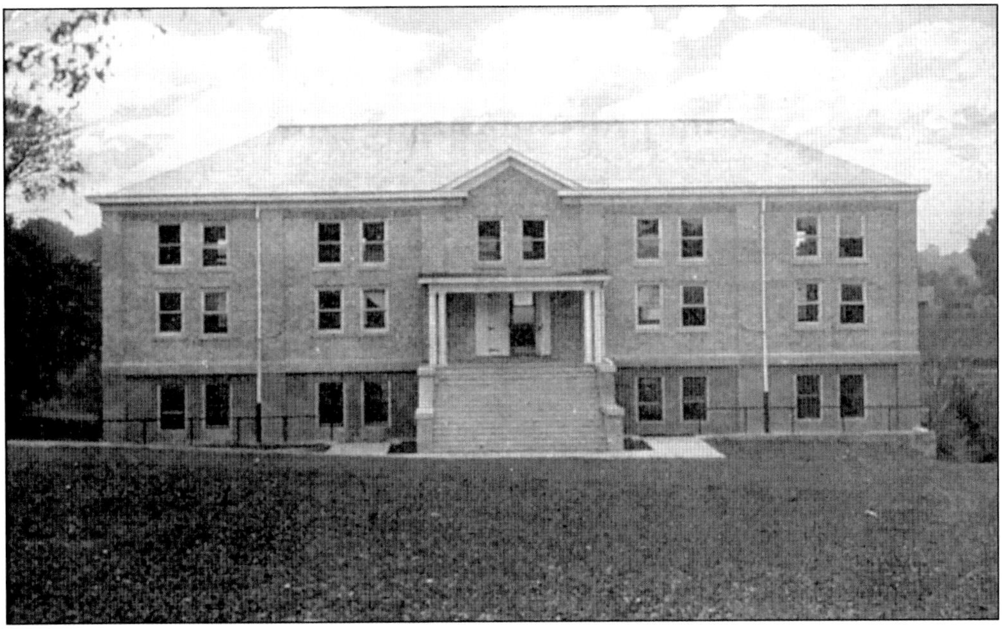

GYMNASIUM, L.W. J. COLLEGE, *c.* 1924. This gymnasium was built in 1922. It included a dining hall seating 300 with a kitchen in the lower level. During the same time, a president's home was purchased, 50 acres added to the campus, and a dairy barn erected. The school changed its name to Lindsey Wilson Junior College in 1923.

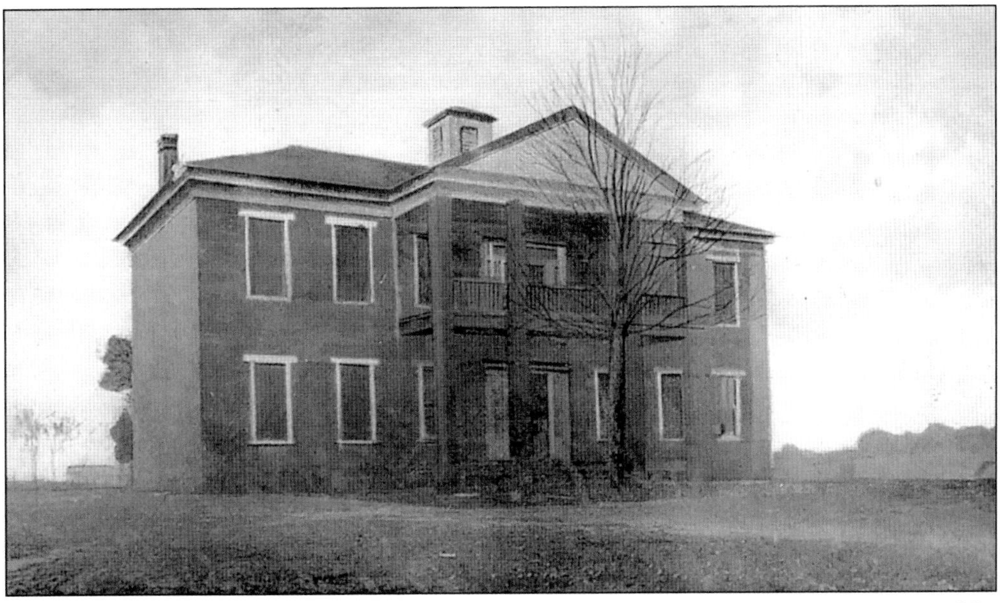

M & F HIGH SCHOOL, *c.* 1909. Interest in having good schools in Columbia resulted in the erection of this building about 1855 at the top of what is now known as Guardian Street Hill. Funds were raised by a joint stock company and through popular subscription to purchase land and erect the building. The following year the Transylvania Presbytery agreed to run the school. Rev. John L. McKee, pastor of the Presbyterian church, was the principal. The school continued until 1908 when trustees transferred the property to the Graded School District.

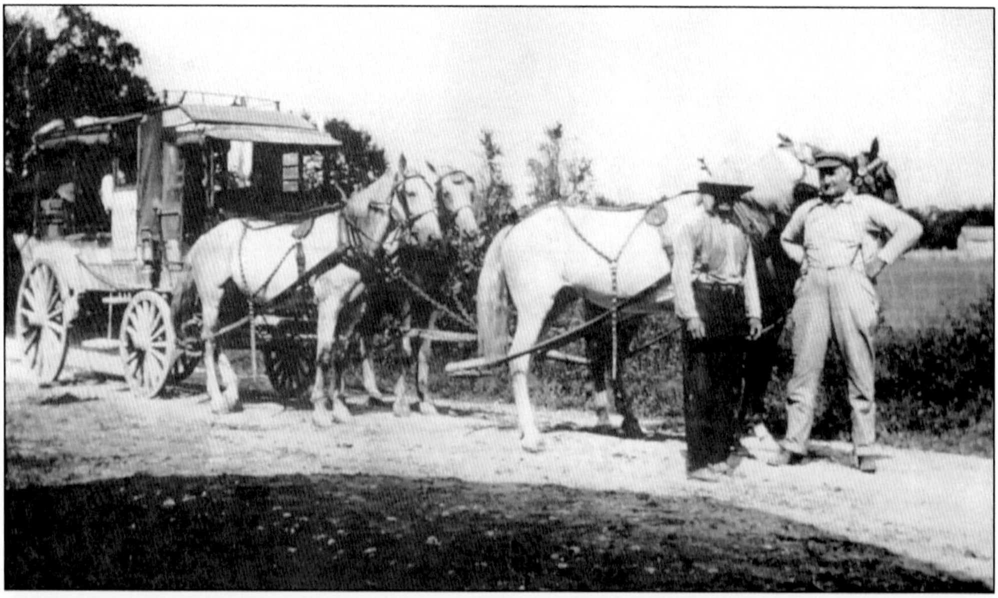

Columbia-to-Campbellsville Stagecoach, c. 1910. In the late 1800s, Columbia and Campbellsville were on the national mail stage route from Zanesville, Ohio to Florence, Alabama. These stagecoaches, which also carried passengers, continued in areas not serviced by trains until about 1914 when they were replaced by mail trucks. Shown in this image are J.R. "Buck" Barbee (left), the owner of the stagecoach, and Bob Parrott (right), a stagehand.

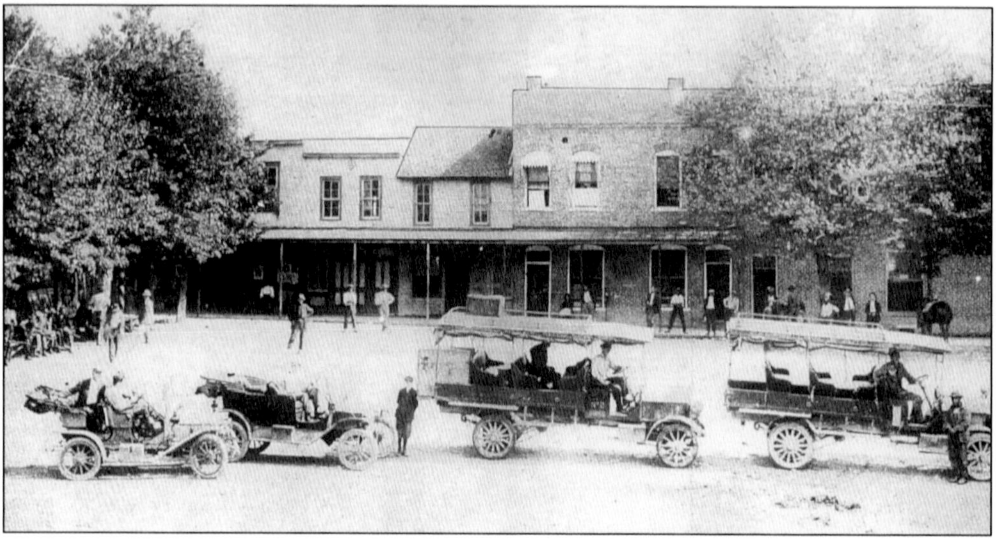

Columbia-to-Campbellsville Mail Run, 1914. These four mail trucks, manufactured by the Indiana Truck Company, replaced the horse-drawn stagecoaches in carrying mail and passengers between Columbia and Campbellsville. Seymour Shaw, Walter Cook, and Omer Barbee are among the truck drivers shown in this photograph made in the Columbia town square. J.R. "Buck" Barbee sold the mail contract to W.R. Marr, who later sold it to a Mr. Noe. The mail had to be gathered at 2 a.m. in Columbia to reach Campbellsville in time to make the morning train. Mail was collected at 10 a.m. in Columbia to catch the train leaving Campbellsville at 3 p.m. Passengers paid $1.50 to ride between the two towns.

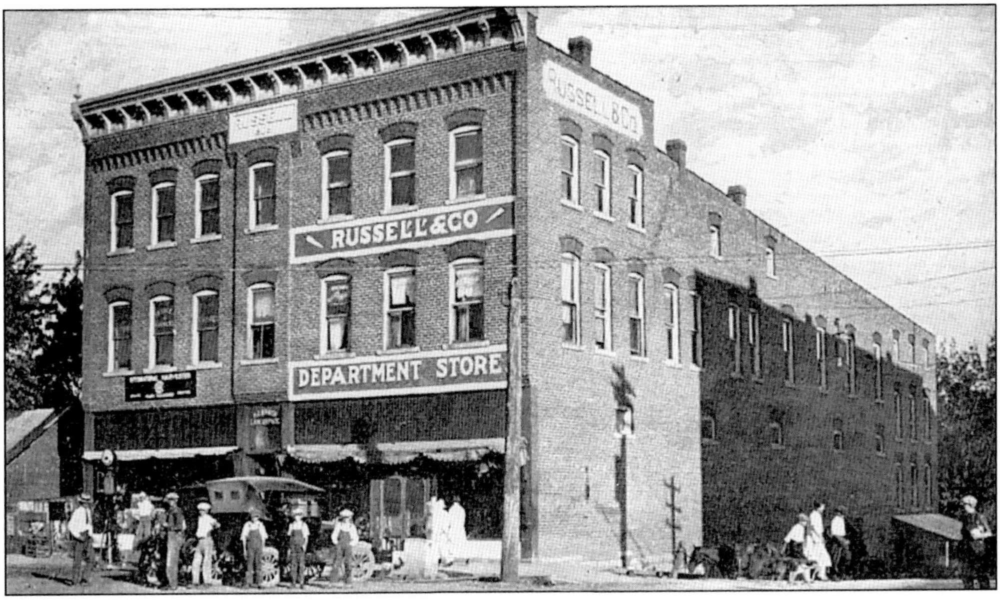

Russell and Company Building, c. 1920. In January 1909, the *Adair County News* advertised the close-out sale of stock in J.O. Russell's Department Store in preparation for the erection of a new three-story brick storehouse. It replaced an 1807 frame building that housed a saddle shop, restaurant, and bakery on what was known as "Isenberg Corner," the corner of Jamestown Street and Public Square. Russell also purchased the undertaking building directly behind his store in order to enlarge his lot. He employed J.T. Phillips of Campbellsville to design and E.G. Shaw of Columbia to erect the new building. W.T. Jefferies & Son purchased all of Russell's inventory, giving them "the largest stock of hardware in the county." In this view, an International Harvester sign is on the left half of the building.

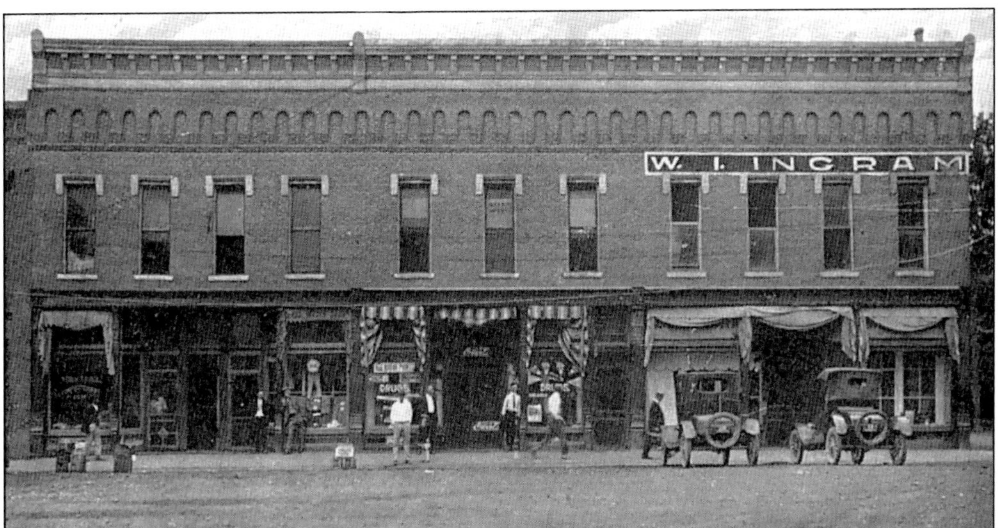

Southwest Corner of Public Square, c. 1920. This is the third view of the large commercial building on the southeast corner of the square. Three or four businesses utilized the first floor. W.I. Ingram was a bookstore and sold other general merchandise. A drugstore occupied the center business. Twenty years before the time this image was made, horse and buggies parked where these autos sit. A mounting block located near the right corner of the building has been removed, as it is no longer needed.

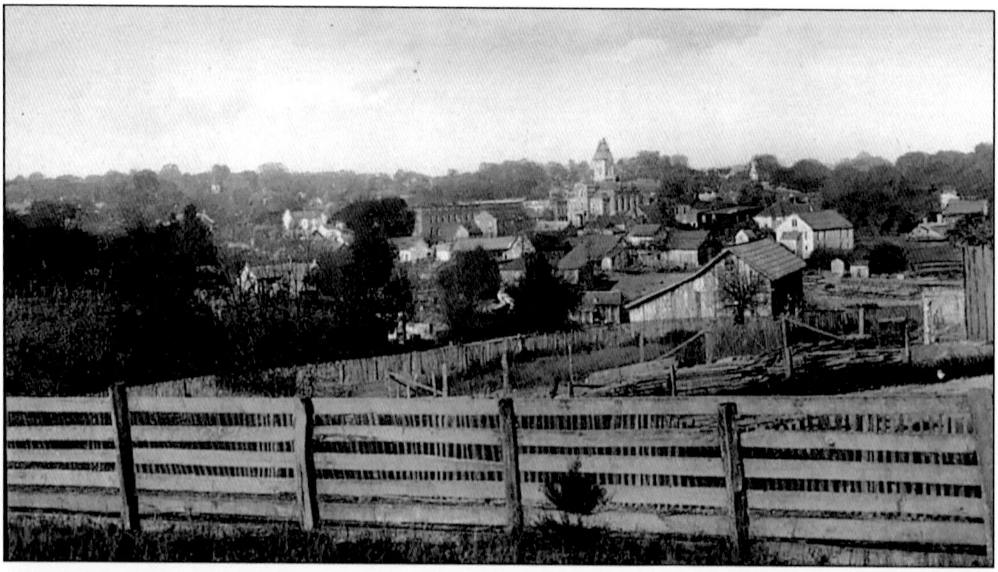

Bird's-eye View of Columbia, c. 1909. Albert Kraemer of Cincinnati captured this view of summer at Columbia when he took this picture from the campus of Lindsey Wilson College in 1909. In the center, the courthouse tower soars above the rest of the structures. The rectangular building to the left of the courthouse is the Jefferies Building. The light-colored building in front of the Jefferies Building is the Isenberg Building, which was erected in 1807. A close inspection of the fence in the foreground shows two fences with a passage between them. The first is made of horizontal boards and the second is a paling fence with small uprights placed close together to prevent small animals from passing through.

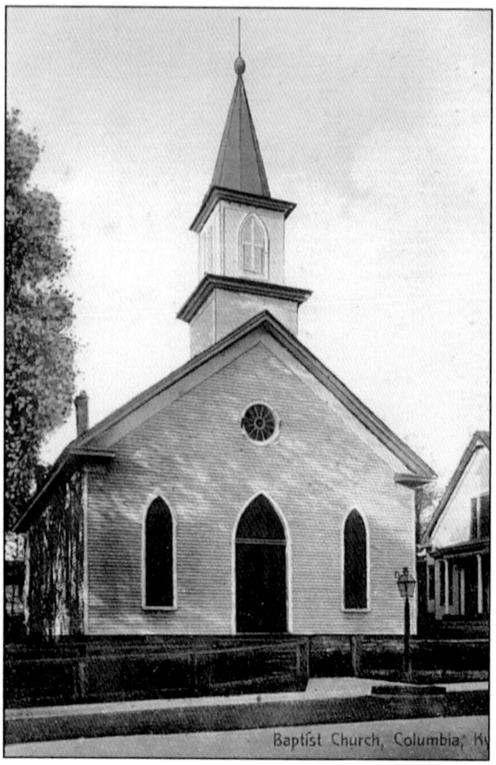

Baptist Church, c. 1909. This church was organized on July 6, 1827, but services were held in the courthouse until a building was erected in 1844. During the Civil War, Federal troops used the church for a hospital. This new church was built in 1874, and pews, which had been taken from the earlier church, were installed. Note the street lantern in the front and the parsonage on the right that was erected in 1907. A new brick church replaced this building in 1915; it burned in 1928.

Presbyterian Church, c. 1909. This is the oldest church building in Columbia. The church was organized in 1827 and held services at Robertson's Academy. This building, located on Burkesville Road, was erected in 1857. The bell tower served as a lookout post in the Civil War, and the attic area, where bullet molds were later discovered, is believed to have been used to manufacture bullets during that time. The original plain glass windows were replaced with gothic-style, stained-glass memorial windows in 1908. The balcony, formerly used by slaves, was also removed at this time.

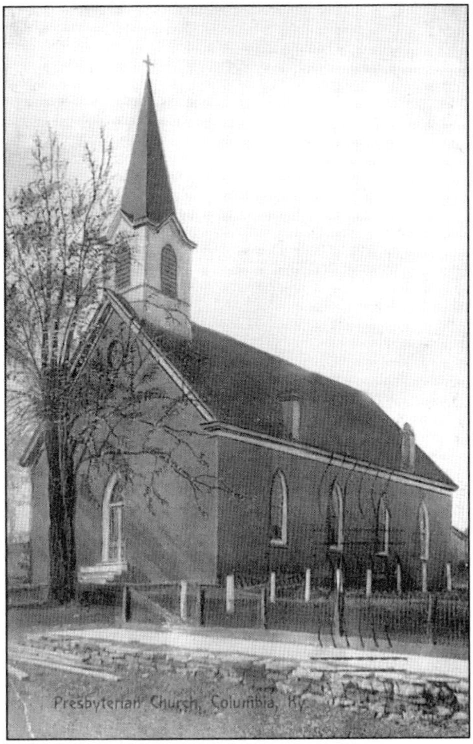

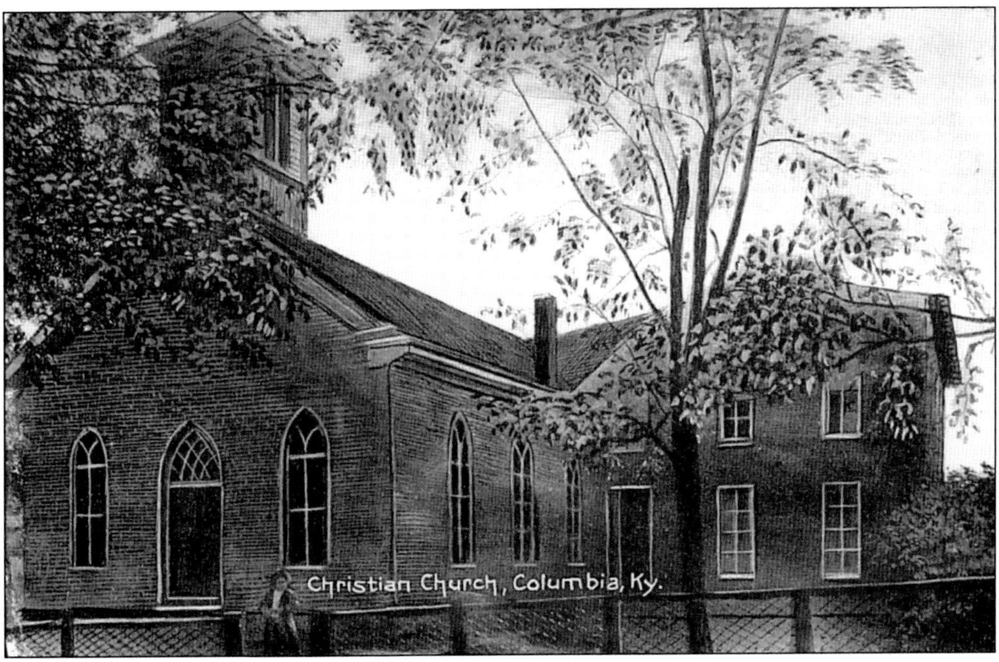

Christian Church, c. 1909. This church was organized about 1866. Worship services were held at the courthouse until this building was constructed. Attached to the church is Columbia Christian College, which was in use by 1874. This building was replaced in 1929 and remodeled in 1938. A new structure was built in 1968.

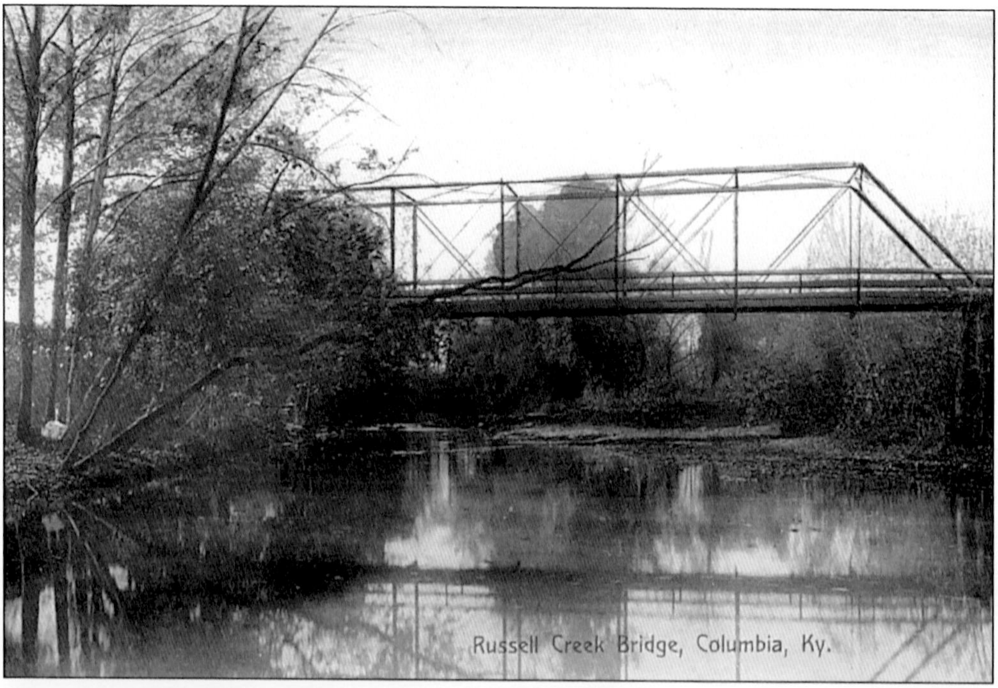

ADAIR COUNTY BRIDGES, *c.* 1909. Navigable waterways and dirt roads provided the first travel routes for the early residents of south central Kentucky. Primitive log bridges, fords, and ferries were the primary means of travel from one side of a river to the other. Noted Cincinnati photographer, Albert Kraemer, published these two Adair County postcards that typify the many metal and wooden bridges that were constructed across rivers and creeks in the mid- to late 1800s and early 1900s. The bridge over Russell Creek is pictured above and the Sulphur Fork Bridge is shown below. Reflections of both bridges can be seen in the water.

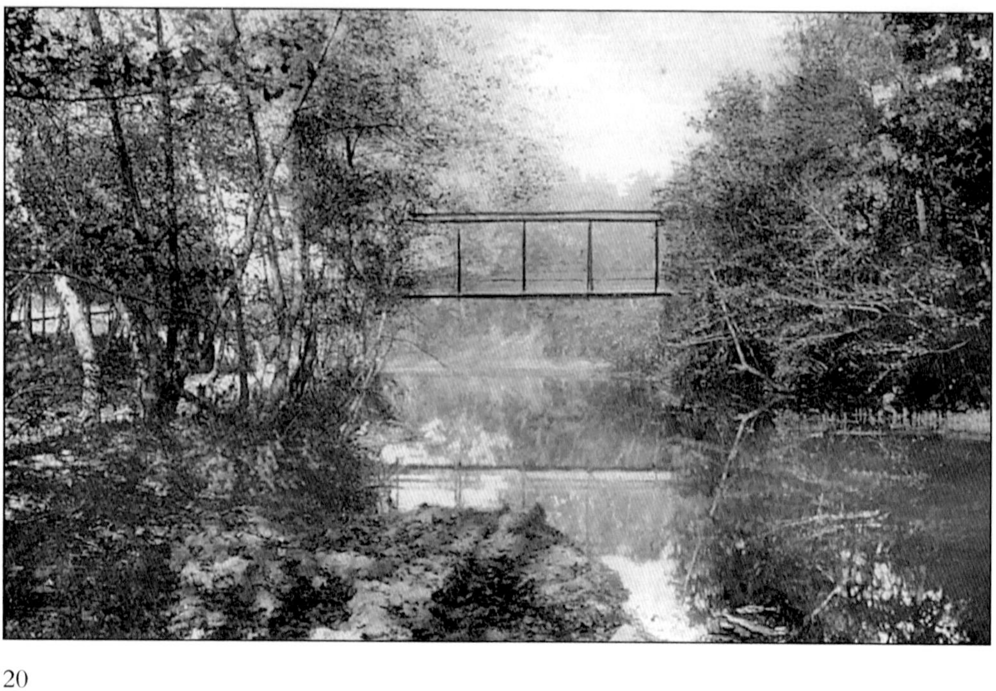

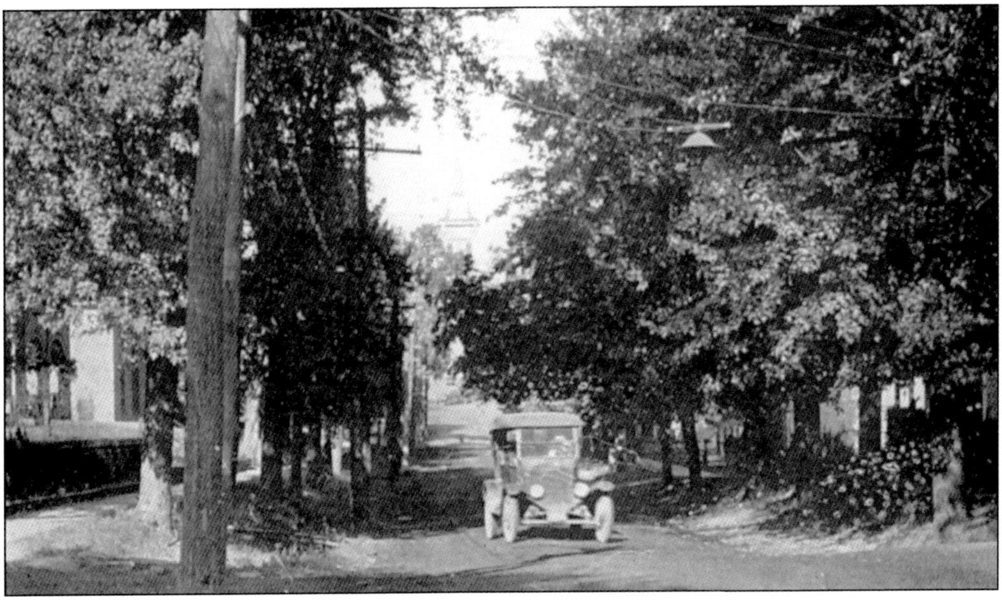

Burkesville Street, c. 1920. Published by Auburn Post Card Mfg. Co. in Auburn, Indiana, as are several other images in this chapter, this view reveals a Model T Ford traveling down the center of Burkesville Street. Sidewalks on both sides of the dirt road and a hanging streetlight attached to a cable can be seen. The top portion of the Adair County Courthouse is barely visible in the clearing at center.

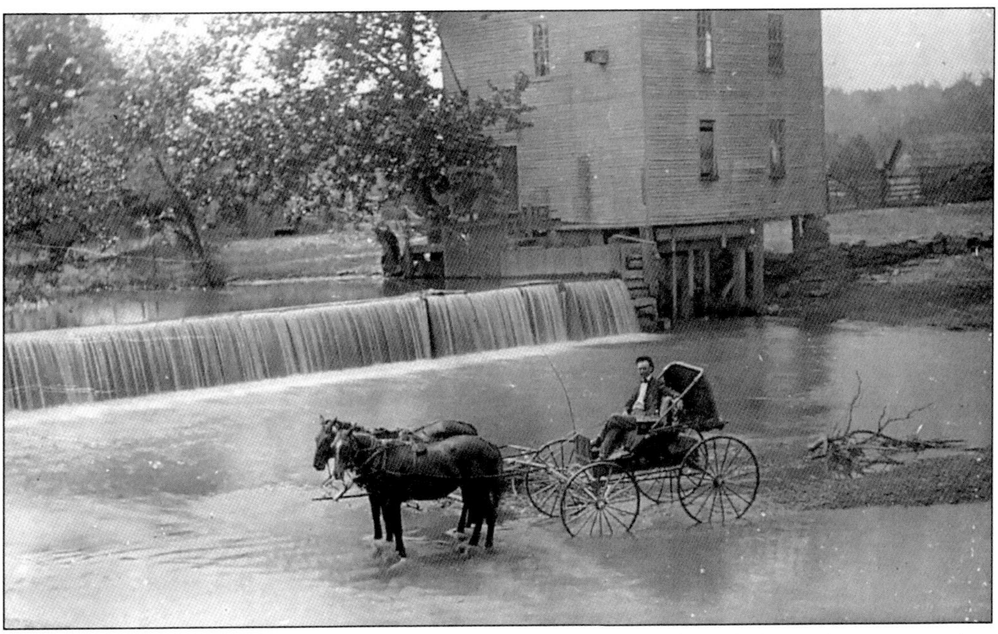

Casey Creek, c. 1910. General stores and local hardware stores depended on sales representatives such as Oma Goode. A native of Adair County, Goode worked for Belknap Hardware in Louisville for 42 years. He is shown here on his route near Dunnville in Casey County. Note the Belknap catalog on the carriage seat beside him.

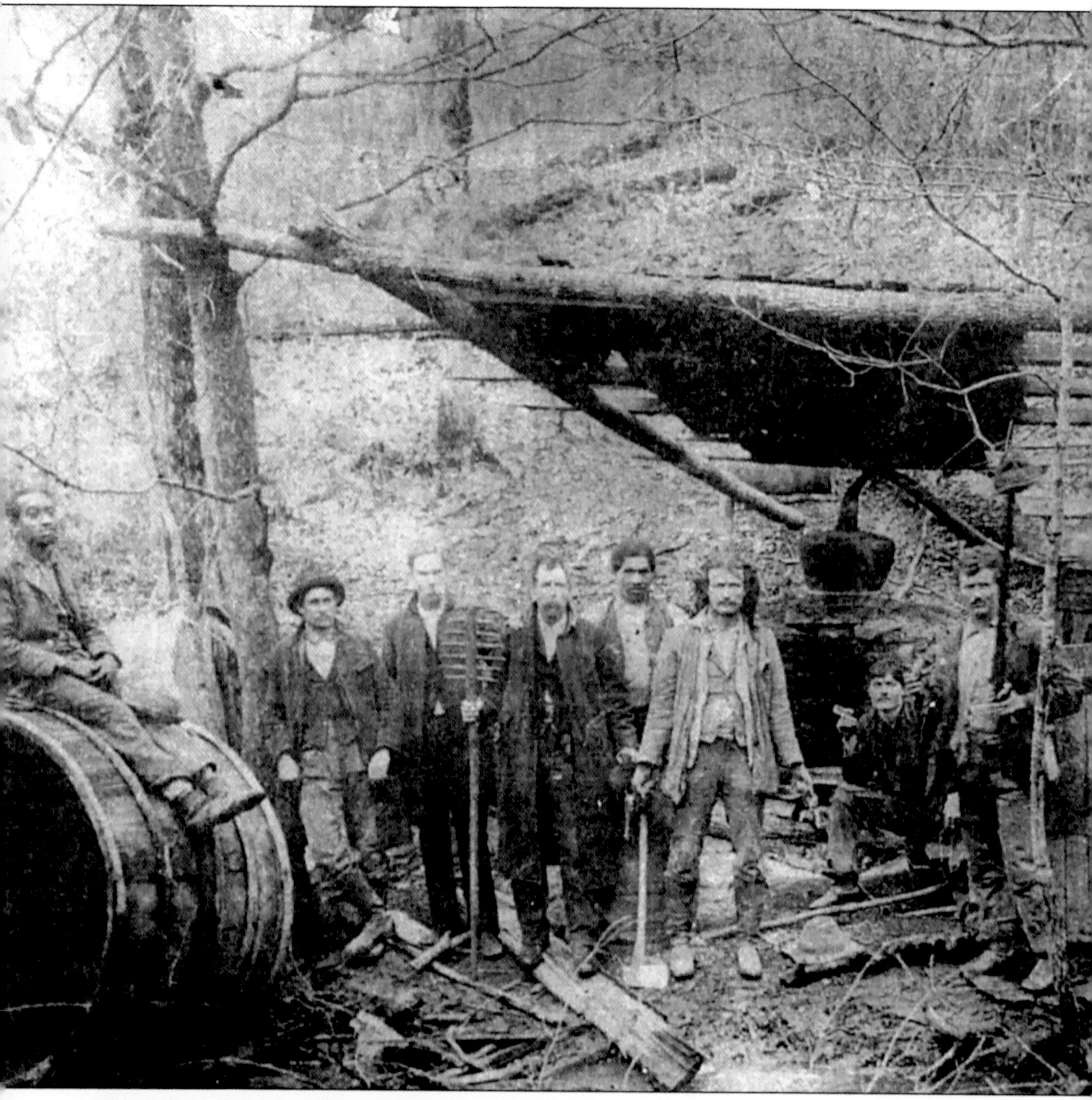

Moonshine Still, c. 1905. Owned by Joe Thomas and operated for about 40 years, this still was located near Pollard's Chapel/Sulphur Springs Methodist Church. Wood Henderson and Roland Pyle operated the still until it ceased production in 1908. Posing in front of the still are, from left to right, Peggie Vaughn (seated on barrel), West Skaggs, ? Downey, Wood Henderson (holding a homemade tool to stir the mash), Bill Frazier, John Lane (holding pistols), Roland Pyle (seated), Frank Lane, and Sam Ed Squires.

Two

Barren County

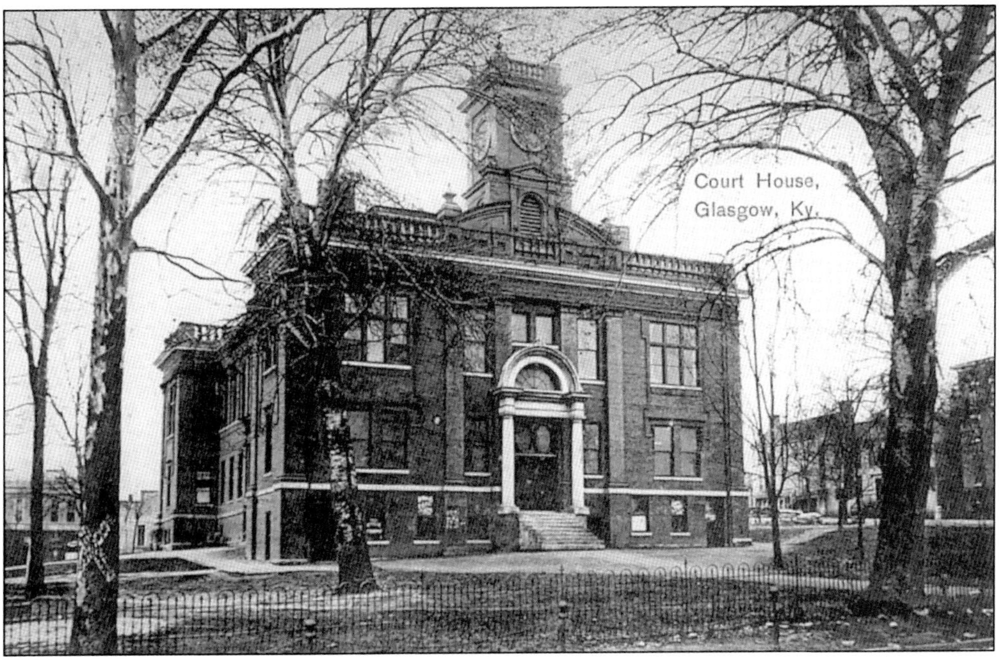

Court House, c. 1910. Created in 1798, Barren County became the state's 37th county. It was named for the barrens, or meadowlands, which cover the top northern third of the county. Glasgow, the county seat, was named for Glasgow, Virginia. This courthouse was built during Judge G.M. Bohannon's administration in 1896. The building committee was composed of Judge Bohannon, J.C. Hutcherson, and E.P. Chamberlain. It was the fifth courthouse and served the county well until it was torn down in 1964. A reunion of the veterans of the Confederate Orphans Brigade was held at Glasgow on July 21, 1899. A photograph published in the *Confederate Veteran* magazine shows the officials of the Orphan Brigade and the Daughters of the Confederacy meeting in the main courtroom at that time.

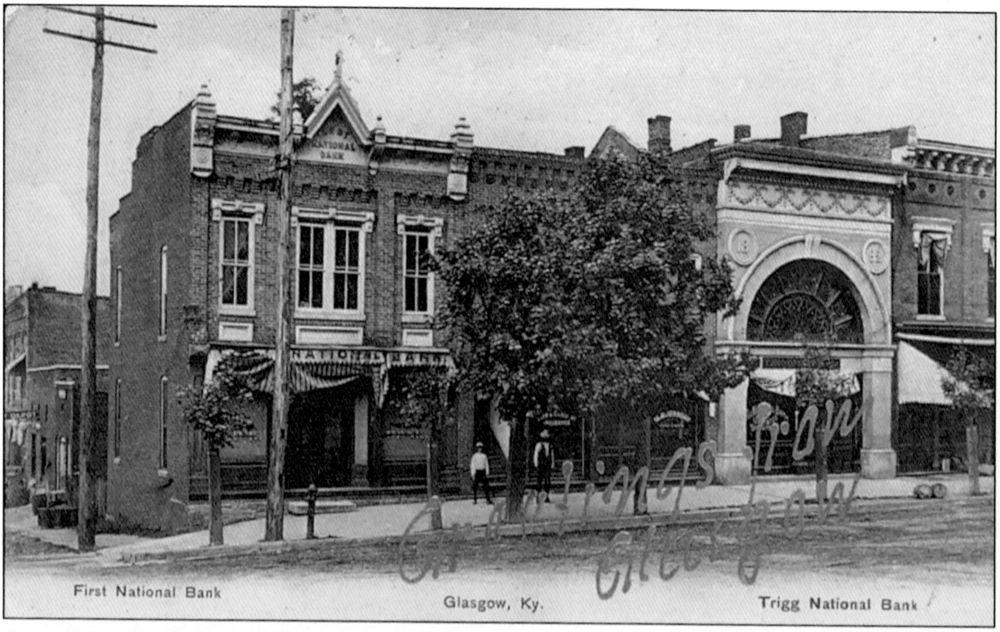

First National Bank and Trigg National Bank, c. 1907. First National Bank succeeded the Deposit Bank on November 8, 1892. A gas explosion blew out the two plate-glass windows and ripped up the tile floor in May 1922, when a man standing in front of the building struck a match. The Trigg Bank was first established in 1874. In 1932 both of these banks closed in spite of heroic efforts to save them during the early years of the Depression.

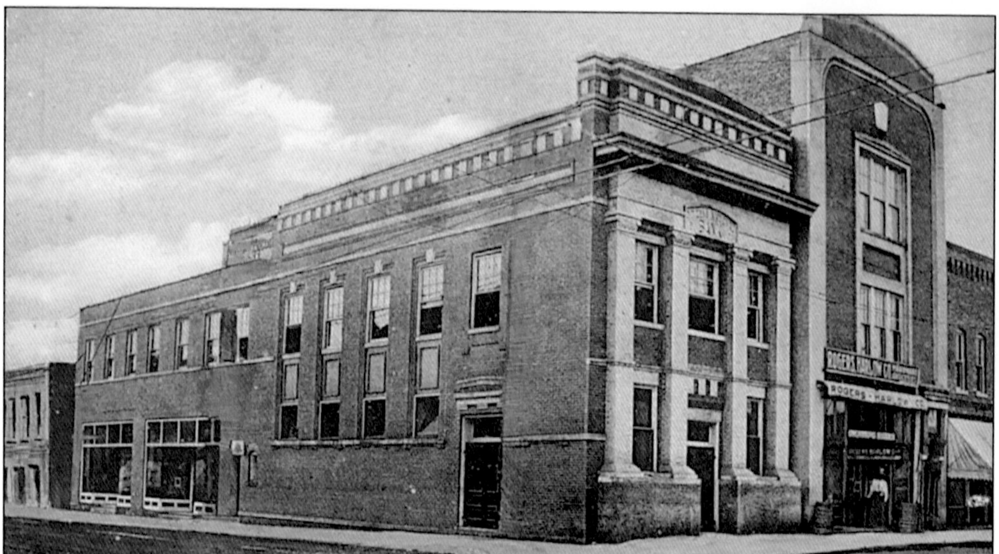

Citizens National Bank and Masonic Building, c. 1909. The bank was organized in 1906 and this building was constructed soon afterward. The post office leased the space in the back of the building, with the "large plate glass front" for a period of ten years, according to a July 1907 newspaper article. In the *Glasgow Republican* of September 27, 1906, Rogers and Harlow Co. announced the leasing of the Masonic Building then being erected on Green Street and stated that the company would move in as soon as it was finished. The members of Allen Lodge #24 built the structure.

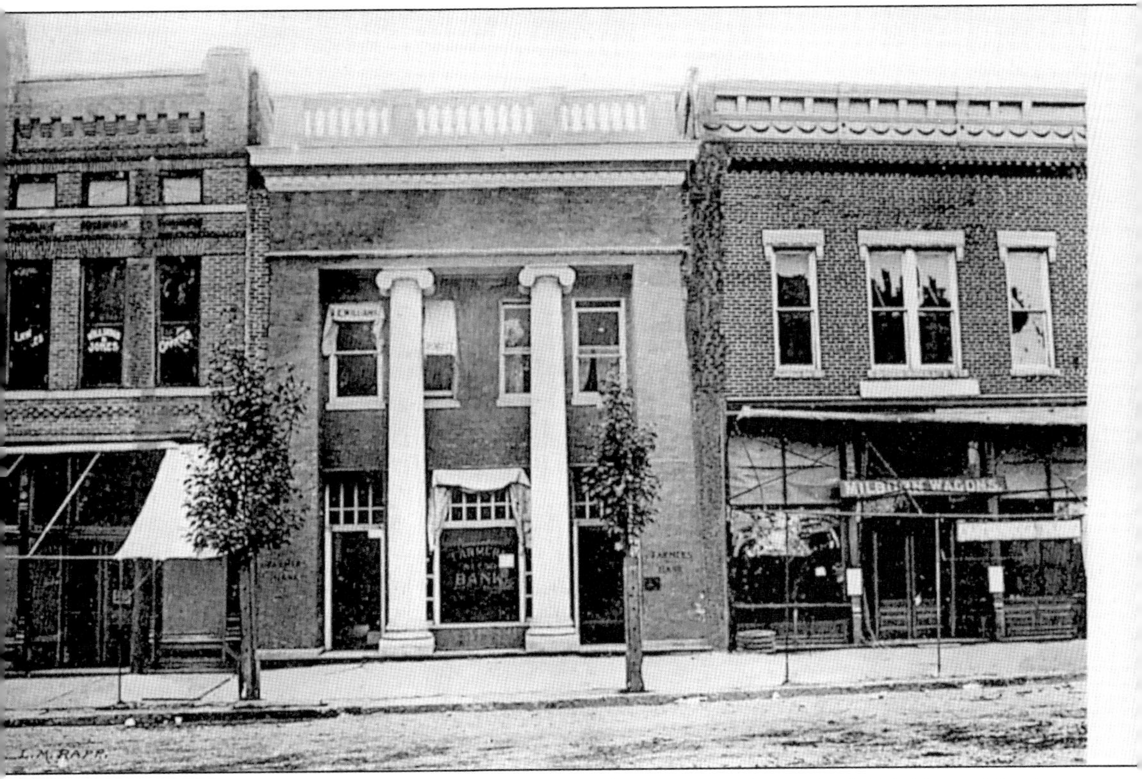

FARMERS STATE BANK, c. 1909. This bank was organized two weeks prior to the Third National Bank receiving its charter in 1903, and John Lewis was its first president. Later in the year the bank acquired all of the assets and assumed all obligations of the Glasgow Trust Company. The new bank was located on the east side of the square until the new headquarters building was opened on Columbia Avenue in 1972. The building is still in use on the square although the columns were removed to the cemetery and a new facade was added. The Farmers State Bank and the Third National Bank consolidated in 1910 to become Farmers National Bank. "Williams and Jones, Lawyers" occupied the second floor of the building to the north and Milburn Wagons occupied the building to the south of the bank.

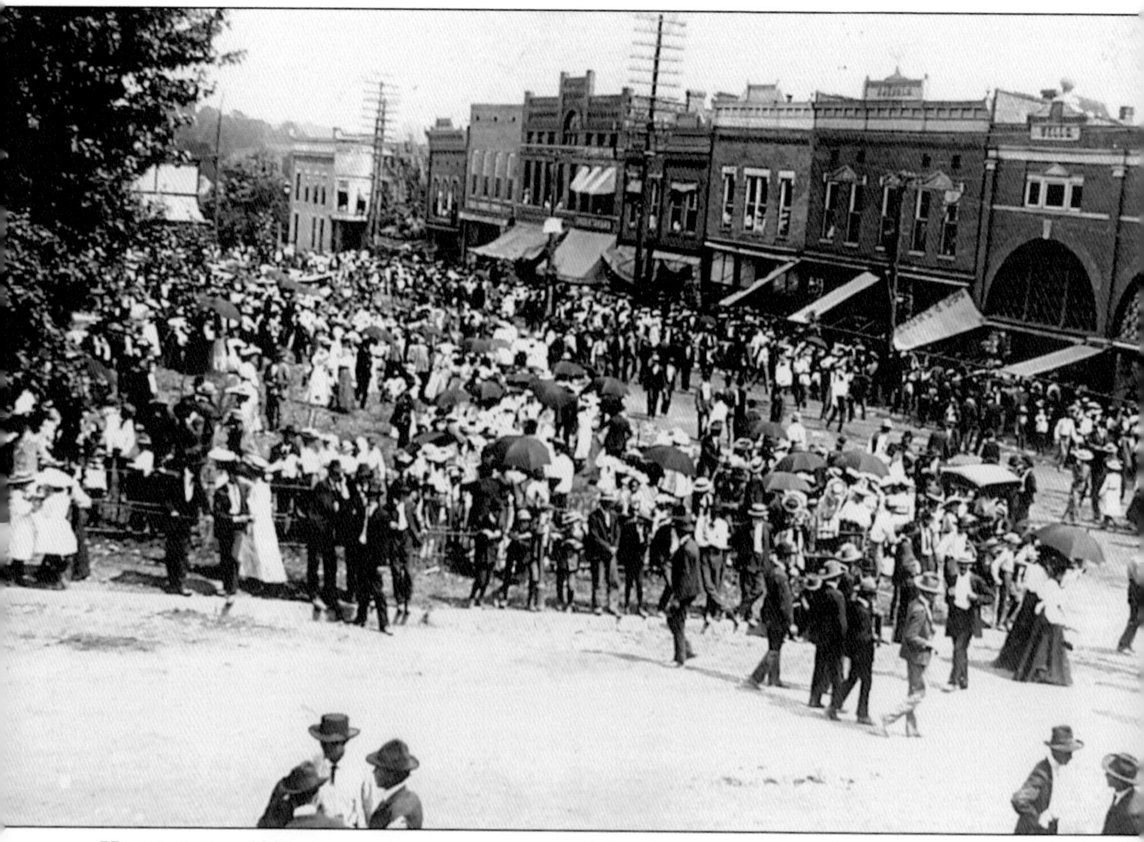

Homecoming, 1906. A newspaper account reported that the Homecoming of June 1906 was the largest crowd to gather in Glasgow since 1897 when William Jennings Bryan spoke at the courthouse. Mailed invitations and widespread publication resulted in a crowd of about 15,000 people. They came early to listen to popular music, view a horse parade, and listen to speakers from Louisville, New York, Bowling Green, and Meridian, Mississippi. The first of two weddings was celebrated at 1 p.m. when Usa Thomas and Sam Cooksey of the Dry Fork country were escorted from the Murrell Hotel by a band playing the wedding march. The party passed into the rotunda of the courthouse and out the north door onto a platform for the ceremony. A basket dinner followed with 188 spaces (752 feet) on the tables in the courthouse yard, but even that was not enough room. Others spread their dinner on the ground. It appeared that each one had tried to bring enough to feed the entire crowd. On the east side of the yard was a 100-foot-long table from which was served 500 gallons of burgoo and 1,000 loaves of light bread for the great throng of people that was unable to go into the courthouse yard. After the second wedding of Gertrude Denunzio and Scott H. Walker of Louisville, an old-fashioned handshaking and general levee was held that lasted several hours. Houses on the square were decorated with flags and bunting.

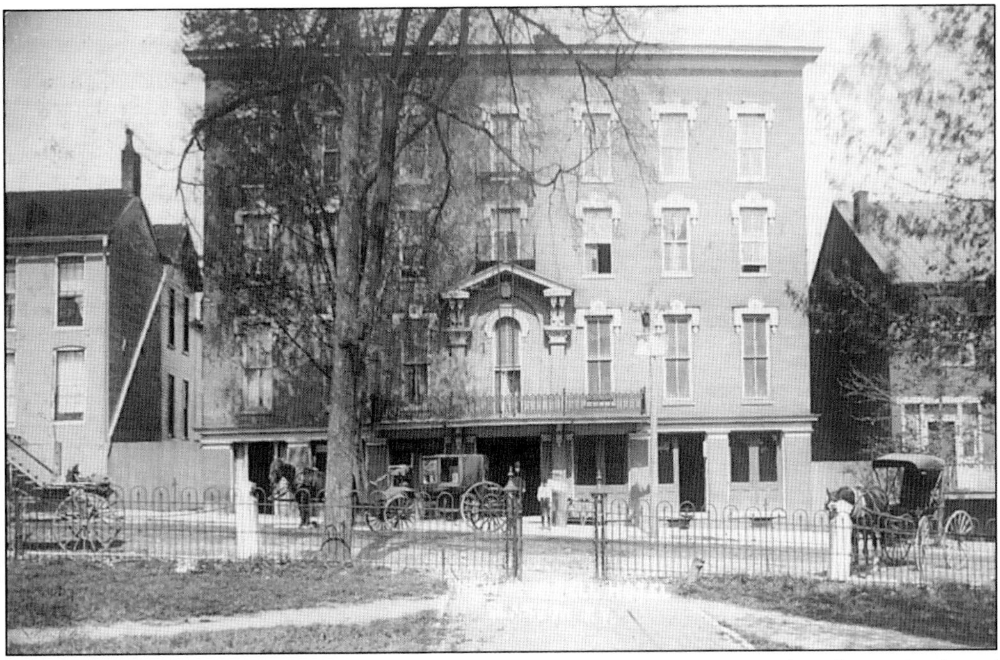

Murrell Hotel, c. 1909. This three-story brick hostel was later known as the Liberty Hotel, and in 1929, the newly modernized building was given the name Spotswood Hotel. In 1906 when Edwin Hatcher was the hotel proprietor, he advertised a pressing club at the New Murrell Hotel for a fee of $1 a month. One local young man was unable to attend church when he realized his only good jacket was still at the pressing club.

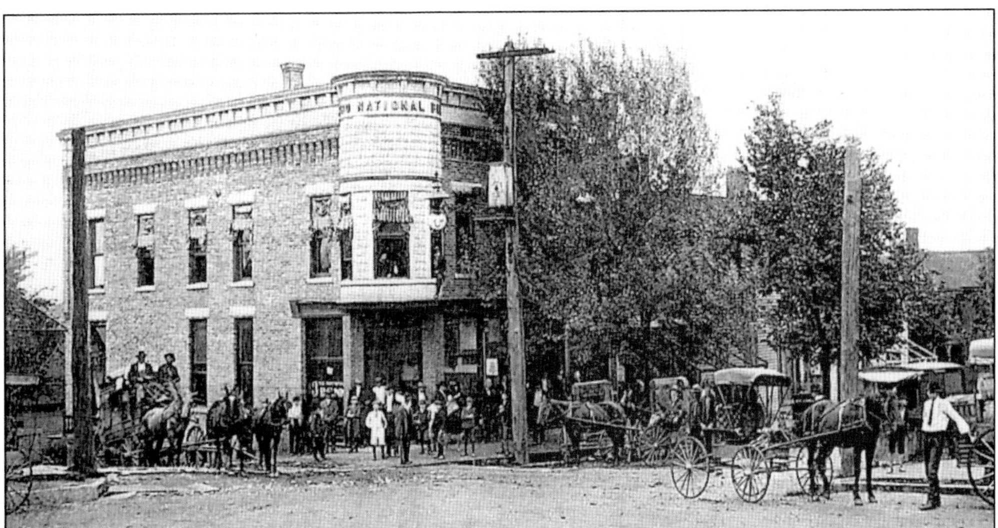

Post Office and Third National Bank, c. 1905. Third National Bank was organized in 1903, and S.T. Young served as its president. It consolidated with the Farmers State Bank in 1910. The Burkesville Stage Coach is seen arriving on the left. Operated by Glasgow Livery Stable owners, P.E. Tandy and Theodore Lockies, the stagecoach made daily trips to transport and deliver both mail and passengers. A newspaper article in 1907 indicates that the post office shown in this view later occupied space in the Citizens National Bank for ten years.

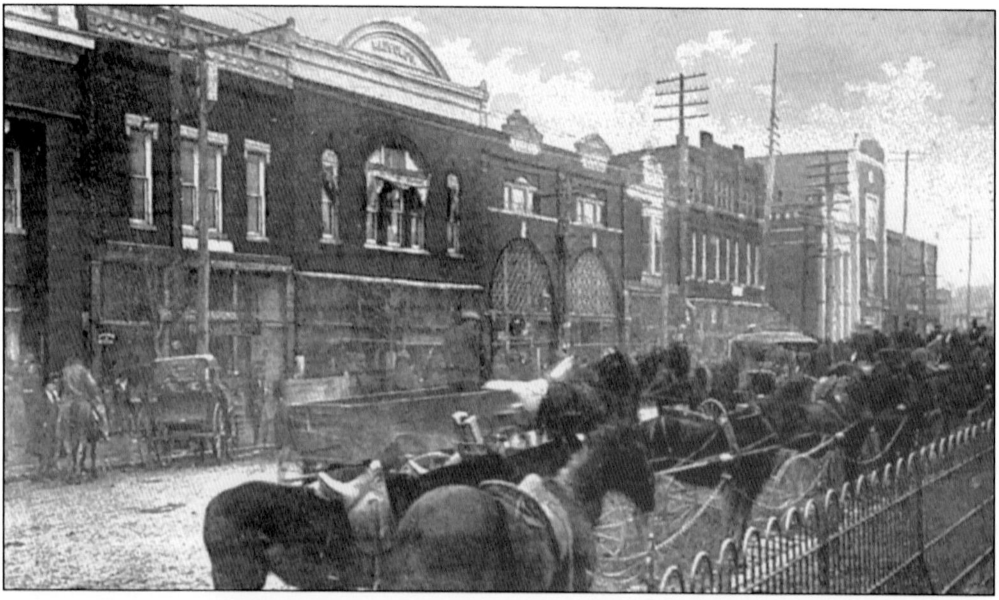

County Court Day, c. 1911. During much of the 1800s and before the automobile became commonplace in the 1900s, travel on horseback or by horse-drawn wagon or buggy from one's home in the country to the county seat once or twice a month for court day was an eagerly awaited adventure. Farmers in Barren County would meet in Glasgow to swap or sell horses, mules, and other livestock. Practically anything that could be transported—produce, corn, tobacco, liquor, leather goods, etc.—was hauled to town to be sold by individuals and families who resided in rural areas.

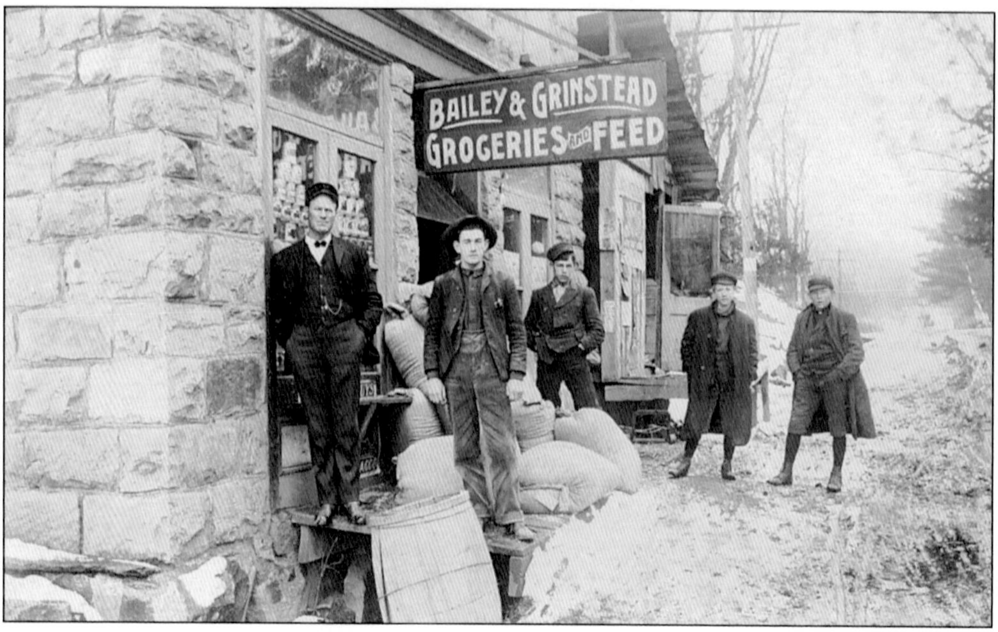

Bailey & Grinstead Groceries and Feed, c. 1905. This building still stands on Main Street but it is now covered by siding. A four-foot section of the front was removed when the highway department widened Main Street. This photograph was made by the Rapp Studio as shown by the impression on the corner.

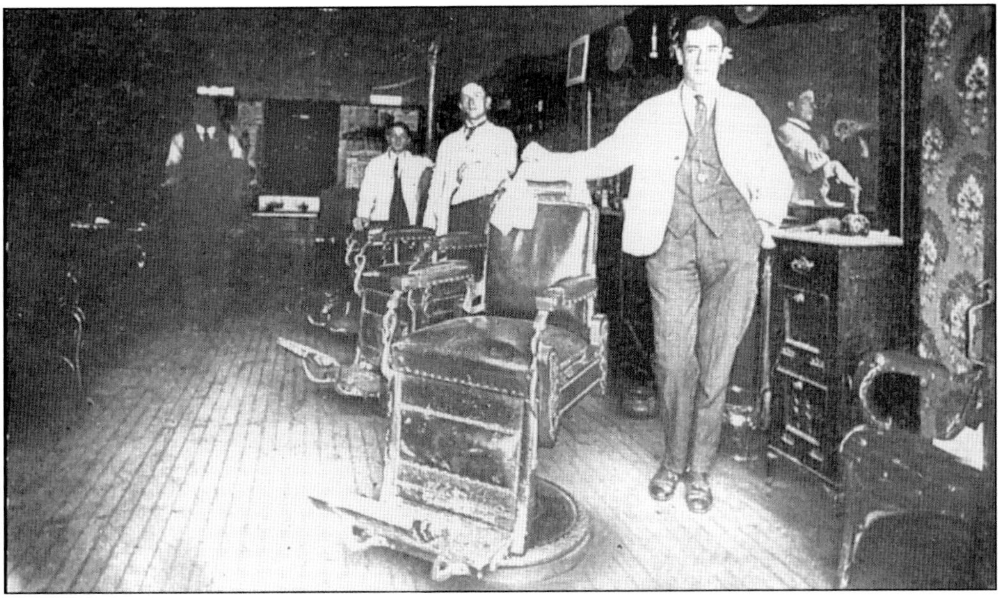

INTERIOR OF PARKE & SETTLERS BARBER SHOP, C. 1910. This turn-of-the-century Glasgow barbershop was more than just a place to get a haircut. It was a popular retreat that provided a relaxed and comfortable, for-men-only atmosphere that could not be found elsewhere. Men would congregate to discuss the weather, crops, and current events while they waited for a shoeshine, haircut, and/or a 15¢ shave. Amid the reek of cigarettes and cigar smoke, tobacco juice that had been spat in a brass spittoon, and bay rum, others would browse the pages of the latest spicy magazines. After tiring of this activity, they would verbally critique the ladies who often provided the primary attraction when they walked past the large barbershop window. Standing next to their new, state-of-the-art reclining chairs, these three barbers proudly pose for their picture to be taken prior to the beginning of another workday.

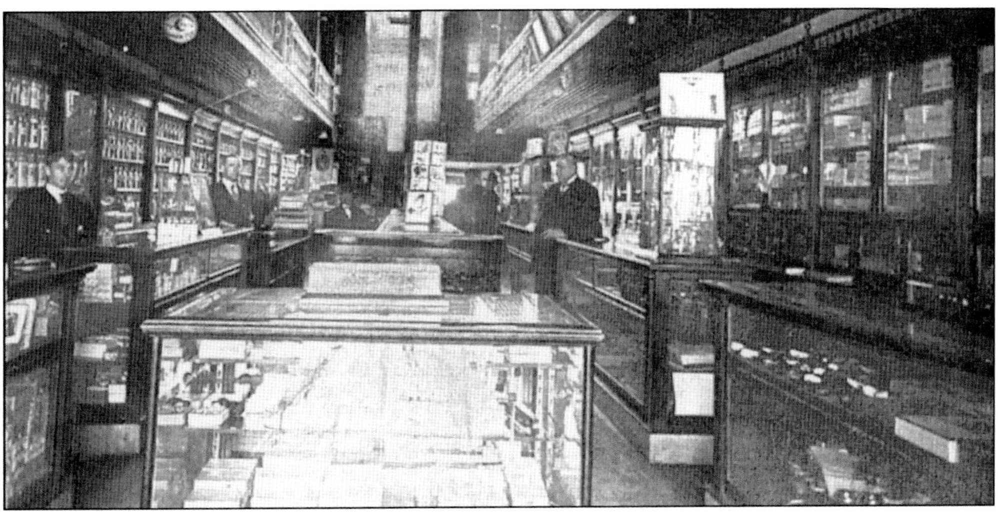

INTERIOR OF LEECH & ELLIS DRUG STORE, C. 1910. This firm was known as the Leech & Ellis Drugstore and Booksellers from 1899 to 1910. In 1907, stock and poultry feed were also sold. The owners advertised Prickly Ash Bitters for turning "a poor, tired, discouraged woman into one of sparkling good health and cheerfulness." Leech & Ellis also had postcards printed of local attractions. In 1911, the Leech & Davis partnership was formed, and Winn Davis operated this business for 40 years.

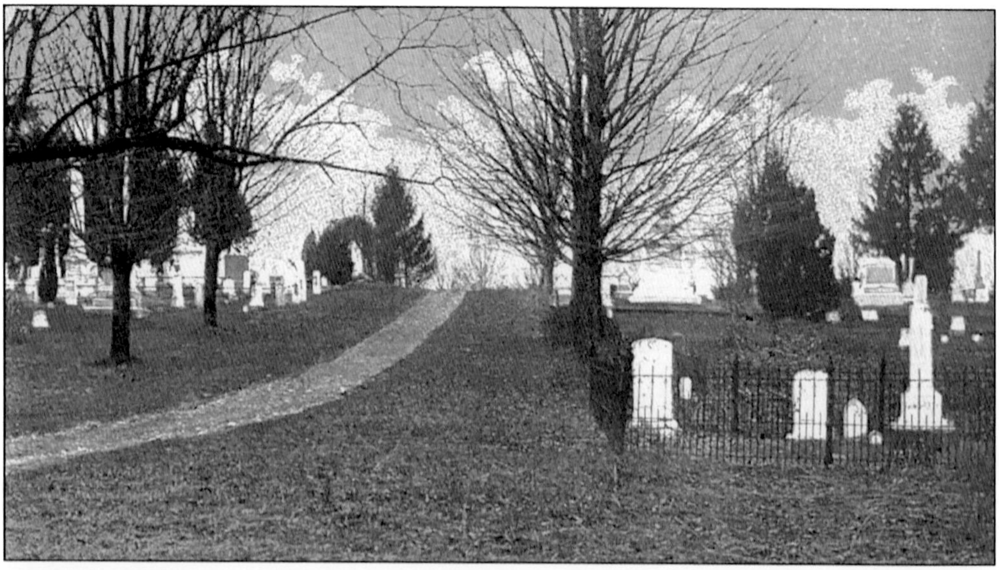

MUNICIPAL CEMETERY, C. 1910. At the top of this view were the earthworks of Fort Williams, a Civil War field fortification. Brig. Gen. J.T. Boyle (USA), in command of the Western District of Kentucky, directed the building of the fort at Glasgow in March 1863. Field guns were placed to cover the northeast, east, and west approaches to the fort, which was named for Brig. Gen. Thomas Williams who was killed in 1862 at Baton Rouge. On October 6, 1863, Col. John M. Hughes (CSA), commanding the 25th Tennessee Infantry, attacked Glasgow with 120 men. The fort was garrisoned by the 37th Kentucky Mounted Infantry of about 420 men. Infantrymen who led the surprise attack captured 142, killed 9, wounded 26, and captured or destroyed ordnance and stores worth about $250,000.

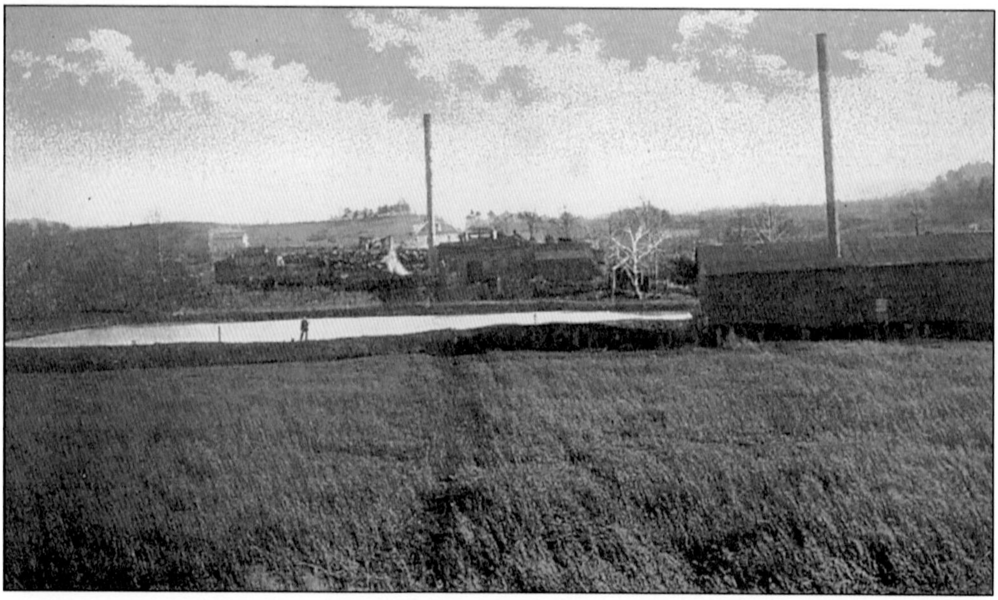

ELECTRIC LIGHT & ICE CO., C. 1910. Advertised as "Manufacturers of Artificial ice from pure distilled water," this plant had cold storage for approximately 100 tons of ice in 1903. Located on South Fork Creek, about one-half mile from the square, the plant produced electricity for 2,500 lights in the Glasgow area. It also furnished power for the Electro Roller Mills on the next lot.

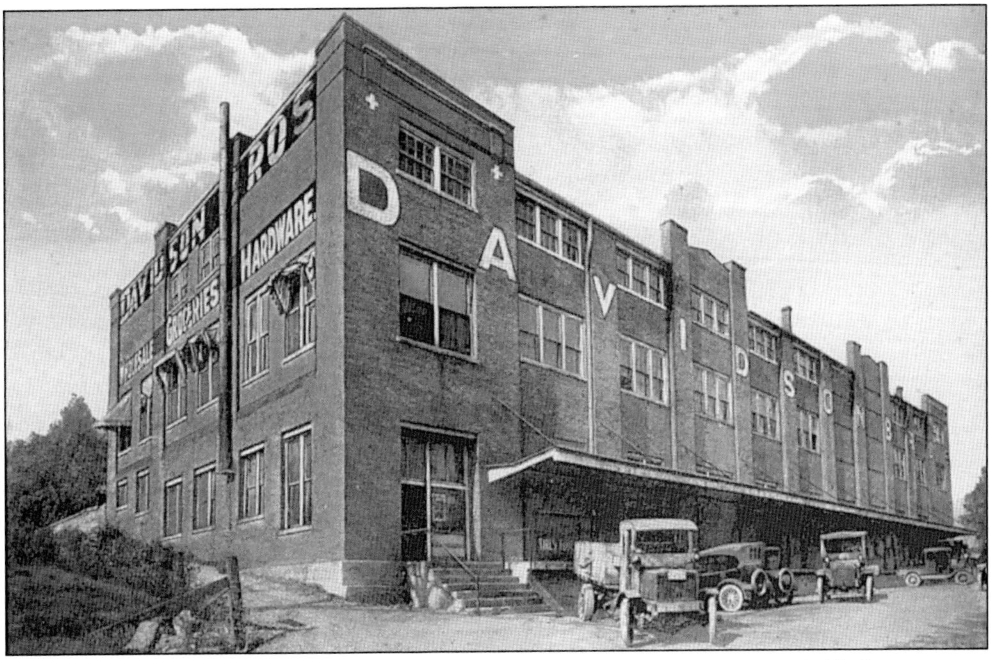

Davidson Brothers Wholesale Grocery, *c.* 1925. In 1933, the owners of this large grocery warehouse on West Main Street suffered a great financial loss when it burned. Davidson Brothers was the largest wholesale grocery business in this part of Kentucky when it went out of business in 1934. They also distributed tobacco products produced by Samson Tobacco Company of Glasgow.

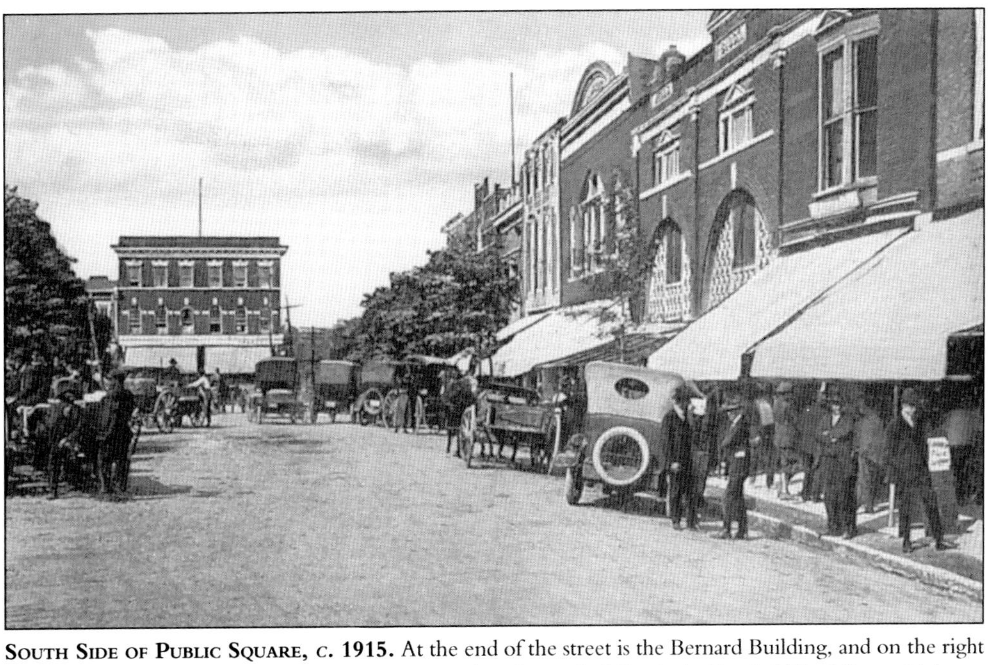

South Side of Public Square, *c.* 1915. At the end of the street is the Bernard Building, and on the right is the corner drugstore of Ellis & Ellison. The round pediment building is the Raubold Building, which was built after the 1900 fire that destroyed most of the east side of the square. Offices used by lawyers, doctors, photographers, and a newspaper business occupied the upper floors of these buildings.

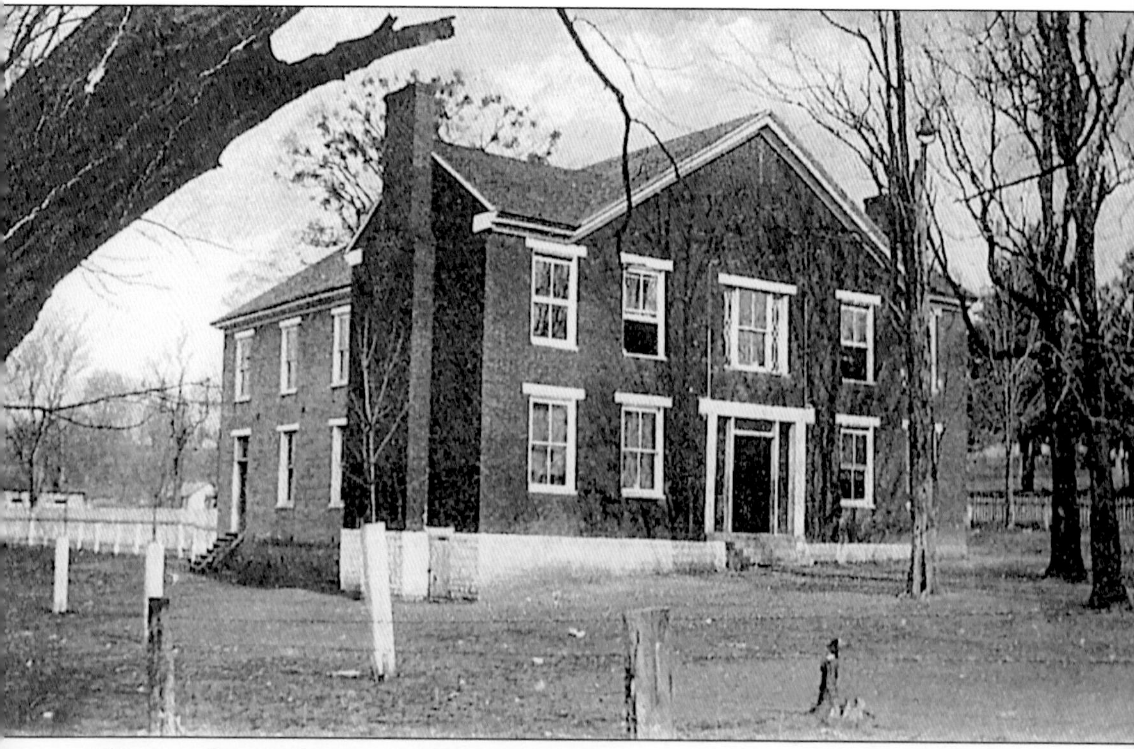

GLASGOW GRADED SCHOOL, c. 1906. Urania College was organized in 1831. This building was soon erected and housed the college until the beginning of the Civil War. During the war, the United States government used it as a hospital. Government payments allowed the construction of the back wing. E.B. Terry established the Glasgow Normal School here in 1901. In 1907, the front part of the building was torn away and a ten-room addition was built with steam heat and electric lights. After the school trustees purchased Liberty College from the Baptist Association, this property was sold and converted into the Jacksonway Hotel.

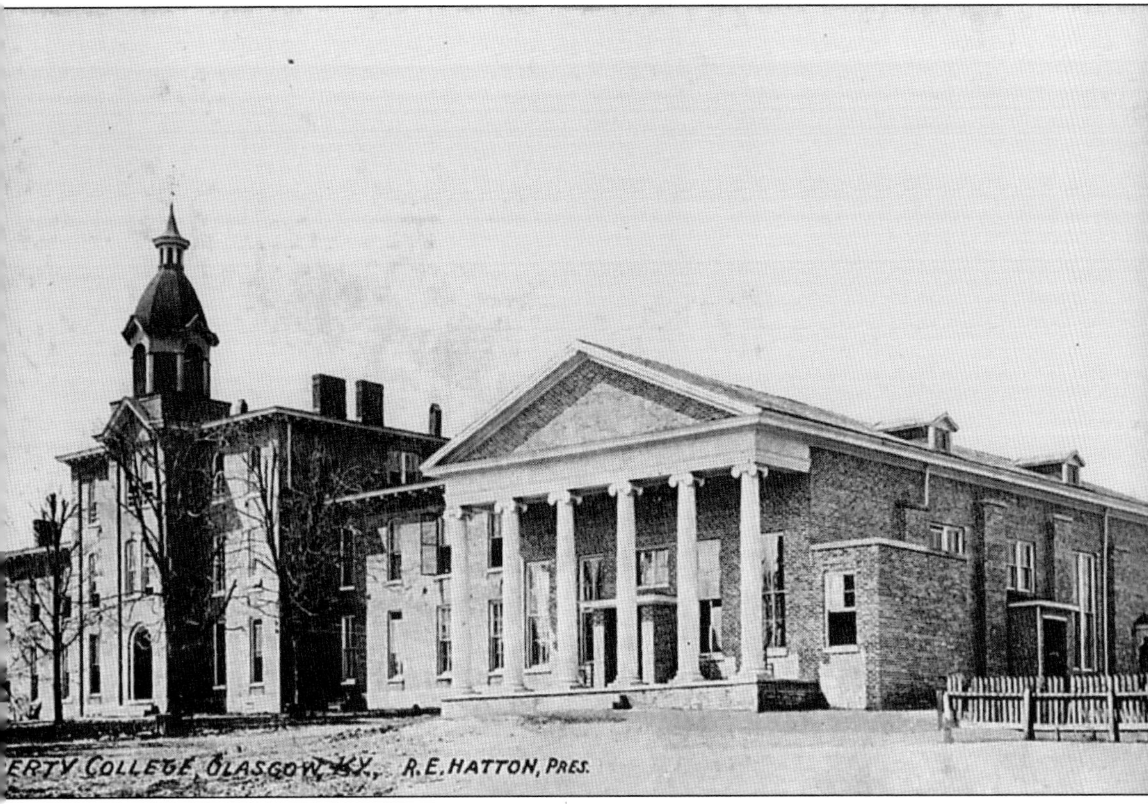

LIBERTY COLLEGE, C. 1907. Liberty Female College was founded in 1875. In the 1905–1906 school year a newspaper advertisement noted that it had 14 teachers and gave degrees in three subjects: music, art, and business. Pres. George J. Burnett announced that a steam heat plant would be added by winter. In 1907, the new president, Robert E. Hatton, advertised the addition of a library, gym, and laboratories. A newspaper article about the addition to Liberty College, described the new facilities as follows: The first floor housed an auditorium 39 feet by 80 feet that could be divided by "vertical flex fold doors" into three rooms. The center room was used as a chapel and a study hall. On the second floor were six large bedrooms, bath and toilet rooms, and a trunk room. Contractor W.C. Moss completed it in less than four months, and trustees gathered money to purchase new desks and electric light fixtures that were missing from the completed structure. Liberty College operated under the sponsorship of Liberty Baptist Association from 1875 until 1913. In 1931, Liberty College was dismantled and a high school building was erected.

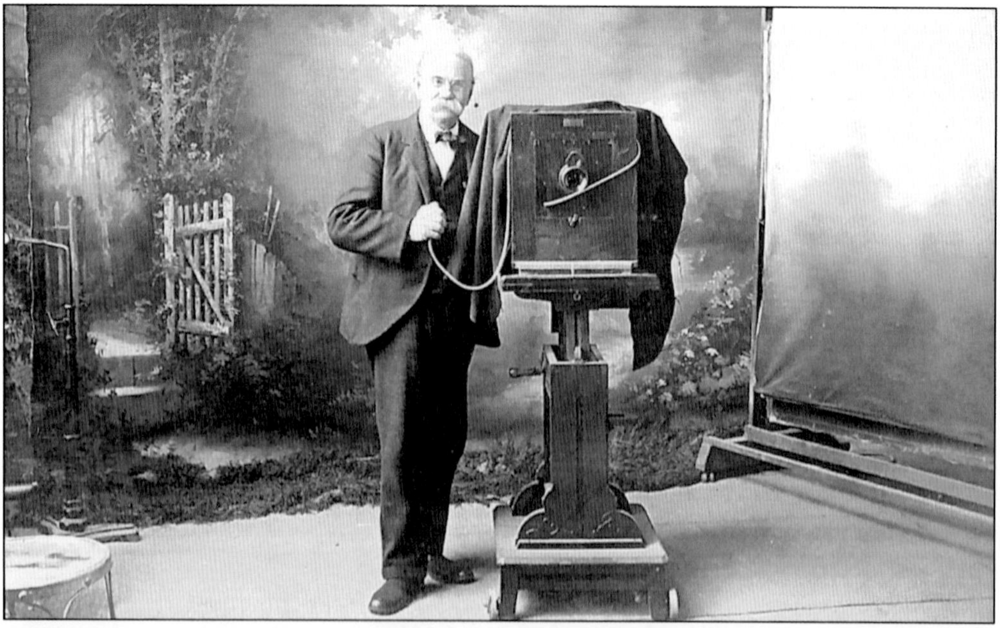

ADOLPH RAPP, C. 1910. This is a self-photograph of local photographer Adolph Rapp in his studio. The *Glasgow Times* in 1898 noted that Adolph Rapp operated "an elegant photography studio on the corner of Main and Green over Bradford's Saddle Shop." Before opening his studio, Rapp operated several businesses including a restaurant and a bakery. He arrived in Glasgow about 1870. Rapp was also an artist and left behind numerous paintings and sketches. Many of his photos were printed on postcards and now provide many of the images found in this chapter.

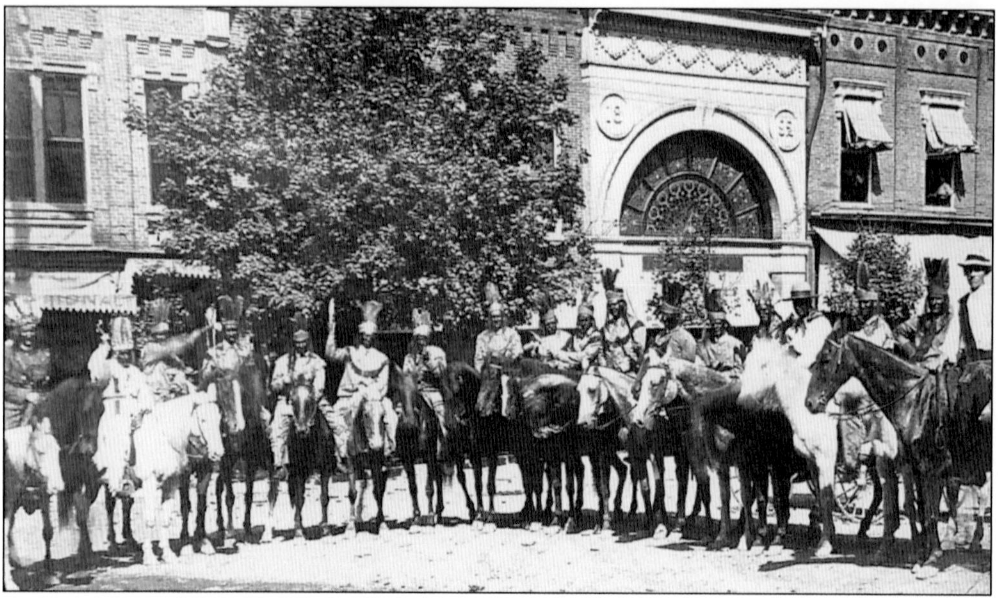

RED MEN, C. 1907. Research failed to explain why 18 men, 16 of which are dressed in "Indian attire," posed on the north side of the court square in Glasgow for this photograph. The only man identified is "P.E. Satterfield on white horse." Which white horse? The words "red men" are penciled on the back of the image. Trigg National Bank is in the background with the arched window.

The Davis Hotel, c. 1910. The Davis Hotel was located on the west side of the square, north of the Murrell Hotel and four buildings up from the corner. When it was advertised for sale in 1925, the hotel was listed as having "22 rooms, hardwood floors, hot and cold water in each room, lighted by electricity and heated by gas." It was destroyed by fire in 1932. Note the "Ladies Entrance" on the door at the left of the picture.

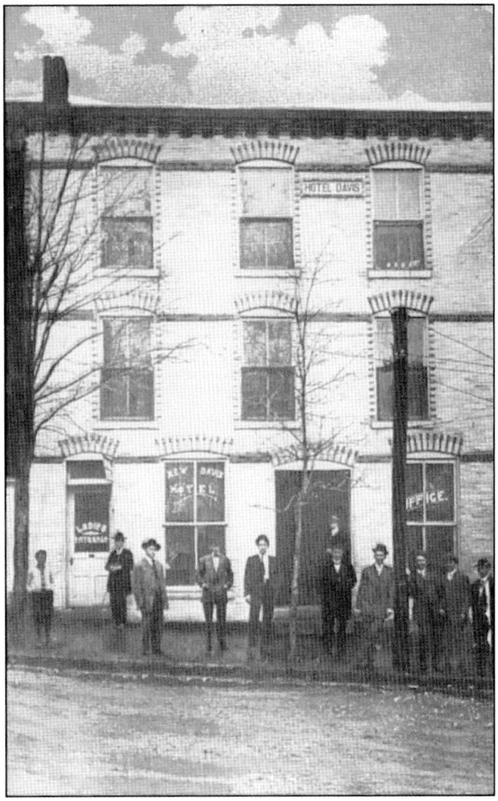

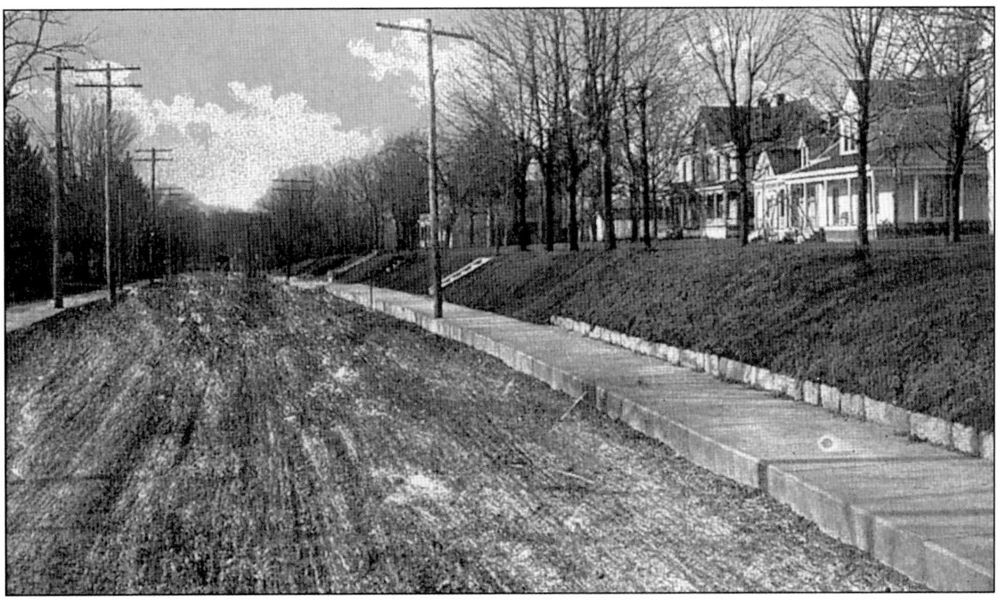

East Main Street, c. 1910. The second house on the right, at 513 East Main Street, was the home of Gov. Preston H. Leslie. Leslie was an attorney in Glasgow when he was elected the 27th governor of Kentucky in 1871. He was appointed by President Grover Cleveland to serve as the territorial governor of Montana in 1887.

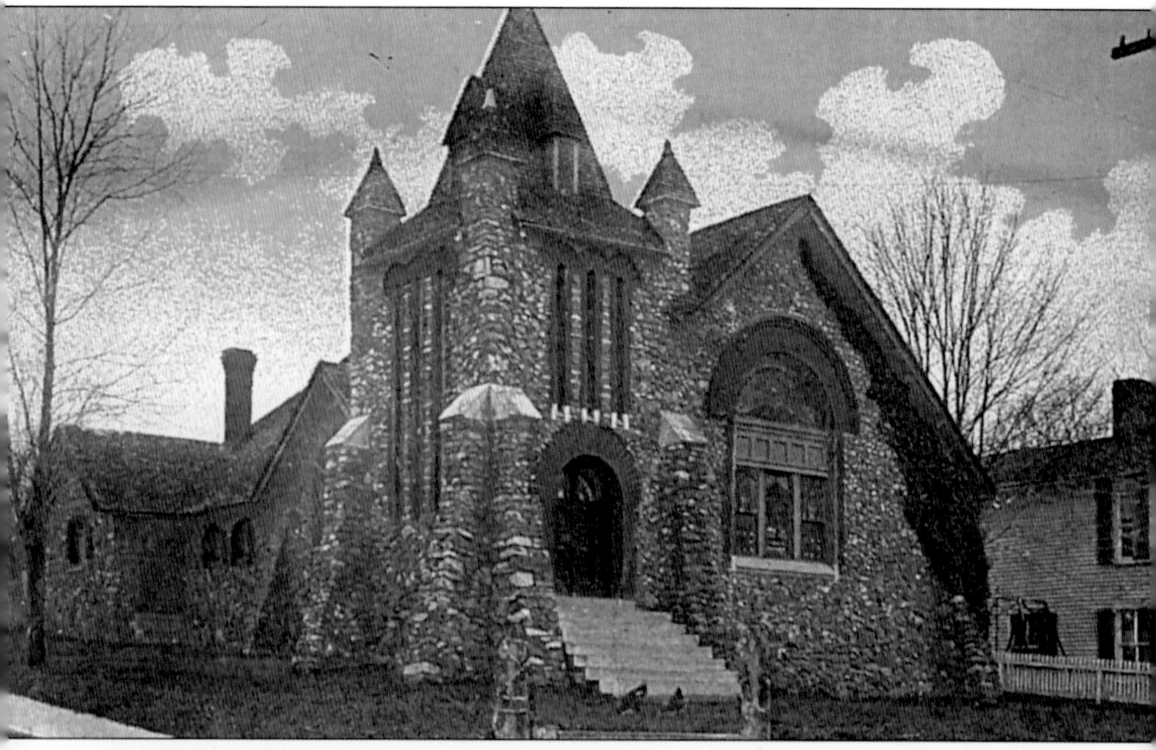

St. Helen's Catholic Church, c. 1910. This church was built under the leadership of Rev. William Dunn and dedicated in October 1893 by Bishop William G. McCloskey. It was built of rough field stones collected by the church's few parishioners. The church is located at 103 Brown Street on a lot donated by the Duke of Norfolk, known as "the highest and most outstanding Catholic member of the English Peerage and House of Lords." A memorial window recognizes the gift. Staffed by a priest from Louisville for many years, the church welcomed Rev. Joseph Wheatley in 1948. He became the resident priest and served in this position until 1956 when he became a monsignor and was recalled to Louisville. The Fathers of Mercy of Brooklyn, New York were given charge of St. Helen's at that time.

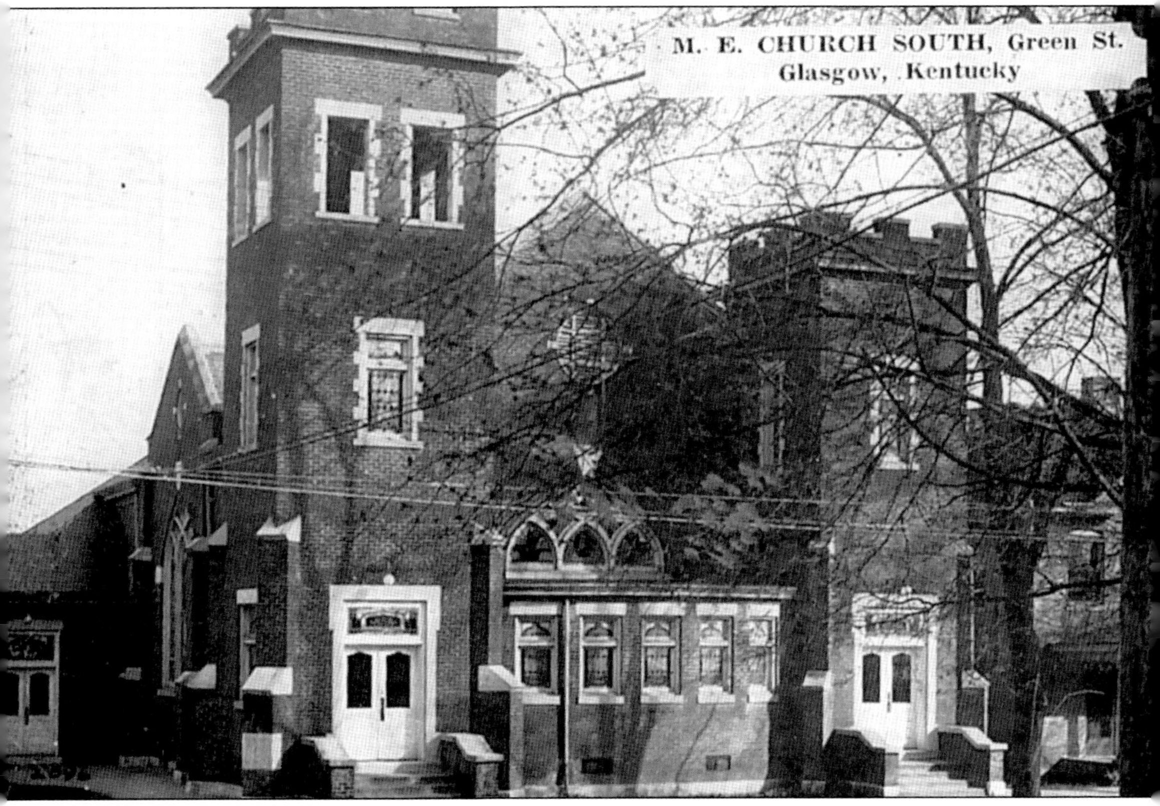

METHODIST EPISCOPAL CHURCH SOUTH, GREEN STREET, *c.* 1920. The first Methodist Society was formed in 1822 and the first building was erected in 1829. This church was torn down and later rebuilt in 1858. The society decided to relocate and constructed a new church on East Main Street near the courthouse square. In 1900 the buildings on the east side of the square burned and the church suffered great damage. Members worshiped in the courthouse until they purchased the old Christian Church on Green Street. In 1909 a committee purchased this site, and in 1911, a subscription for $15,500 was made for the new church pictured above. The old church was sold for $1,200. The cornerstone for the new church was laid on October 31, 1911, and construction began. There were insufficient funds for the windows, but a successful drive resulted in the purchase and installation of memorial windows for the entire building. Bishop A.W. Wilson dedicated the church in September 1913.

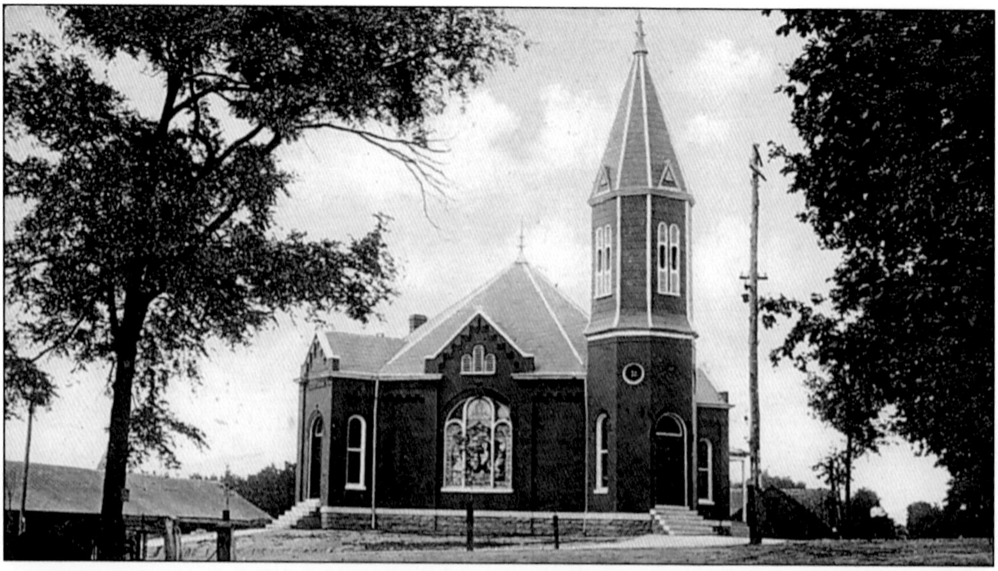

Christian Church, c. 1906. A visit to Glasgow by Alexander Campbell in 1831 signaled the beginning of the Christian Church in Glasgow. In the late 1880s the Christian congregation became divided over authority of the elders. Several members left and established the Second Christian Church in 1891. They reunited in the late 1890s and decided to purchase land, sell their two churches, and build a new one large enough to accommodate the full congregation. On June 22, 1902, this new building on the square was dedicated. The beautiful stained-glass windows were all memorial gifts.

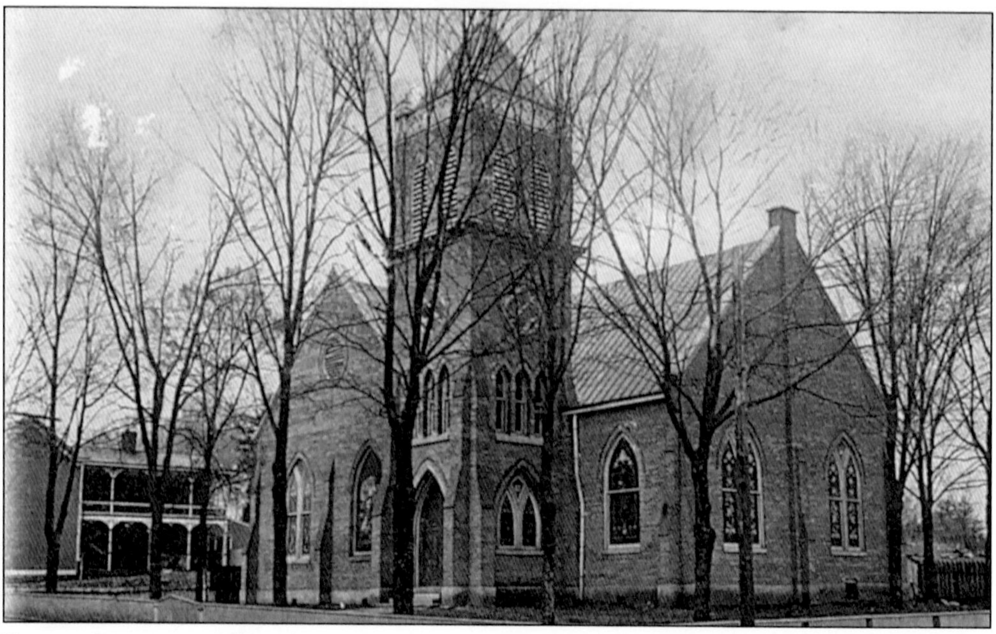

Baptist Church, c. 1906. The congregation was organized in June 1818 but their first church was not completed until 1851. They worshiped at that church until the building was torn down in 1894. This was the second church constructed at this site. It was dedicated on June 30, 1895 by T.T. Eaton of Louisville and replaced the earlier building. By 1918, heating, lighting, a pipe organ, and interior decorations modernized the above building.

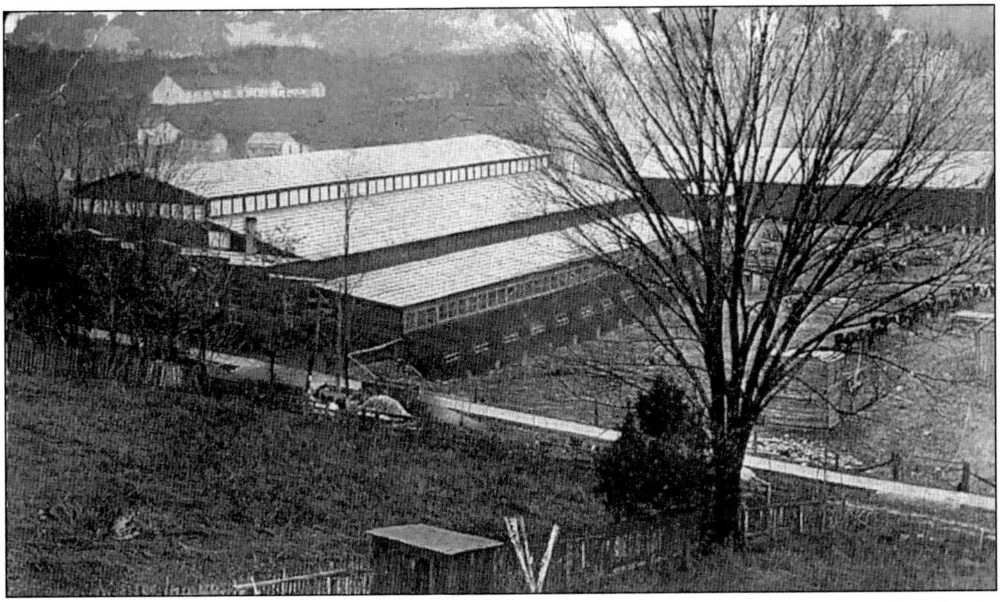

Planters Loose Tobacco Warehouse, *c.* 1910. Glasgow opened the second loose-leaf market in Kentucky in 1909 when Carl Bridgewater of Glasgow and Robert N. Barton of Knob Lick established the Planters Warehouse. Loose-leaf marketing became the preferred alternative to packing tobacco into hogsheads; however, both types of marketing continued for several years. Another loose-leaf warehouse was established in 1910 by a company based in Louisville and in Danville, Virginia.

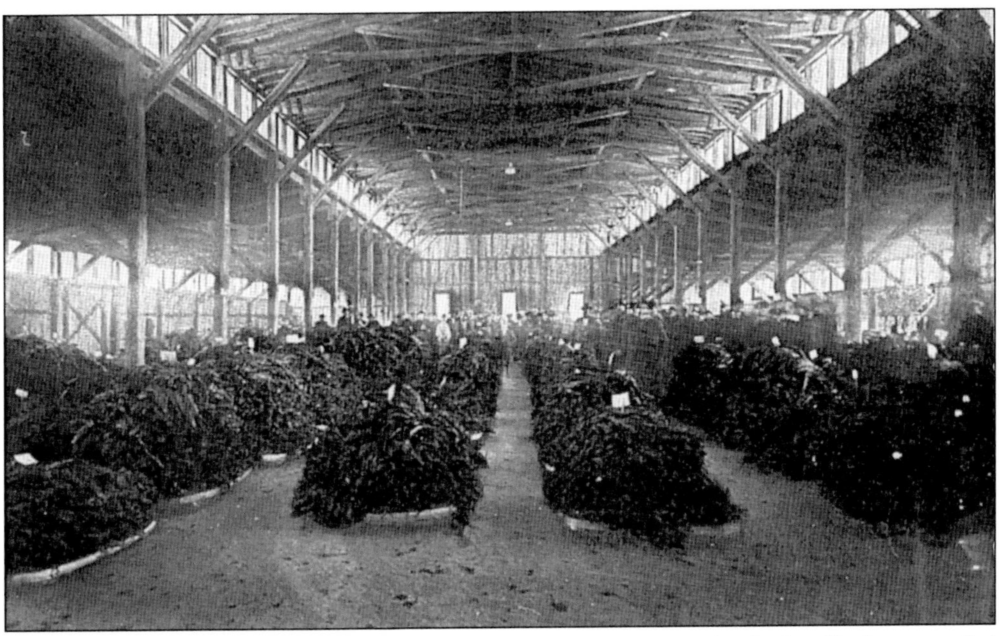

Interior Planters Loose Tobacco Warehouse, *c.* 1910. This postcard and others like it were mailed to local growers from the warehouses located on Lower Depot Street, with the following message on the back: "This is the warehouse that sold four million pounds of Burley and Dark tobacco last season at satisfactory prices. So don't sell at home but bring your tobacco here where you have competition and get the best price. Don't miss our big Tobacco Fair, October 15, 1910."

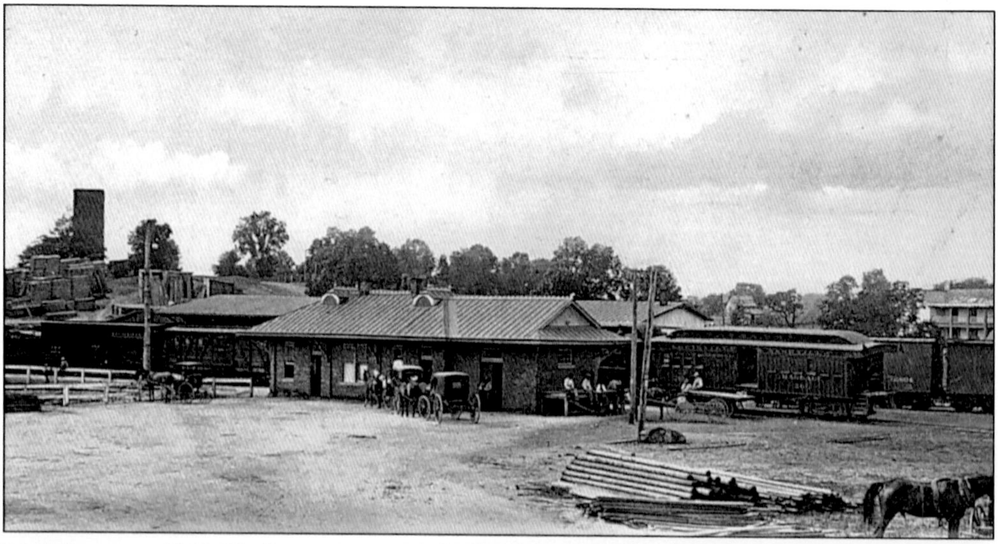

L&N Depot, c. 1906. The Barren County Railroad Company was incorporated in 1856 with the intention of building a rail line to connect with the main L&N line at Glasgow Junction, ten miles from Glasgow. Controversy over a railroad tax for funding delayed the construction, and by November 1865, the tracks had been extended only half way to Glasgow Junction. Bell's Tavern of Glasgow Junction was perhaps the largest single contributor of funds to keep the construction going. The Glasgow Railway line was completed by September 1, 1870 and was taken over by the L&N, which still operates the line even though it is privately owned.

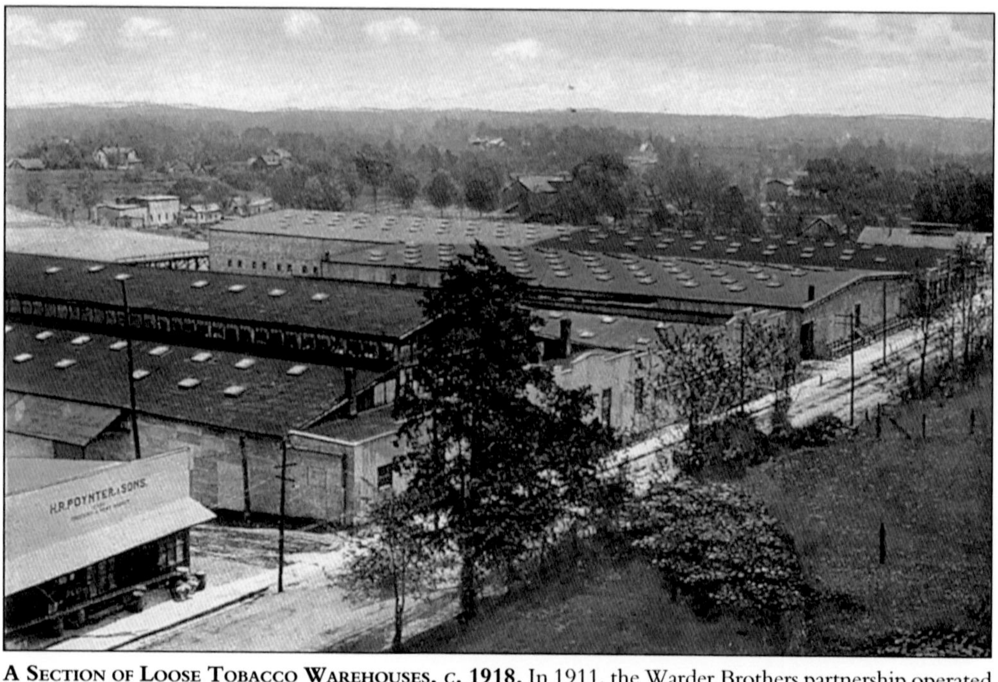

A Section of Loose Tobacco Warehouses, c. 1918. In 1911, the Warder Brothers partnership operated a warehouse behind Planters Warehouse and bought all available pooled dark tobacco. The "pooled" tobacco referred to the accumulated tobacco from cooperatives that tried to get a higher price by controlling the amount sold at low prices.

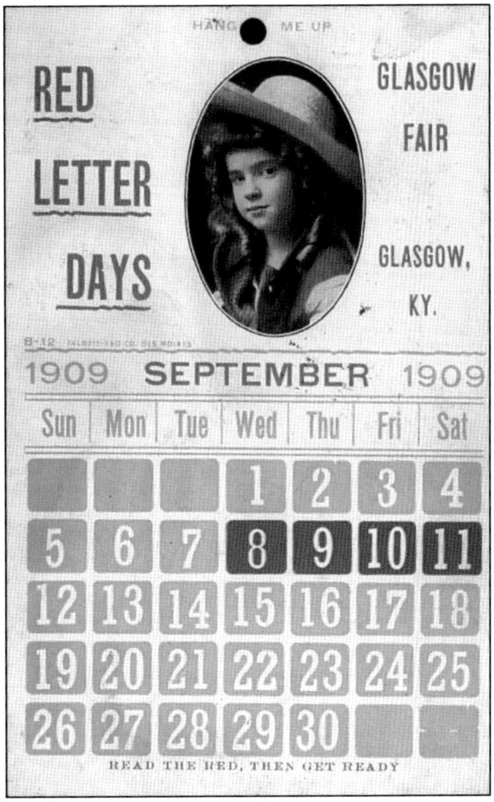

GLASGOW FAIR CALENDAR, *c.* 1909. "Come on over to the Glasgow Fair, Glasgow, Ky., Sept. 8-11, 1909," proclaimed another postcard, this one mailed to a resident of nearby Edison in Metcalfe County on August 10, 1909. To further entice attendance was the following announcement: "Great New York Hippodrome–The World's Greatest and Most Progressive Attraction has been secured for the Fair. Also Chariot Races, Ladies' and Gentlemens' Races; Running Races." The Glasgow Fairgrounds was located off South Green Street and below Seay Street.

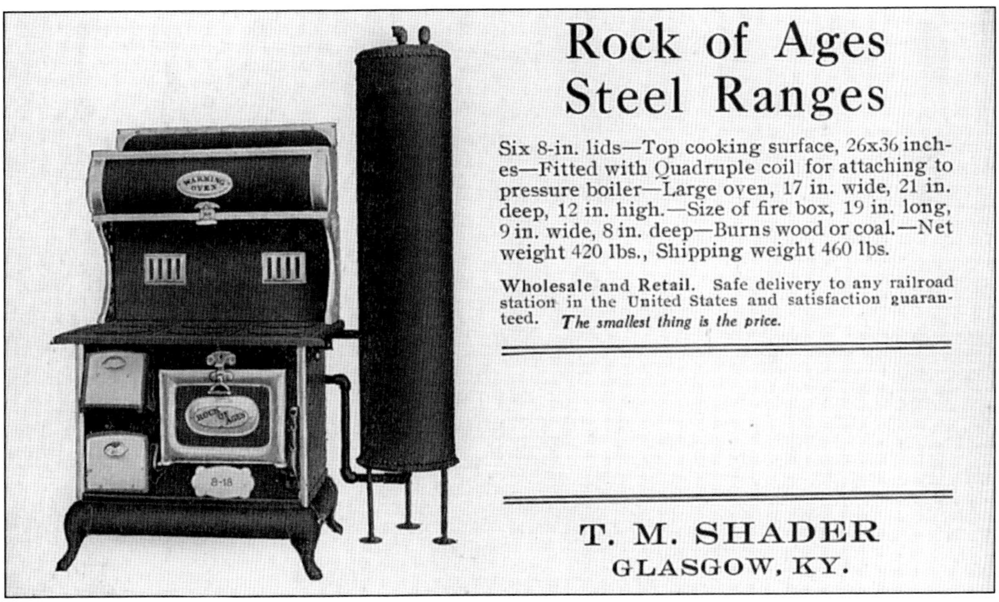

T.M. SHADER CARD, *c.* 1910. Adolph Shader and his son Tom operated a stove and tinware business in Glasgow in the early 1900s. This "Rock of Ages six burner stove" burned either wood or coal and weighed 420 pounds. Hot water could be heated in the attached boiler. Safe delivery was guaranteed to any railroad station.

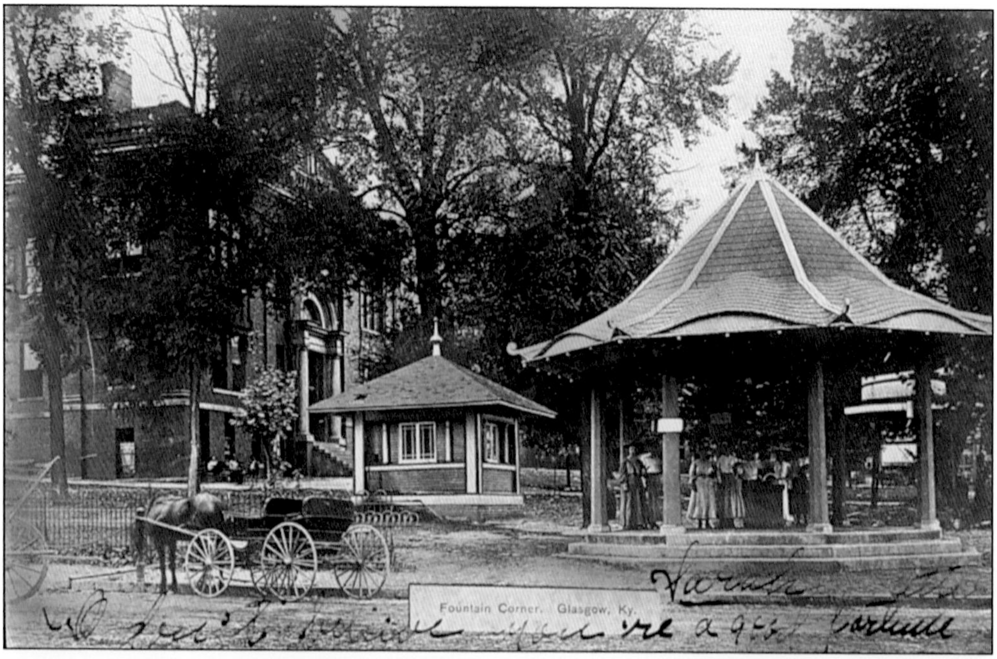

Fountain Corner, Court Square, *c.* 1906. In 1906 there were 3 dry goods stores and 12 groceries around the square. Most visitors used the fountain corner as a meeting spot and partook of the free refreshment of cool water. Twenty-two years later, a new pump was installed at the well so it could continue as a public "watering hole." In the background is the 1896 courthouse. Citizens of the community wanted a clock for the courthouse tower, but the fiscal court would only donate $500 of the $1,500 cost. Community fund-raising collected the necessary funds, and in 1913, a clock was installed so everyone could tell the time.

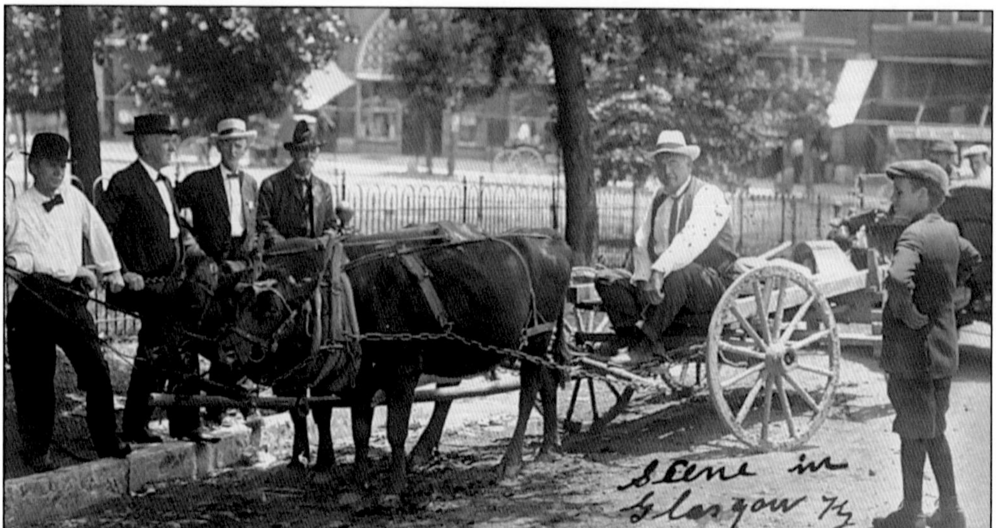

Ox Cart in Court Square, *c.* 1910. Jim Depp drives these oxen, which were broken to a regular harness instead of to a yoke. The spectators, from left to right, are an unidentified man, Lewis Ganter, Judge John Bowles, and Bill Read.

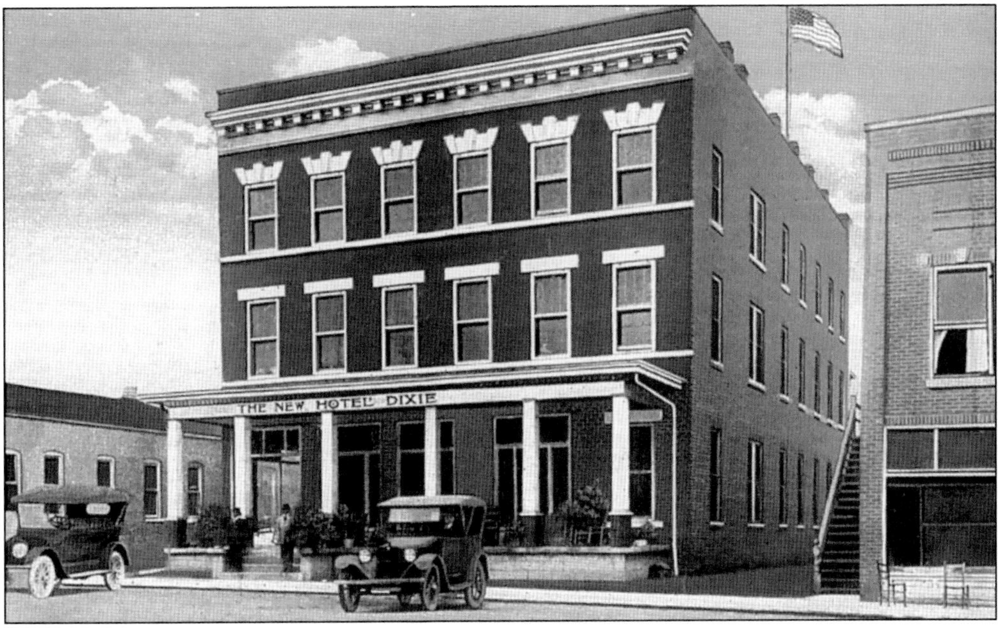

Hotel Dixie, 1918. This luxurious "railroad hotel" in Cave City served as the hub of activities for visitors and media alike during the time Floyd Collins was trapped in Sand Cave in 1925. Below, calendars published by the H.Y. Davis State Bank (upper center) and the Peoples Bank (upper right) adorn the walls of the hotel lobby. William M. O'Neal, wearing the dark coat and narrow tie behind the counter, was the hotel manager and Shug Bethel (far right) served as bellhop for many years.

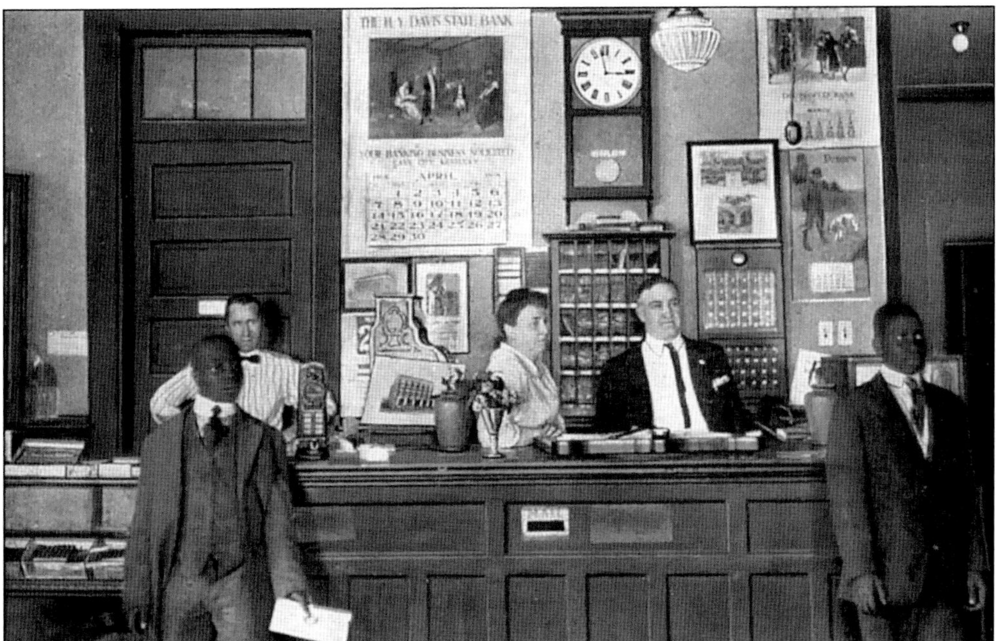

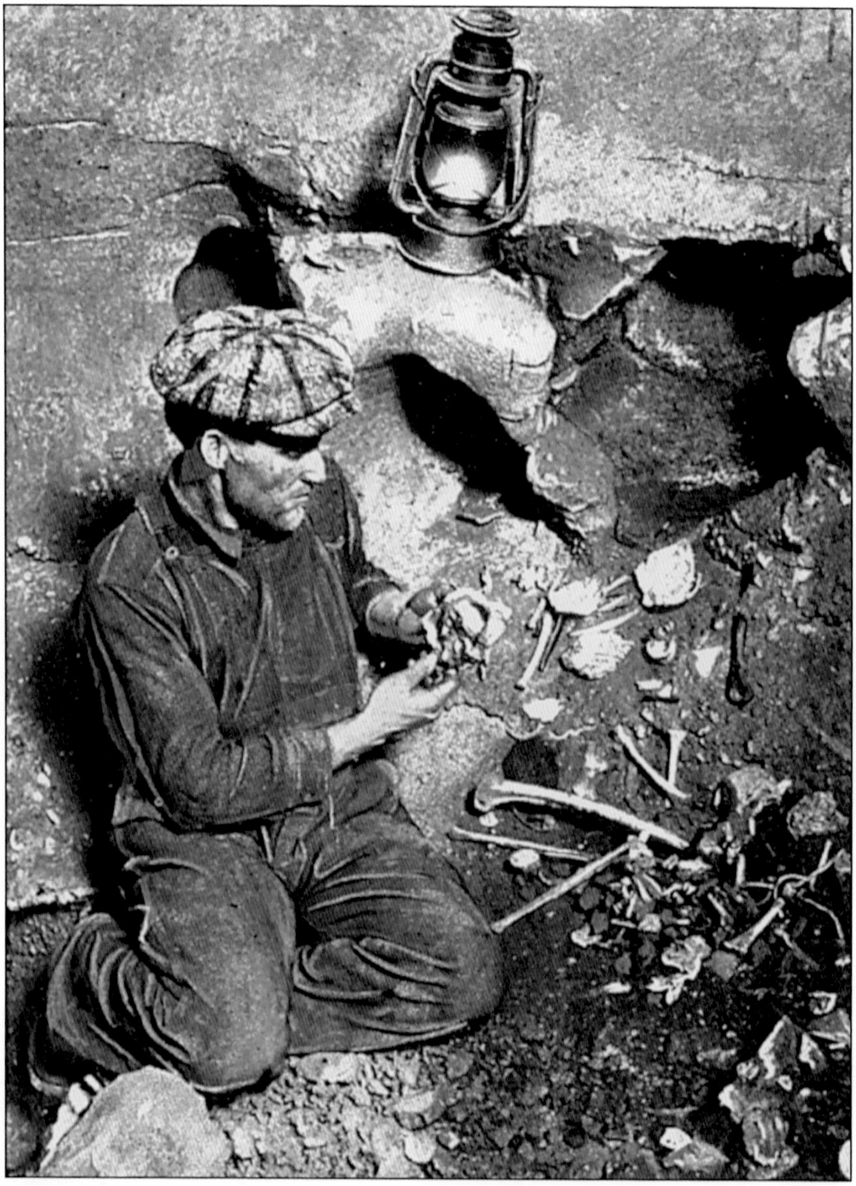

Floyd Collins, March 15, 1922. Using a lantern for light, Floyd Collins examines bones and artifacts at a site believed to be Crystal Onyx Cave, which is located in the Cave City area. According to Homer Collins, Floyd's brother, the photo used for this printed postcard was taken on March 15, 1922. While exploring Sand Cave on January 30, 1925, Floyd Collins was trapped on his way out by a fallen rock in a narrow passage about 150 feet from the cave's entrance. The next morning, farmers found his coat at the entrance and a small boy went inside the cave and discovered his entrapment. Collins's family was alerted, and within a few hours, the world knew of his tragedy. Unorganized rescue attempts began that served to weaken the cave walls that caused a cave-in in front of him. When a 60-foot shaft that had been constructed finally broke through 18 days after his entrapment, he was found dead. The shaft was sealed and funeral services were held on the surface near the cave entrance. The dramatic effort to rescue Collins was one of the most widely reported news stories during the 1920s and became the subject of a popular Kentucky ballad. Collins's remains now rest in the Mammoth Cave Baptist Cemetery.

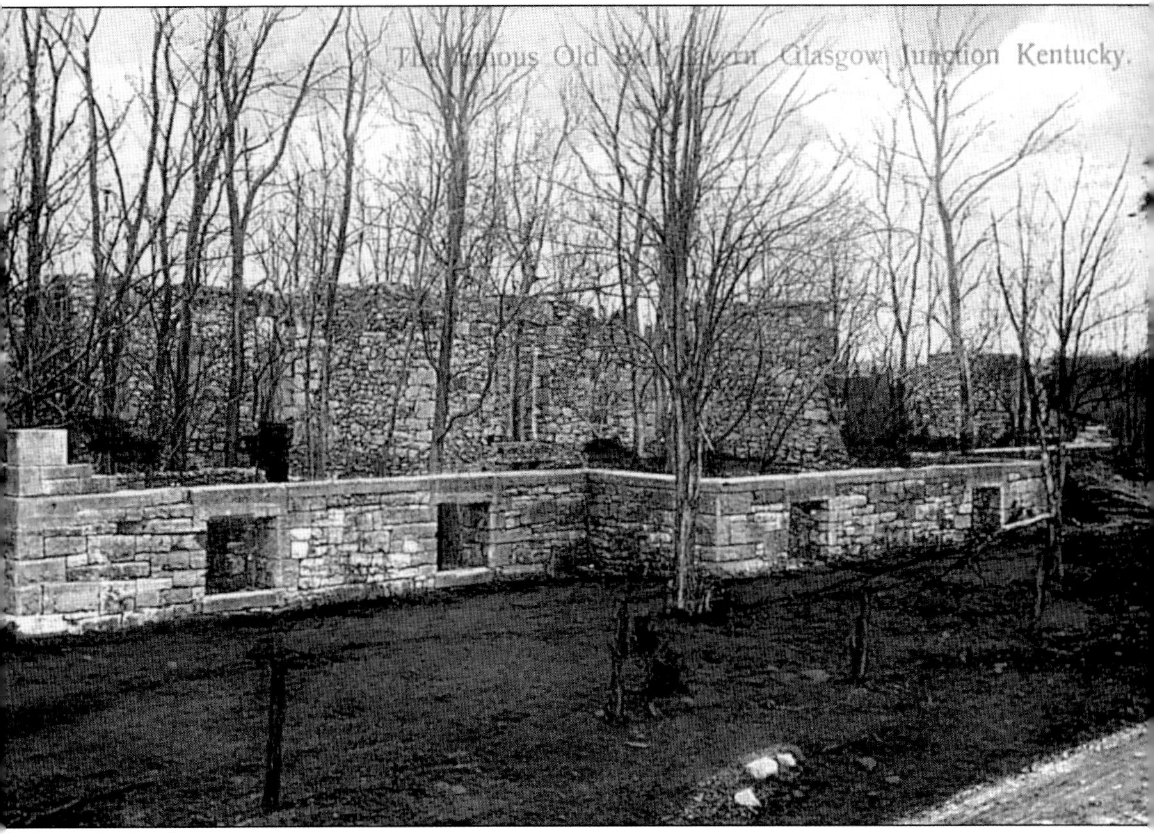

THE FAMOUS OLD BELL TAVERN, *c.* 1910. Bells Tavern at Three Forks was a noted stop for travelers going to and from Tennessee during the early 1800s. William Bell built a large brick structure in the 1820s where three roads, one to Nashville, one to Louisville, and one to Lexington, forked. The tavern was a popular spot for stagecoach passengers and the many travelers who wanted to visit Mammoth Cave but it was destroyed by fire shortly before the Civil War. Construction was begun on what was to be a larger and more magnificent tavern structure. Financial difficulties prevented its completion and these stones are all that remain of the new Bells Tavern. In 1859, the L&N Railroad had just arrived and a new post office for the community of Bells Tavern was established. By 1868, a railroad was reaching southeast to Glasgow, and Col. George M. Procter laid out the streets of the growing community. It was incorporated in 1871 as Glasgow Junction.

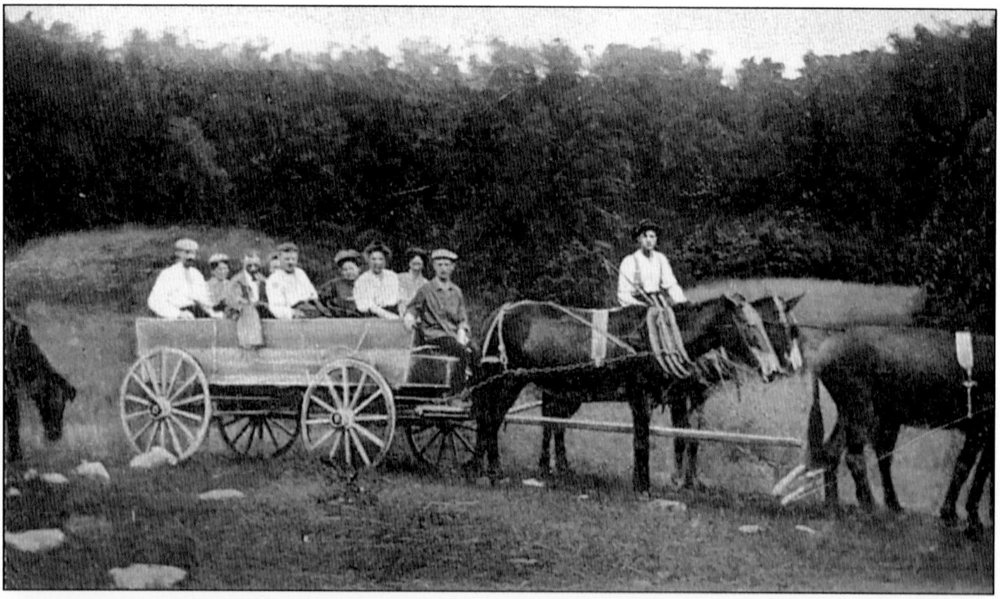

Cave Explorers Traveling to Colossal Cave, c. 1908. Cincinnati postcard publisher Albert Kraemer photographed this local tour guide sitting atop one of the mules pulling a wagon full of cave explorers as they pause during their travel from one cave to another. In the early 1900s, many groups of tourists and weekend spelunkers often traveled to, from, and between caves in the south central Kentucky area via horse and/or mule-drawn wagons.

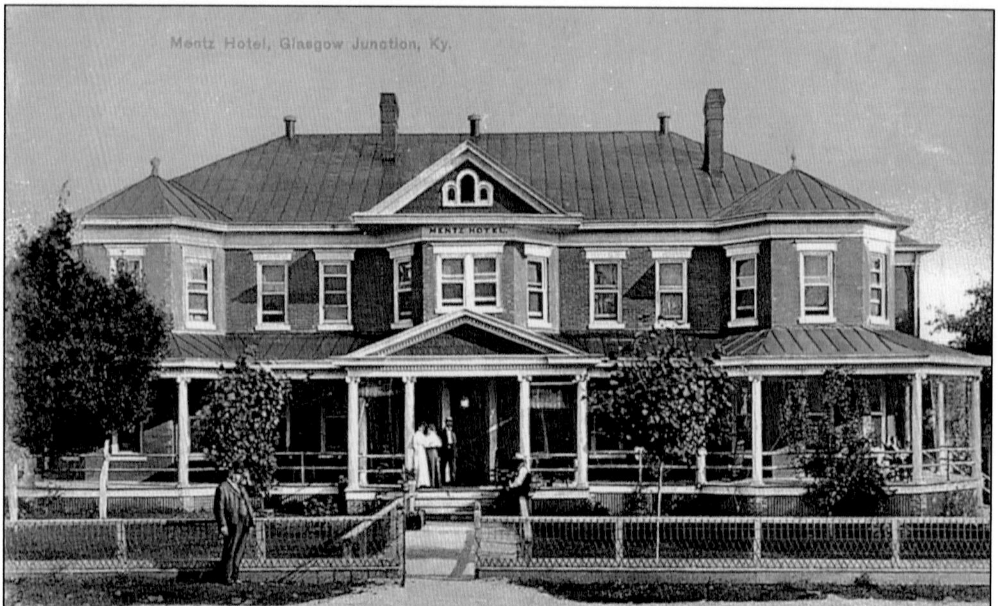

Mentz Hotel, Glasgow Junction, c. 1915. Opened in 1883, the Mentz Hotel was operated by Ed Mentz. An 1880s newspaper reported that "everything connected with the Mentz Hotel at Glasgow Junction is as neat as a pin and the table is always loaded with the best in the market." Mentz was the manager of the Mammoth Cave Railroad in 1898 when all of its assets were advertised to be sold in order to settle a $100,000 judgment.

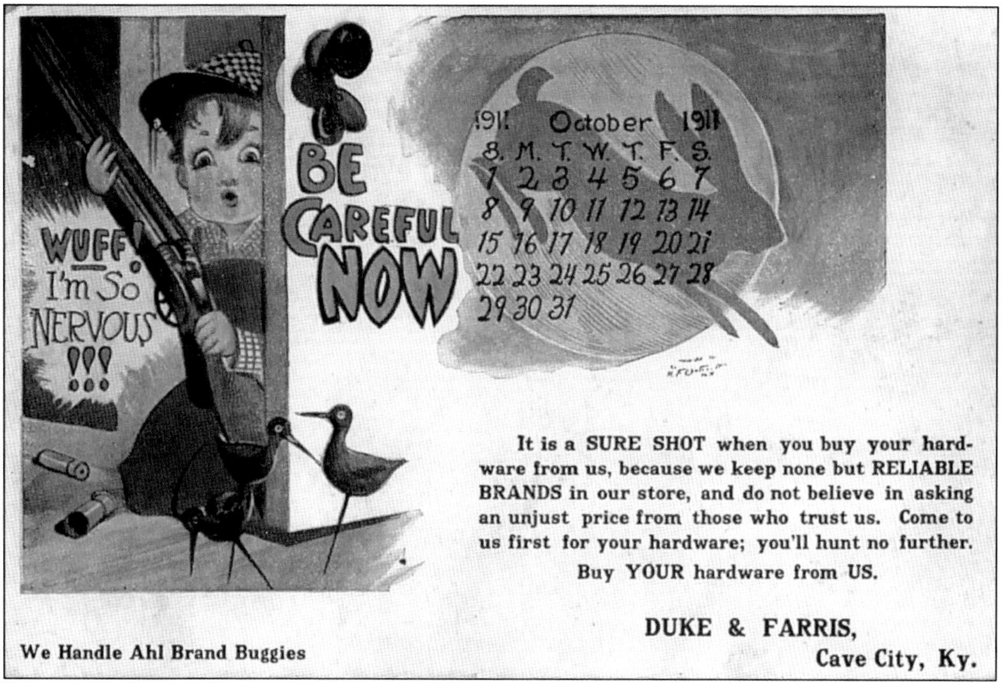

DUKE AND FARRIS ADVERTISEMENT, 1911. During the early 1900s, advertisers often displayed and described the virtues of their products on postcards that cost only 1¢ to mail. Advertising postcards such as the one above were typically used by store owners to invite potential patrons to their places of business. The printed message on the back of this 1911 calendar month Cave City postcard reads, "Our line of stoves are complete. Come to see us and let us show you."

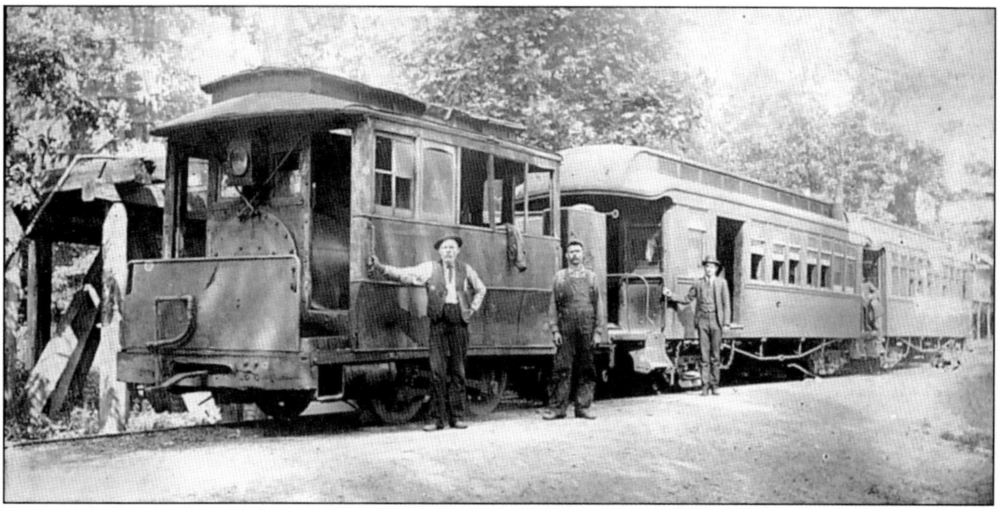

THE DINKEY TRAIN TO MAMMOTH CAVE, 1906. In 1886, an 8.7-mile connector line was constructed from the L&N main line at Glasgow Junction (Park City) to Mammoth Cave. Pictured is the dinkey train that was used on this line for many years to accommodate cave visitors. Although this short railroad line was privately owned, it was operated under L&N protection until September 1931, five years prior to the establishment of Mammoth Cave National Park. The handwritten message on the back stated simply, "The train that met the L&N and took us to Mammoth Cave."

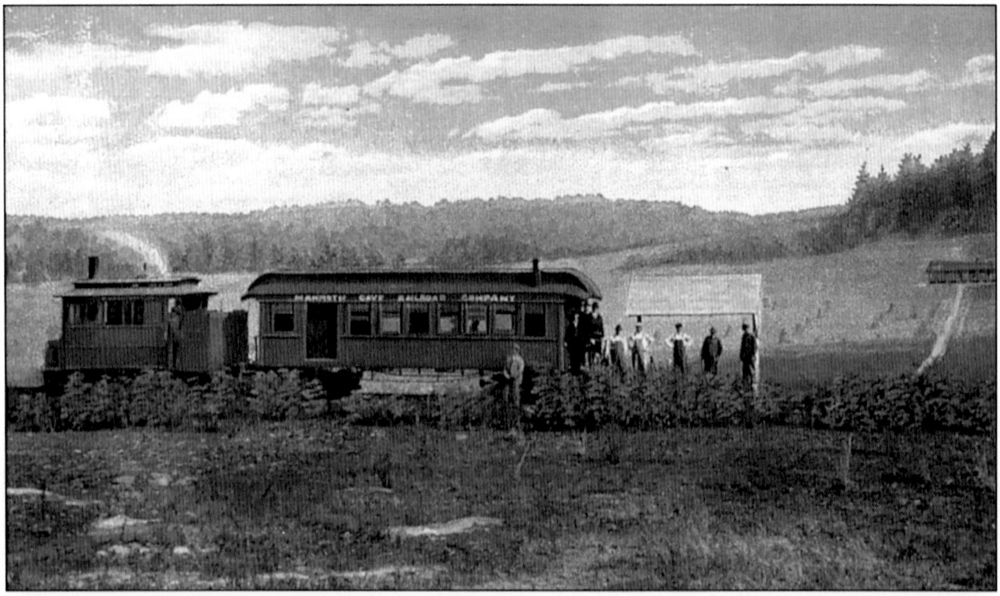

Diamond Caverns Railroad Depot, c. 1908. On July 3, 1886, workers began laying the Mammoth Cave railroad tracks a few hundred feet west of Diamond Caverns along the border between Barren and Edmonson Counties. The depot was constructed about one and a half miles north of Glasgow Junction. This early 1900s view shows passengers leaving the Mammoth Cave Railroad Company train to take the path to Diamond Caverns at right.

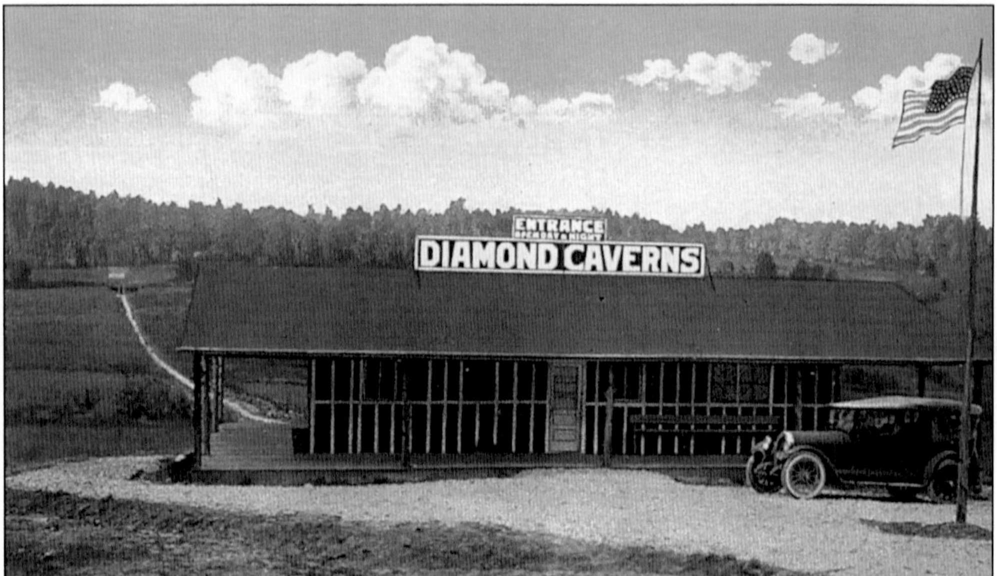

Diamond Caverns Office and Entrance, c. 1908. This view shows the building that houses the office and protects the cave entrance. The same path referred to in the top image can be seen at left leading back to the Diamond Caverns railroad depot. Diamond Caverns has been open to the public since 1859 when the first visitors thought sparkling calcite formations resembled diamonds, thus the name for the cave was born.

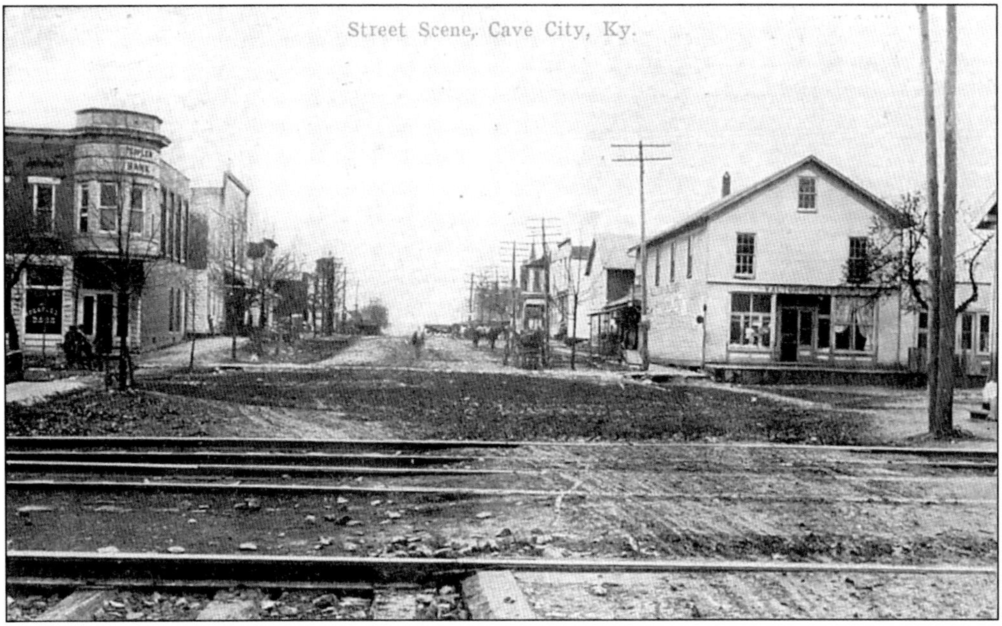

Street Scene, Cave City, 1918. This view looks east across three sets of railroad tracks and shows the Peoples Bank, organized in 1897, at left. S.D. Caldwell was president and R.F. Smith was cashier in 1917. Notorious criminal Tom Slaughter and a companion robbed the bank in 1920. Taking $8,500 in cash only, the pair locked Caldwell in the vault and rode off in a Ford Coupe. They were chased but not caught. The building still stands and houses a gun shop. The building on the right is Walton & Dickey, a general merchandise business, which later became Handy & Reynolds Store.

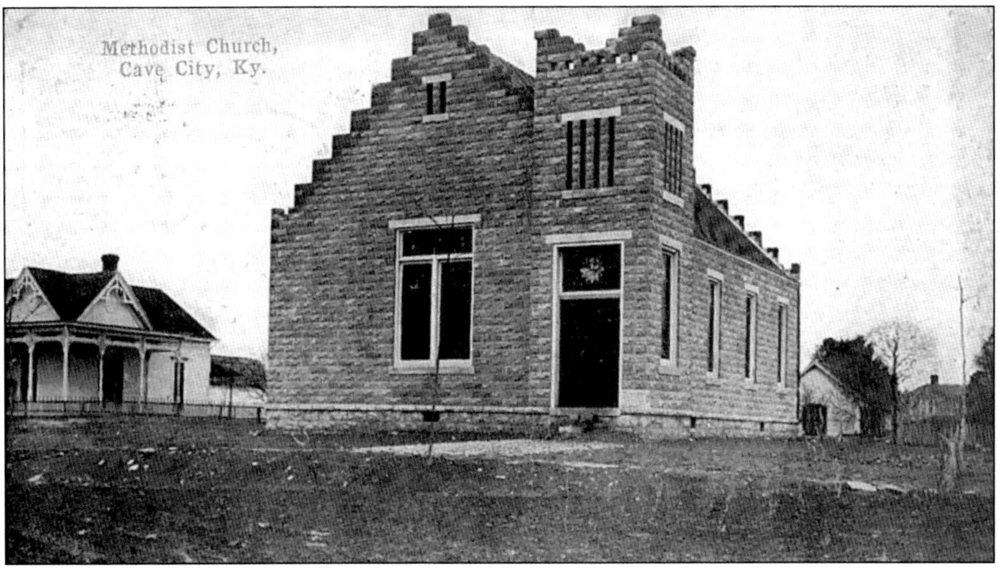

Cave City Methodist Church, c. 1908. The worshipers of this community used a "shared church" until it was destroyed by a big storm in 1870. They rebuilt a Union Church on the present site of Christ Church. The Methodist congregation sold their share of the church and built on land donated by the L&N Railroad Company. Under the leadership of Rev. Ed Goodson, funds were raised and the cornerstone was laid in 1906.

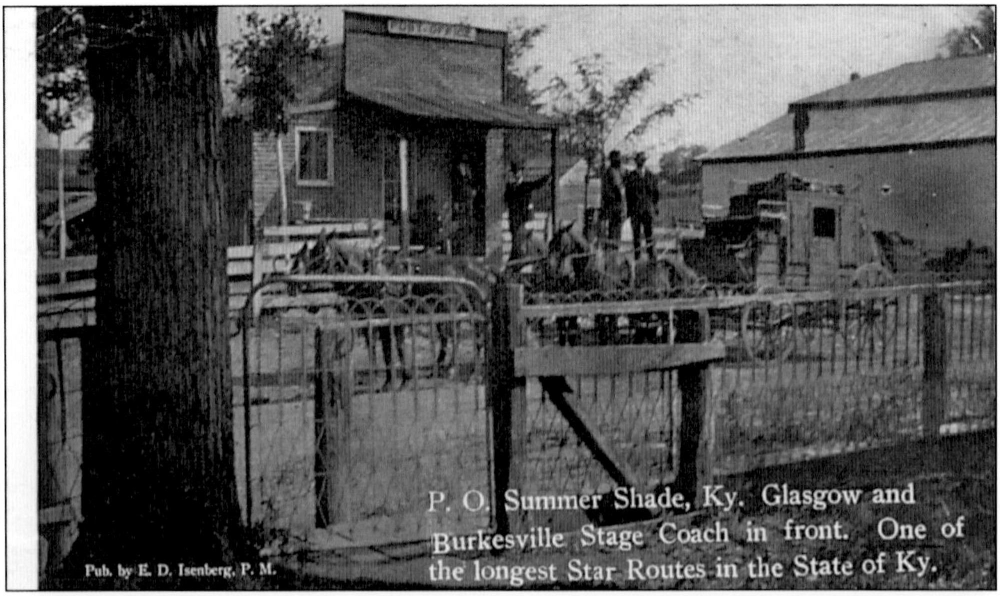

GLASGOW-TO-BURKESVILLE STAGE AT SUMMER SHADE, c. 1910. The Glasgow-to-Burkesville, four-horse stagecoach has stopped to pick up passengers and deliver the mail at Summer Shade in Metcalfe County. It took all day for the stagecoach to travel its 40-mile route and carry the mail to ten post offices along the line. The fare was 10¢ a mile or $4 for the entire distance. When the waters were high, an additional amount was charged.

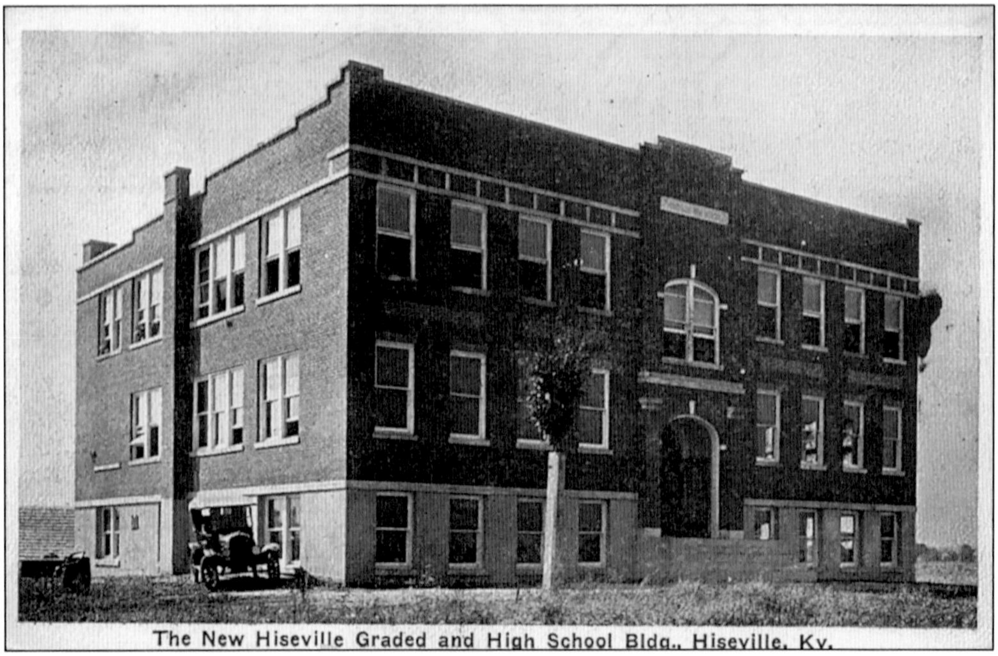

THE NEW HISEVILLE GRADED AND HIGH SCHOOL, c. 1924. The Hiseville Common School originally contained only four rooms. A four-year high school was added to the elementary school in 1924, when this building was constructed. As early as 1907, local parents solicited Prof. J.E. Hastand, principal of Summer Shade High School, to teach the fall term at Hiseville.

Three

Green County

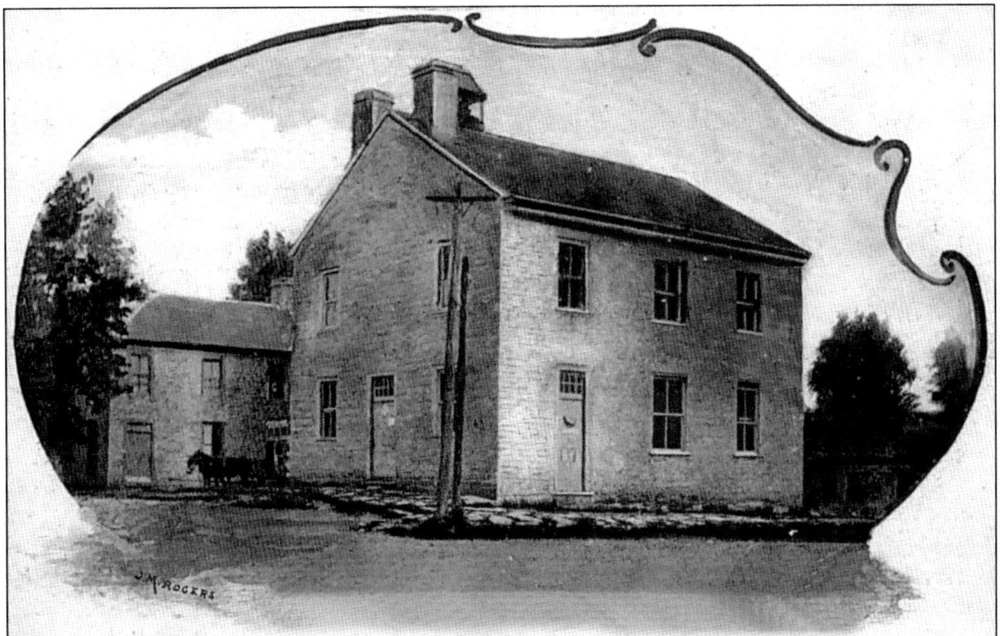

Oldest Kentucky Courthouse, c. 1909. Green County was the 16th county when it was formed in 1792 and named for Rev. Nathanael Greene. This courthouse was built in 1802–1804 by Thomas "Stonehammer" Metcalfe, the tenth governor of Kentucky (1828–1832), who later served as U.S. senator. The building was constructed of native limestone with 22-inch-thick walls and continued in use as a courthouse until 1932. Waller Bullock of Lexington is noted as the builder in charge of the construction. The total payment to Bullock was £918, the unit of money used at the time. Carpenters for the building were Edward J. Bullock and Daniel Lisle, and Robert Ball was the chief stonemason. The two-story, 34-by-40-foot structure had a courtroom on the first floor, with stairs to reach the gallery, and two jury rooms located on the second floor.

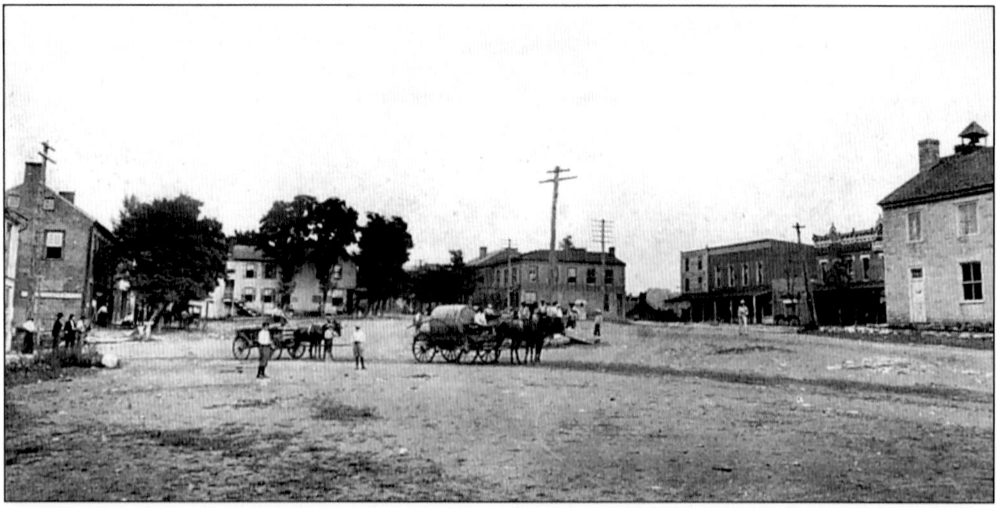

North Square and J.L. Wilson's Drugstore, *c.* 1907. The Green County Courthouse is pictured at right. The two buildings located beyond and to the left of the courthouse were destroyed by fire in 1936. The Pickett Hotel, center, was also destroyed by fire in later years. The J.L. Wilson Drugstore, located across Main Street from the Pickett Hotel, is the present location of Sam Moore's Law Office. Also in this building are several boarding rooms that can be partially seen behind the trees. Shrouded by the trees at left is the People's Bank next to the large building at far left. In the center foreground is a horse-drawn wagon carrying a hogshead of tobacco pressed into a huge barrel. Barely visible behind this wagon in the center are several people sitting and standing around a well that was used by animals for drinking purposes. Frank Cowherd, standing in the doorway at center in the image below, is the only person identified. Several small china dolls are on display in the left window.

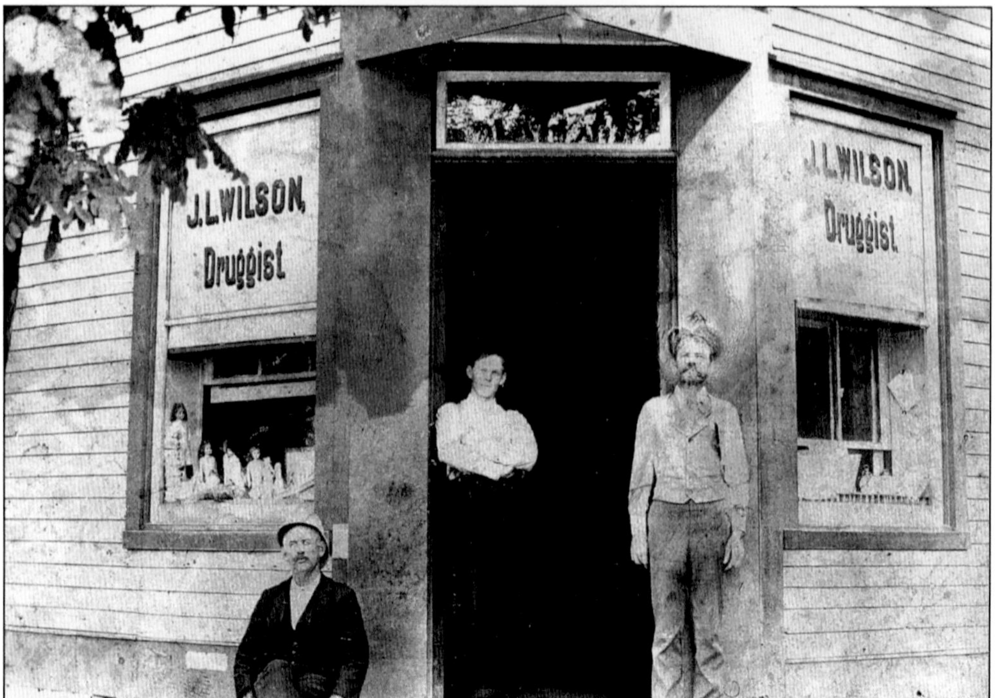

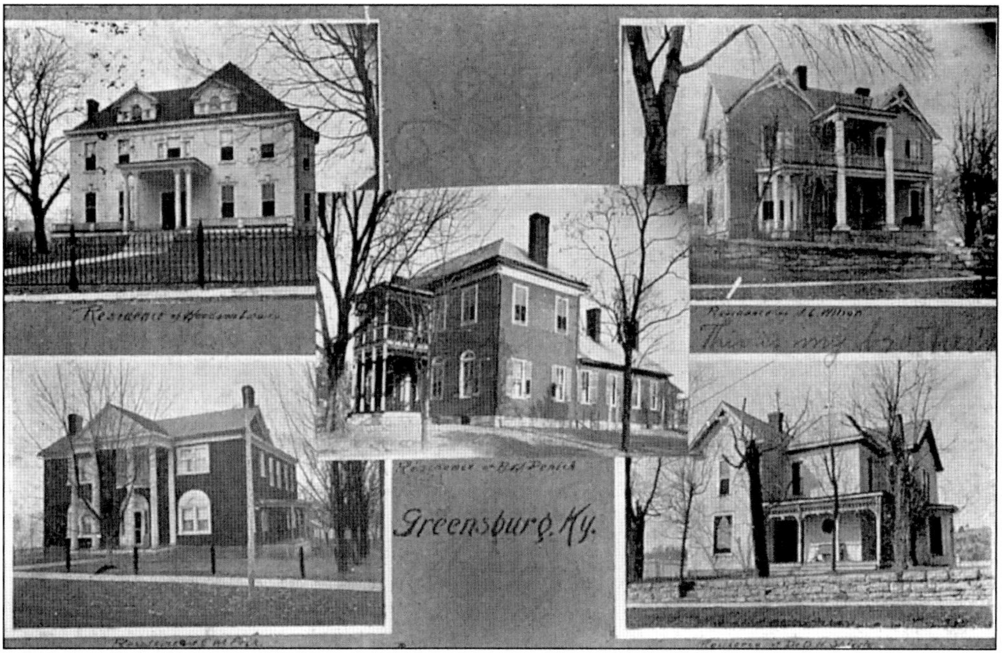

GREENSBURG MANSIONS, *c.* 1914. Built by James Marshall in 1904, the Woodson Lewis residence (upper left) on the corner of North Main Street still stands today. It is in excellent condition, but the iron fence has been removed. The Federal-style house (lower left) on East Columbia Avenue was built for Elijah Creel in the 1820s. Also known as the Pendleton house, it was the residence of C.W. Peck in 1914 and is still in existence today. The house in the center was first occupied by the Richard Taylor family, then the James Louis Howell family, and then the Benjamin Penick family. Dismantled many years ago, it was located on Depot Street across Goose Creek Valley. During the early 1900s, the house located in the upper right was the J.L. Wilson residence, and the home beneath it was the residence of Dr. O.H. Shively, both of which are no longer standing.

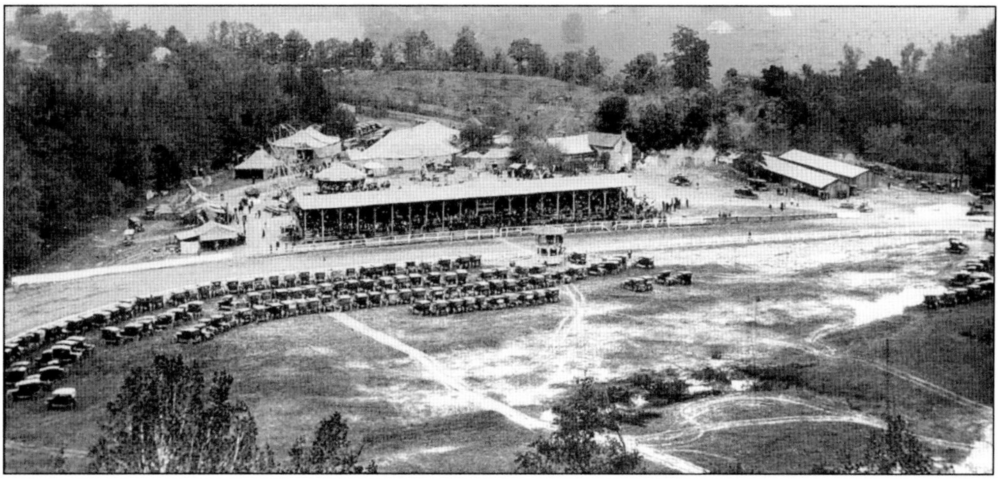

GREEN COUNTY FAIR, *c.* 1921. Taken from a tall bluff on the south side of Green River, this photograph of the Green County fairgrounds reveals the grandstand, which was built about 1919; horse track; and various attractions. This was the second location of the fairgrounds and is the present site of the American Legion Park.

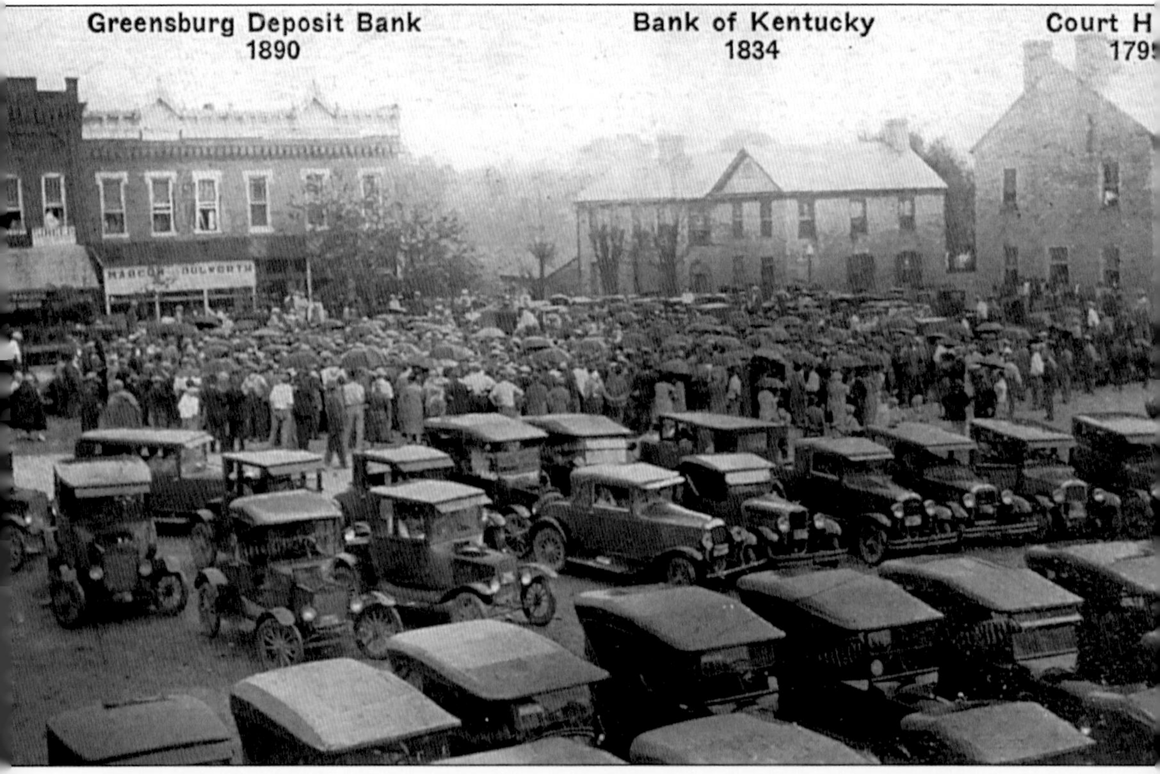

"Cow Day," c. 1930. The first Cow Day is believed to have occurred in Greensburg during the Great Depression. It was begun by local merchants to entice people out in the county to come to town to spend their money. The primary attraction was that merchants gave away a cow to a lucky person whose name was drawn as the winner. The Marcum and Dulworth Store, located in the building that housed the Greensburg Deposit Bank, appears to be the center of attention in this image. It also appears from the large attendance that the rainy weather did not dampen the crowd's enthusiasm. The building next to the courthouse housed the Bank of Kentucky in the right portion, and the Allen Inn, built in 1808, occupied the remaining portion of this building. Andrew Jackson is believed to have spent the night there in 1828. Next door is the Henry Durham Hardware Store, which began operating in 1920. The 1799 date above the courthouse is erroneous as the building was actually constructed between 1802 and 1804. This entire block was destroyed by fire in 1935.

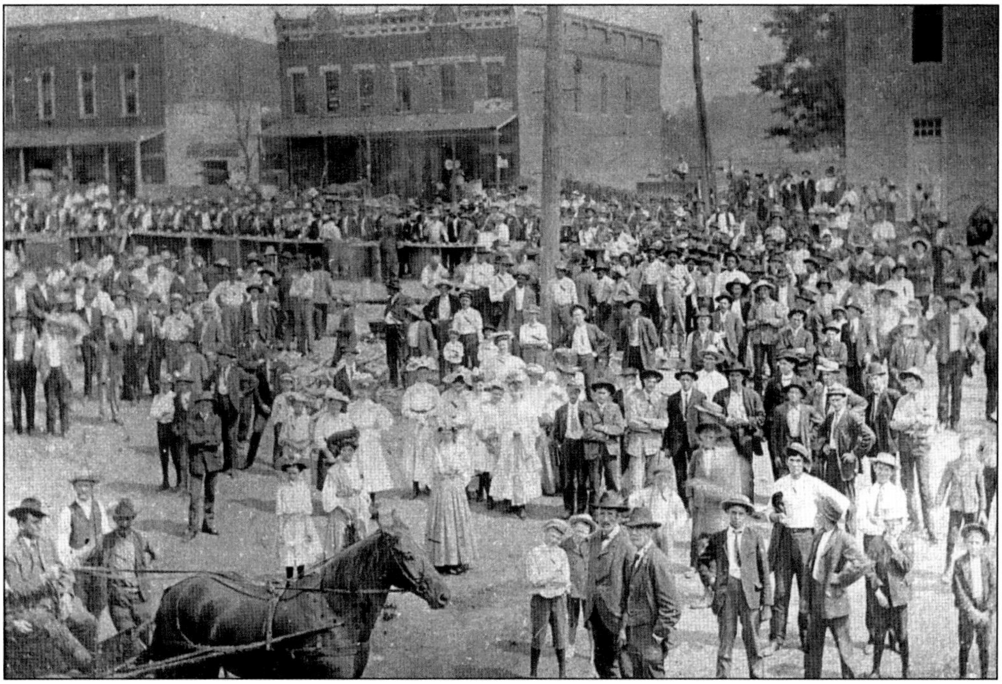

PUBLIC SQUARE, *c.* 1900. Men, women, and children wearing their Sunday finest have stopped to pose for the photographer on the east side of the public square in Greensburg. The two-story brick building in the background was occupied by the Greensburg Deposit Bank on the left and a dry goods store on the right, which was operated by W.W. Mitchell. Later, Lucian Durham had a dry goods store in the same location. The small white frame building to the left of the bank once housed a shoe store run by Arthur Miller. The old courthouse is partially shown at right.

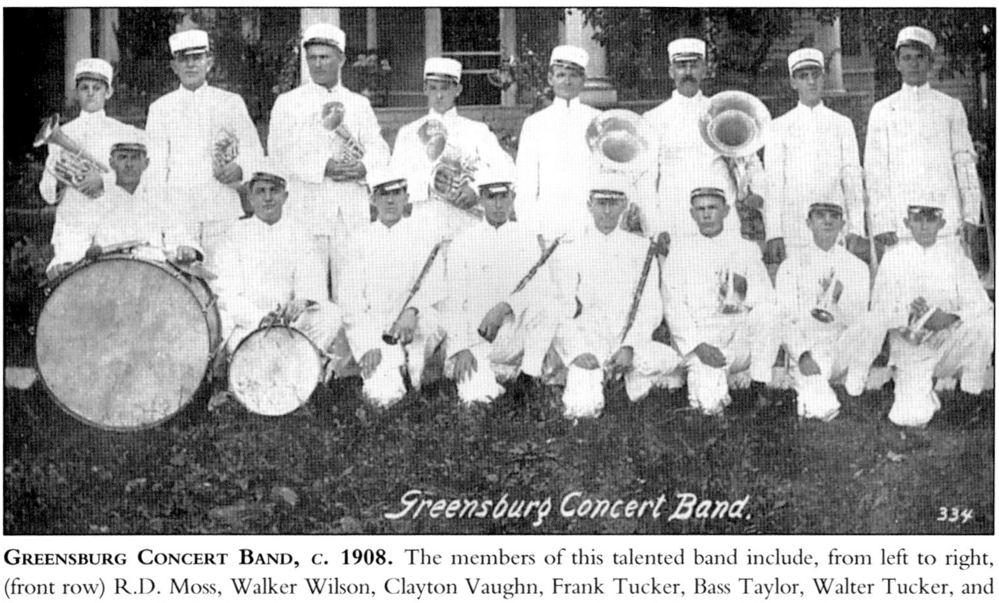

GREENSBURG CONCERT BAND, *c.* 1908. The members of this talented band include, from left to right, (front row) R.D. Moss, Walker Wilson, Clayton Vaughn, Frank Tucker, Bass Taylor, Walter Tucker, and Ammon Hancock; (back row) Otis Moss, J.L. Wilson, J.L. Durham, Billy Sandidge, Bob Buchanan, Dr. ? Helm, Rollin Perkins, and Richard Hagan.

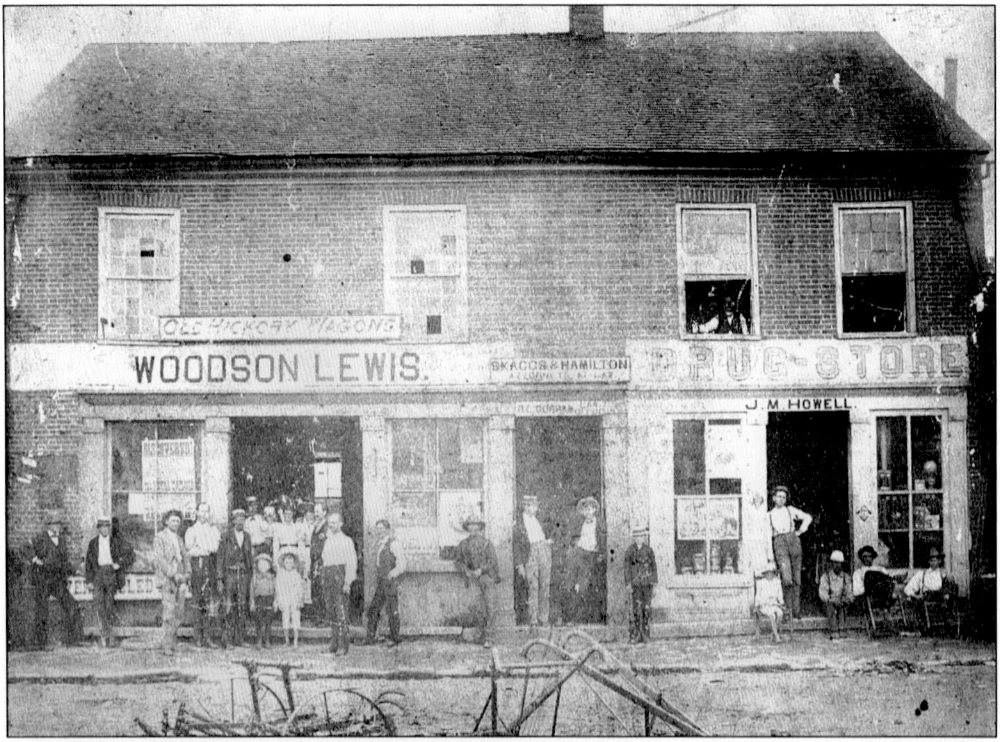

Business Enterprises, c. 1900. Local Green Countians pose for this picture in front of the following businesses, identified from left to right: Woodson Lewis Store, Skaggs and Hamilton Law Offices, R.L. Durham Law Office, and J.M. Howell Drug Store. Various farm implements are visible in the foreground.

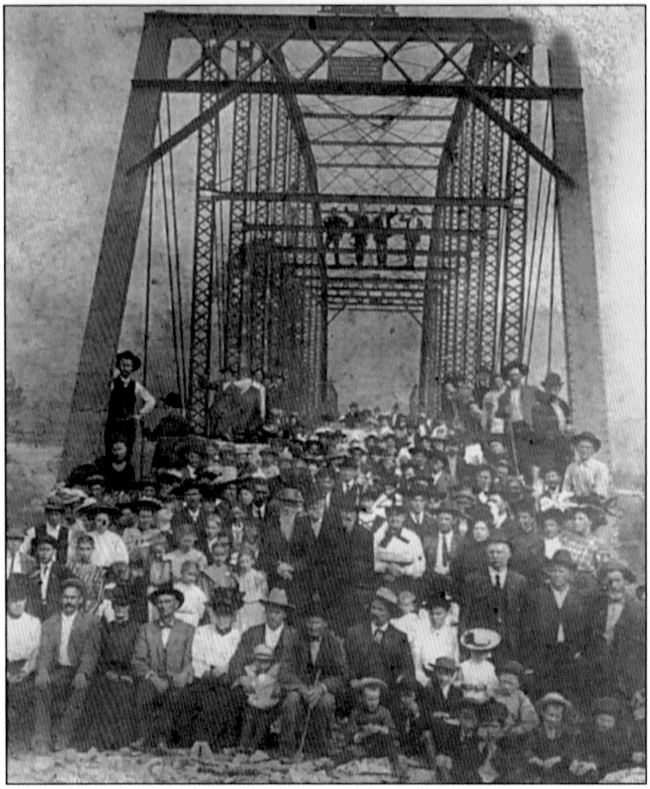

Berry's Bridge, c. 1900. Local citizens proudly pose for this picture at the dedication of Berry's Bridge. Located about two miles south of Greensburg, this bridge crossed Green River and replaced the local ferry that had served the community for many years.

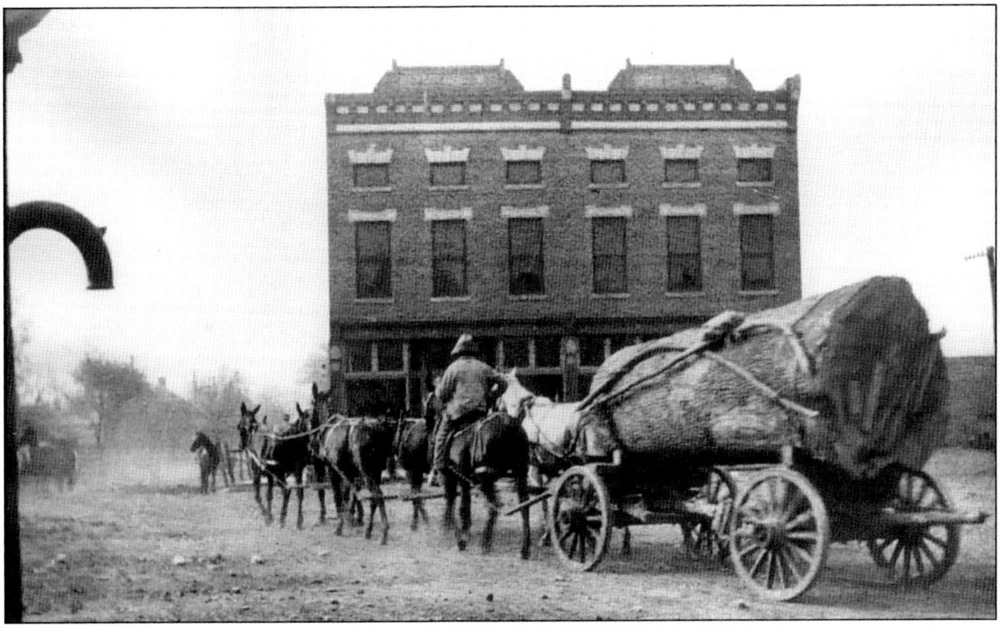

Hauling Log on Horse-Drawn Wagon, c. 1907. This massive log is being hauled by a six-mule team through Greensburg in front of the Woodson Lewis building, which was constructed in 1900. A well spout is visible in the foreground along the left side of the image. This photograph, looking south on the square, was taken near the pump and water trough near Main Street.

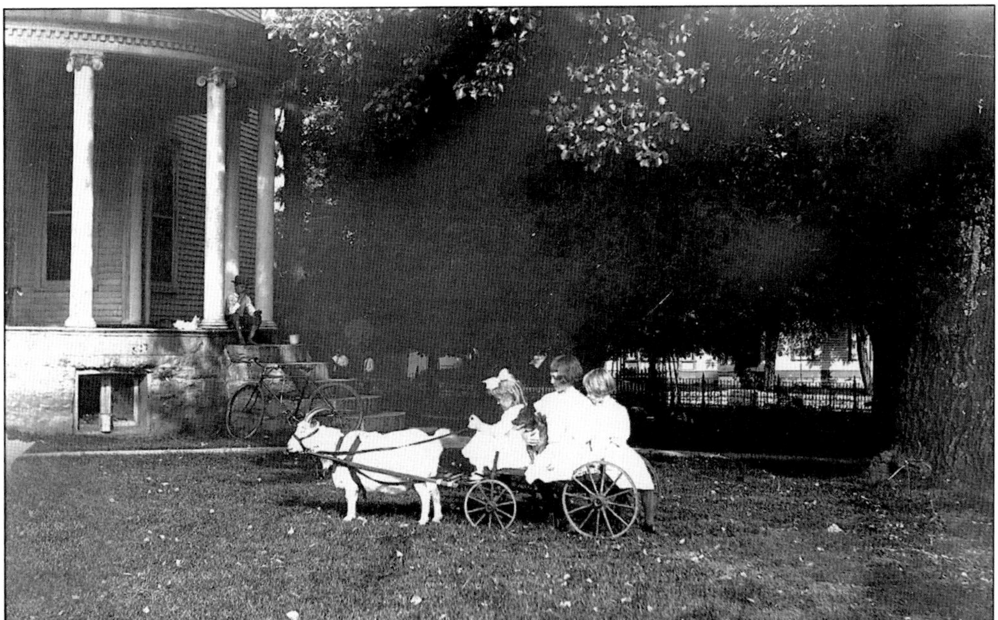

Goat-Drawn Wagon at Woodson Lewis Residence, c. 1910. Pictured in the yard of their North Main Street home and seated in a wagon are Minnie Bremmell Lewis and Hortense Lewis, the children of Woodson Lewis, together with a friend. J.W. Miller, a popular Lebanon, Kentucky photographer, made this real photo picture.

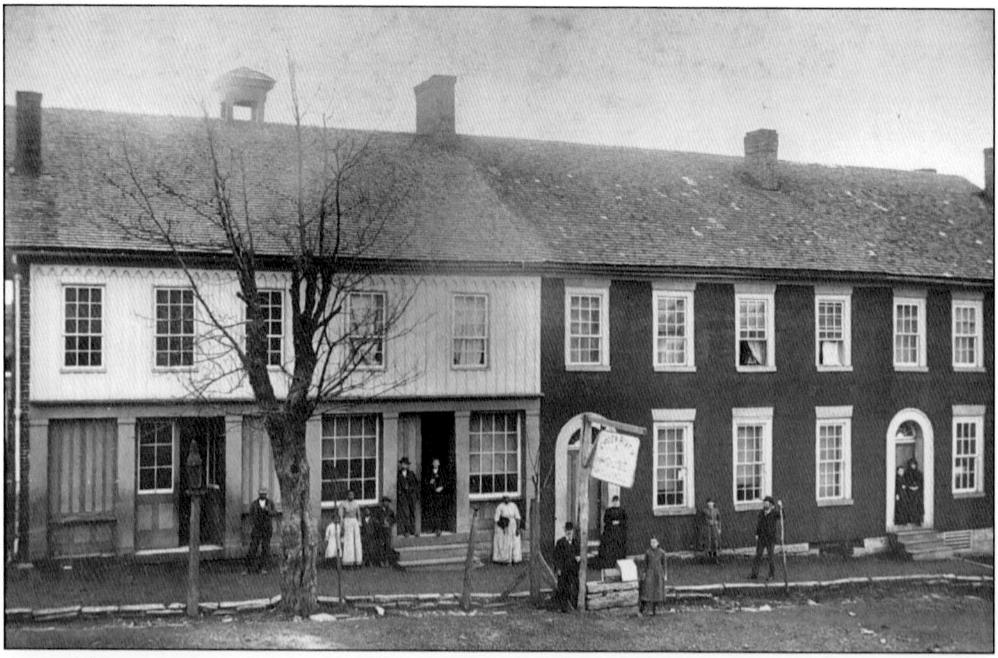

Green River Hotel, c. 1915. Located on South Main Street, the brick building at right was the Green River Hotel, also known as the Howell Hotel. The hotel and adjoining restaurant were managed and operated by Rose Howell for many years. The left portion of the frame building contained a general merchandise business run by Joe Strull. Note the street lantern next to the tree at left.

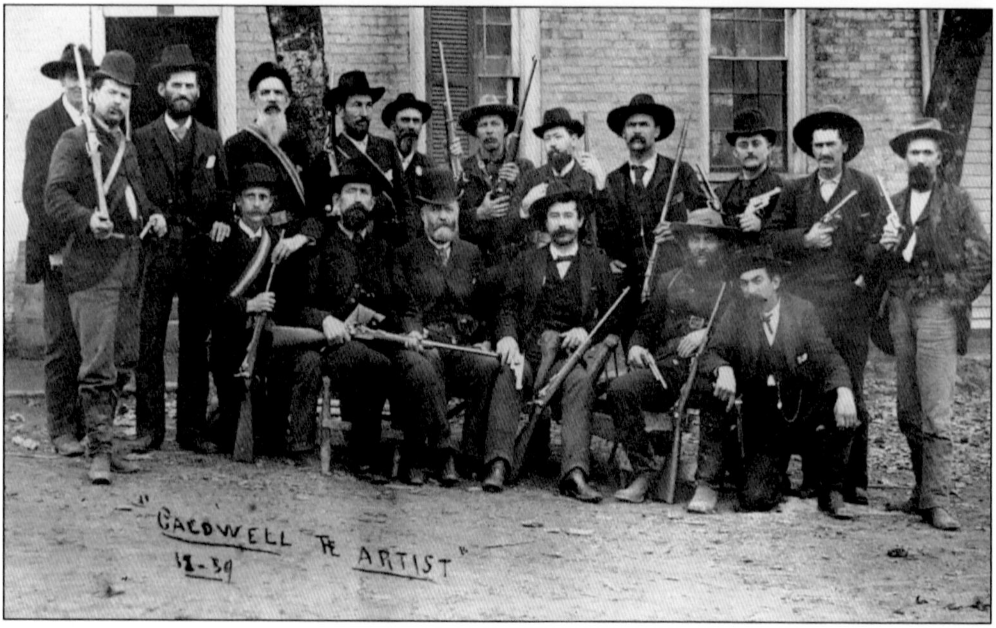

Reunion of Civil War Union Soldiers, c. 1900. These veterans of the Civil War are shown proudly displaying the weapons of their choice as they pose on the square in Greensburg. For many years, Civil War veterans from both the North and South met on an annual basis at a Chautauqua or local fairground to tell tales and renew past experiences of the Great Rebellion.

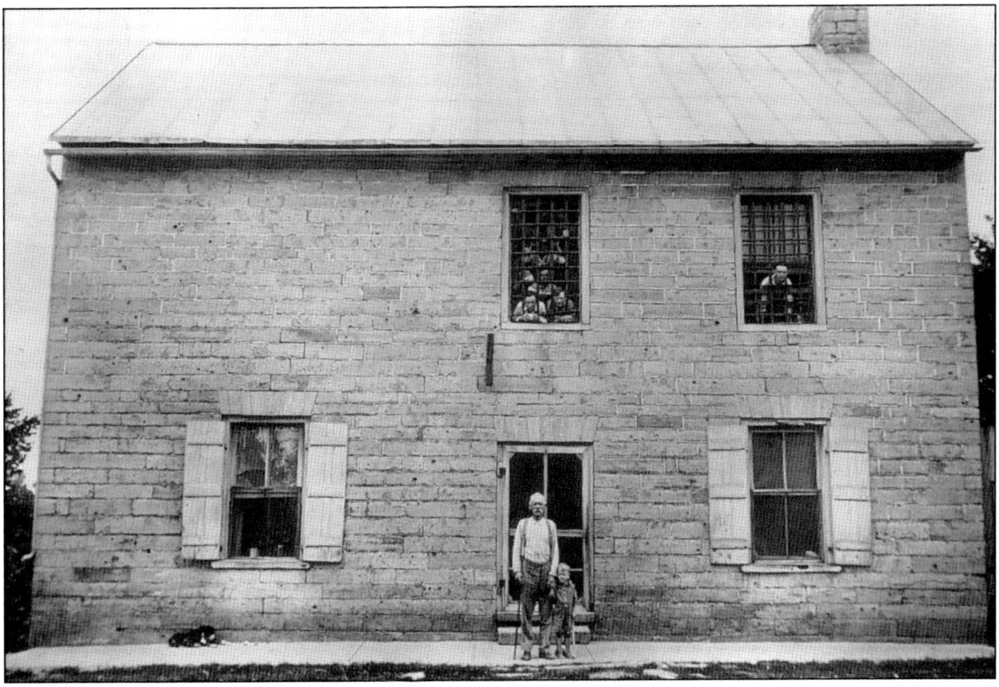

Green County Jail, c. 1910. This old, stone jail, built in 1799 by Henry Embry, stood on the site of the present courthouse on Court Street. The jail cost £200 to build and had a dungeon and debtor's room. Jailer Dick Coffey is the man standing with the unidentified young boy. This building was destroyed by fire on December 17, 1930.

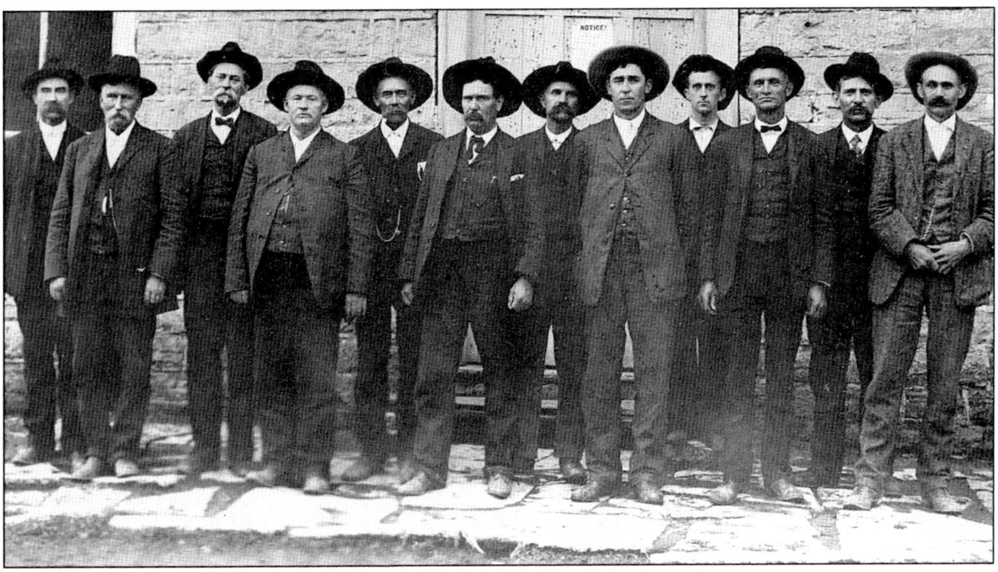

Green County Officials, c. 1905. Posing in front of the old courthouse are the following 12 men, from left to right: Edd Perkins, tax collector; Judge Green Howell; Larkin McGinnis, tax collector; Elliott Graham, county judge; Bill Jones, tax collector; Ed Lewis Chaudoin, magistrate; Rufus Burress, magistrate; Showdy Rhea, magistrate; Vernon Coffee, magistrate; George Durrett, magistrate; Perry Marshall, county clerk; and Dick Coffee, jailor.

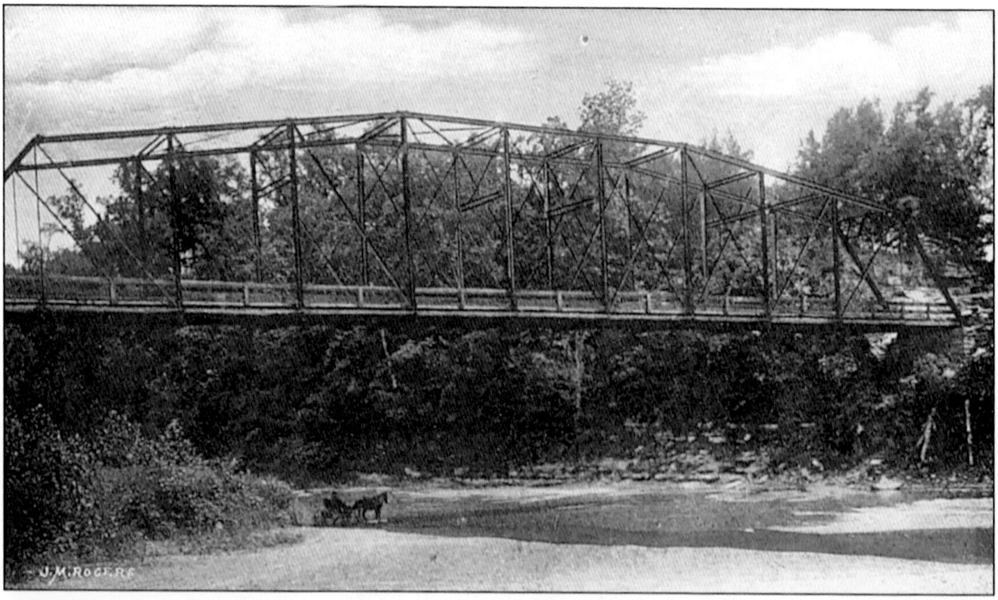

Bridge across Green River, c. 1915. This metal bridge was manufactured by the Vincennes Bridge Company and built in 1913 at a cost of $10,500. It was a triple-span structure with cylindrical metal supports and was the largest of the metal truss bridges in Green County before its collapse. A concrete bridge, which still stands today, replaced it in the early 1950s.

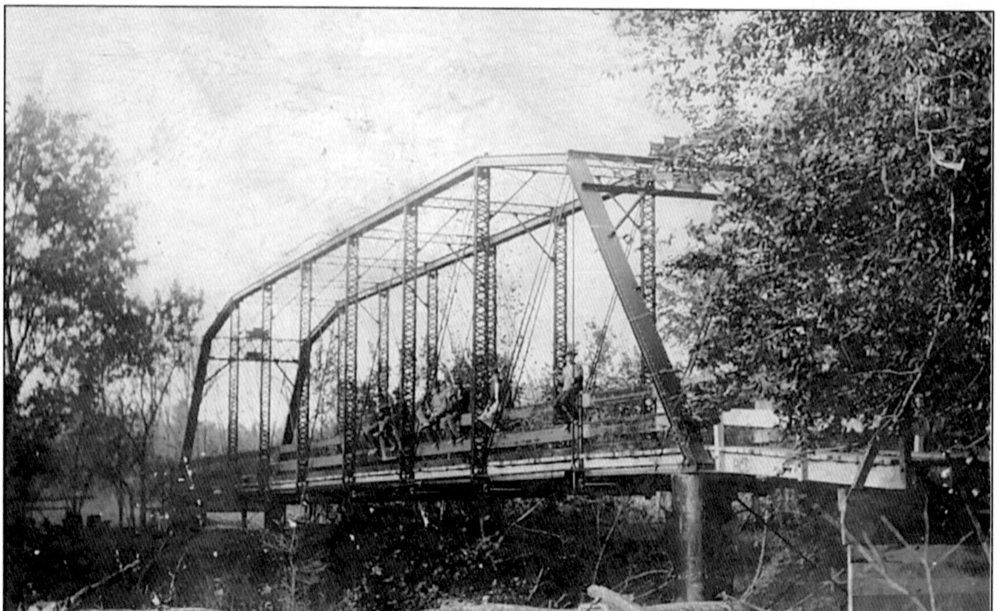

Bridge across Little Barren Creek, c. 1908. Six men are pictured in this real photo image of a steel bridge located about ten miles from Greensburg. Although it no longer stands, this bridge is typical of many of the small bridges that spanned the rivers and creeks of rural areas in south central Kentucky.

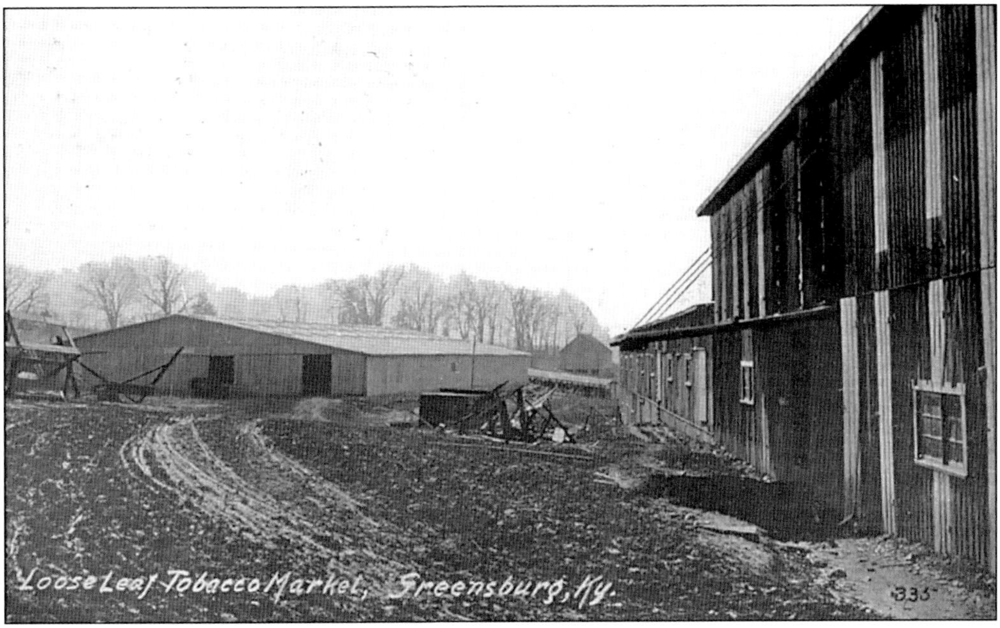

LOOSE-LEAF TOBACCO MARKET, EXTERIOR AND INTERIOR VIEWS, C. 1914. Practically all farmers throughout south central Kentucky raised tobacco each year as their primary cash crop. In the late 1800s, they stripped their tobacco and then took it to a large barn after it had been cured where it was compressed into hogsheads that weighed 750 to 1,000 pounds. The hogsheads were then shipped to Louisville or some other city for sale. By the early 1900s, this method of sale was replaced by loose-leaf tobacco auctions in Greensburg and other central Kentucky towns. The tobacco sales floor is in the building at left and the prize room is in the building at right. Pictured below are many of the buyers and sellers in the floor area during sale season. These warehouses were situated on the property where Greensburg Manufacturing Company is located on North Depot Street.

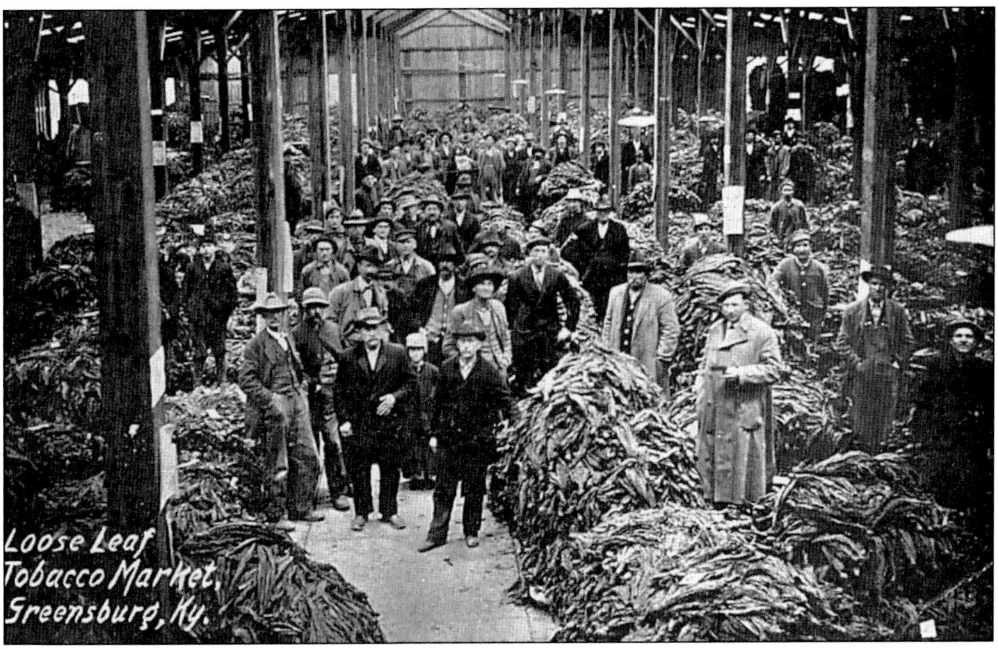

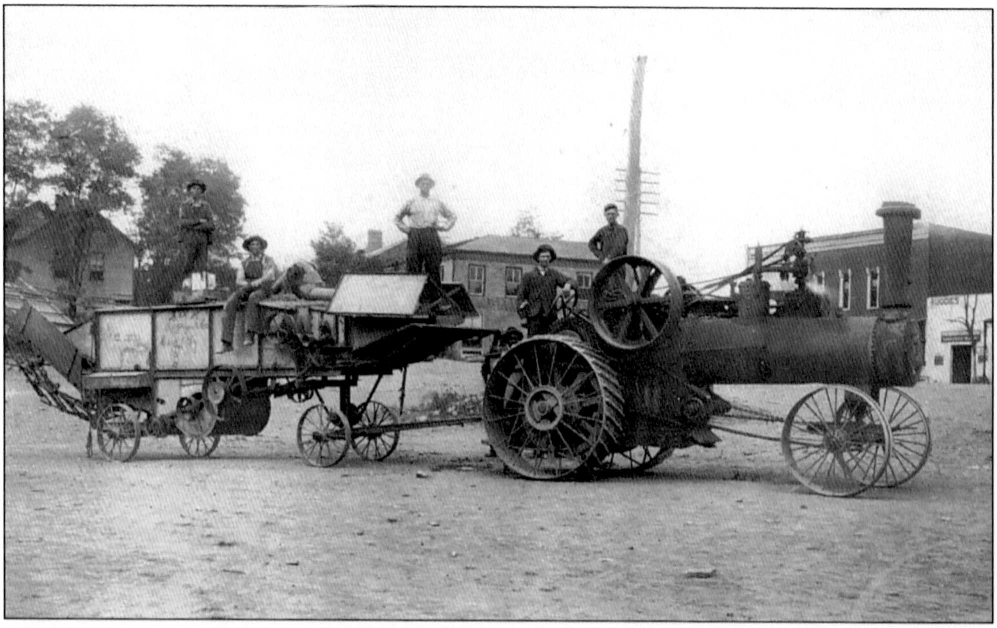

Steam Engine and Threshing Machinery, c. 1910. The men posing for this picture are ready to begin a day's work on a nearby farm in Green County. This image of Greensburg's Public Square reveals the northeast corner of the town in the background. A livery stable that housed and sold buggies is pictured at right.

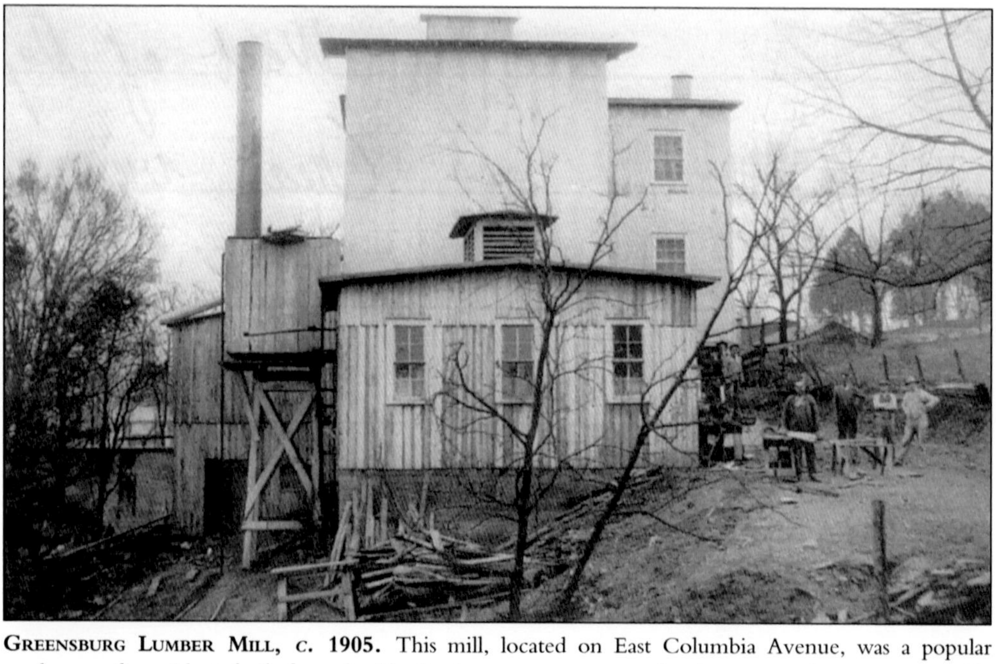

Greensburg Lumber Mill, c. 1905. This mill, located on East Columbia Avenue, was a popular rendezvous for residents both far and wide. In almost every community there existed one or more mills to which the most promising logs were hauled. Coarse rough lumber that was sawed was used in building houses, barns, and fences. Yellow poplar was the area's distinctive and most popular timber, as it was easily worked and relatively light.

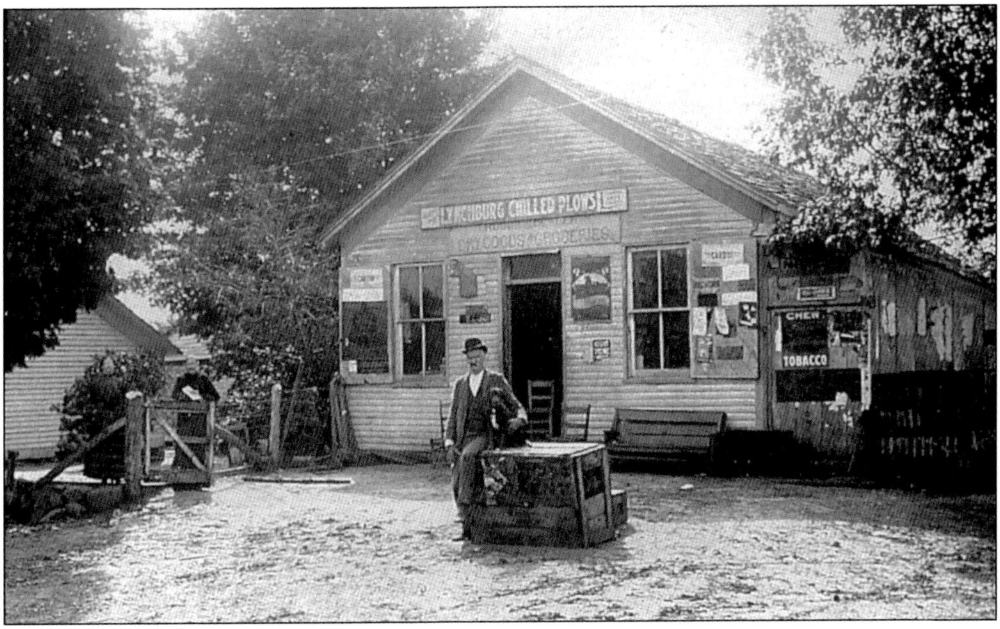

HUDGINS COUNTRY STORE, *C.* 1904. Located on Highway 569 about one mile from the Hart County line, this store was owned and operated by Richard Hudgins, the founder of the town of Hudgins. He holds his dog in this image while his wife, Lucy Close Hudgins, and an unidentified lady, stand by the gate at left. The words "Hudgins, Dealer in Dry Goods and Groceries" appear below the "Lynchburg Chilled Plows" sign. A wide variety of goods were sold at stores such as this one throughout central Kentucky. The country store was a place where adults could congregate, girls could buy calico dresses and cologne, and boys could purchase a baseball glove or their first bicycle. The days of playing checkers, ordering lunch at the meat counter, and relaxing with friends around the pot-belly stove are now gone. This small Green County town had a post office from 1883 to 1958.

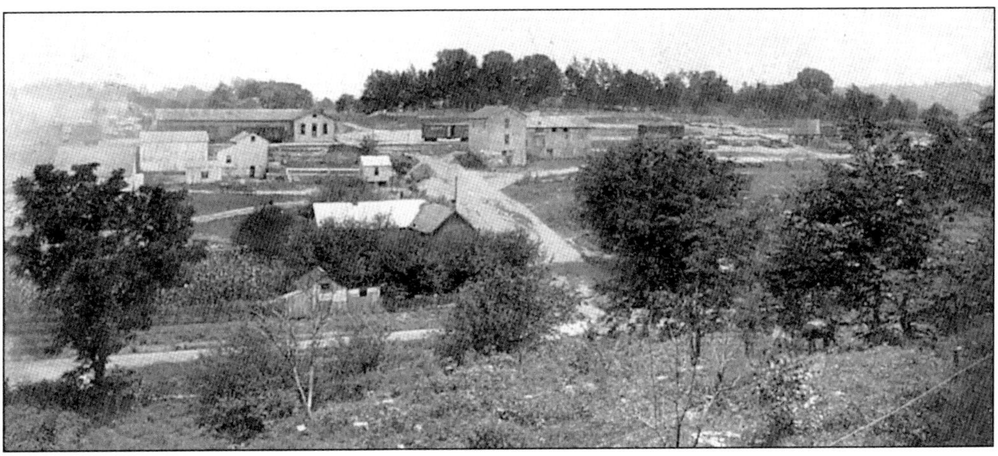

L&N STATION, *C.* 1908. Many attempts were made to bring a railroad to Greensburg before a successful bond issue encouraged the Cumberland and Ohio Railroad Company to complete a line to the town in 1879. Because the rails ended at Greensburg and did not go through Green County as promised, the county refused to pay the bond funds. The sheriff resigned in 1879 due to the controversy, and it was 42 years later, after a compromise was met with the railroad company, that Green County again had a sheriff. The depot was built in 1913 by the L&N Railroad, which had acquired the line.

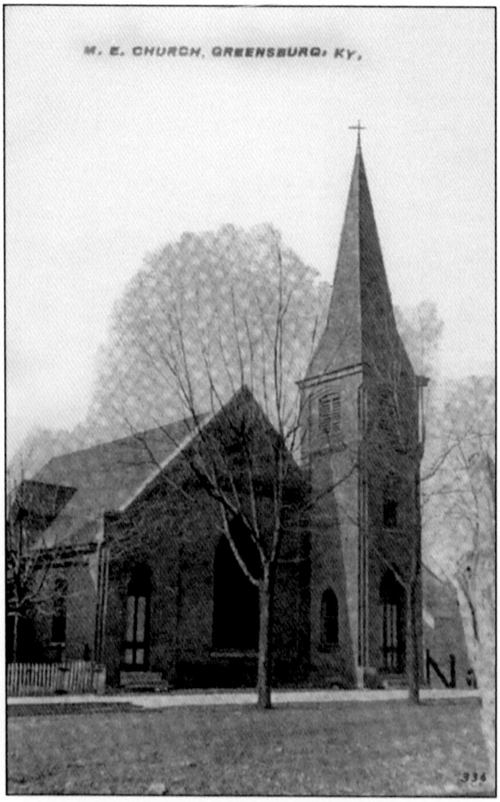

METHODIST EPISCOPAL CHURCH, *c.* 1915. The first Green County M.E. Church was established in 1830, at which time a lot was purchased and construction began. The building was replaced on the same site in 1893 by the church in this image. It remained a Methodist Episcopal church until 1938. A Methodist church building, which still stands, was erected at this location in 1938.

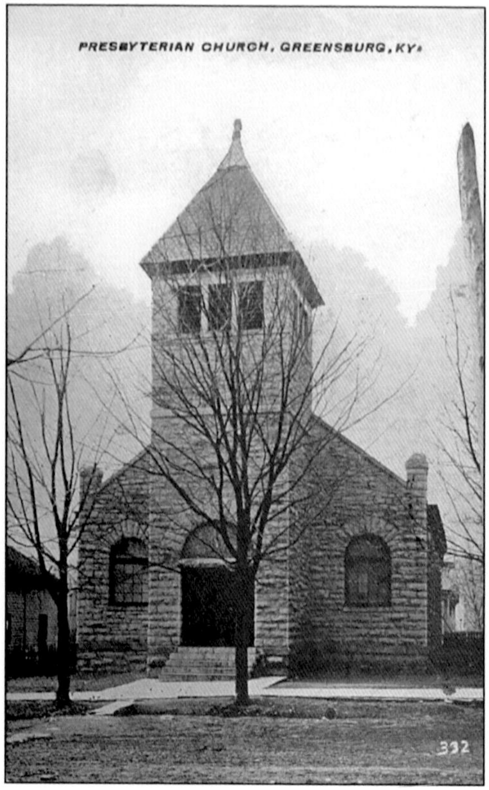

PRESBYTERIAN CHURCH, *c.* 1913. The first Green County Presbyterian Church was established in 1808 after Presbyterians in the Green County area requested a preacher from the Transylvania Presbytery in 1795. Chartered in 1821 by the Reverend David Rice, who is known as the "Father of Presbyterians in Kentucky," the church met in the meetinghouse and in the courthouse. After their first church was built on this site in 1829, they met regularly until about 1840. The congregation then met sporadically until the 1870s. The limestone church pictured here was a gift from John G. Barret in memory of his parents, John Barret and Mary Barret, and was built in 1890.

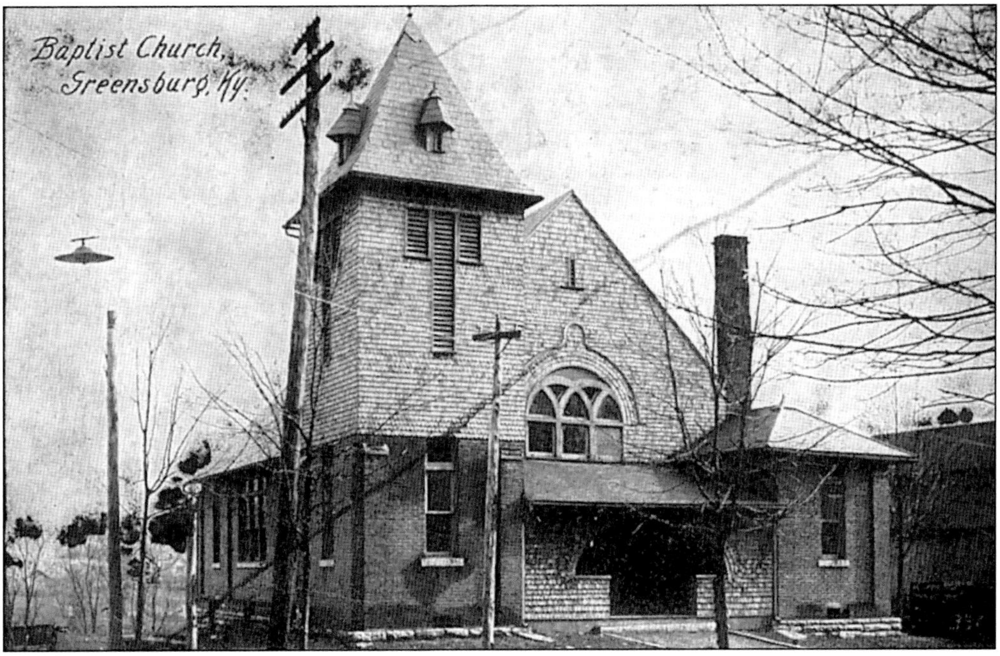

BAPTIST CHURCH, C. 1922. Designed by architect W.A. Crain of St. Louis, this building was erected in 1899 at a cost of $3,700. Since the first church was constructed about 1820, the Baptists have utilized four buildings in Greensburg since their 1820 beginnings. Located across the street from the Greensburg Presbyterian Church, this building was remodeled in 1930 at a cost of $6,500. It was later dismantled and replaced by a new structure in the 1950s.

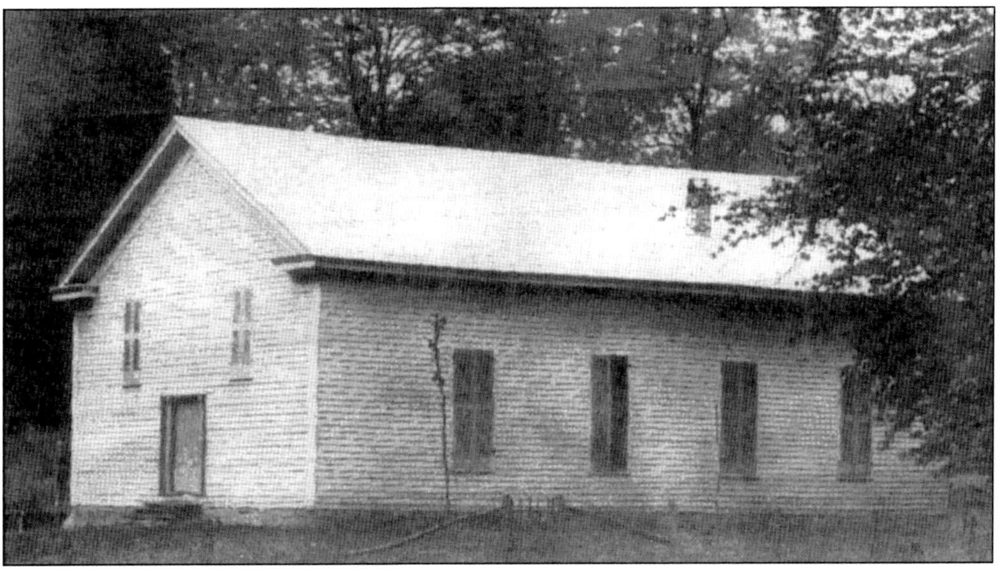

EBENEZER PRESBYTERIAN CHURCH, C. 1906. Residents of Gresham and Pike View comprised most of the membership of this church, located about five miles south of Greensburg. Prior to 1865, slaves owned by church members sat in the second-floor balcony that opened toward the sanctuary. Instead of the weather-boarding exterior, the church now has vinyl siding, a porch in the front, and a Sunday school in the rear. Organized in 1799, the original church was located about one mile west of this site.

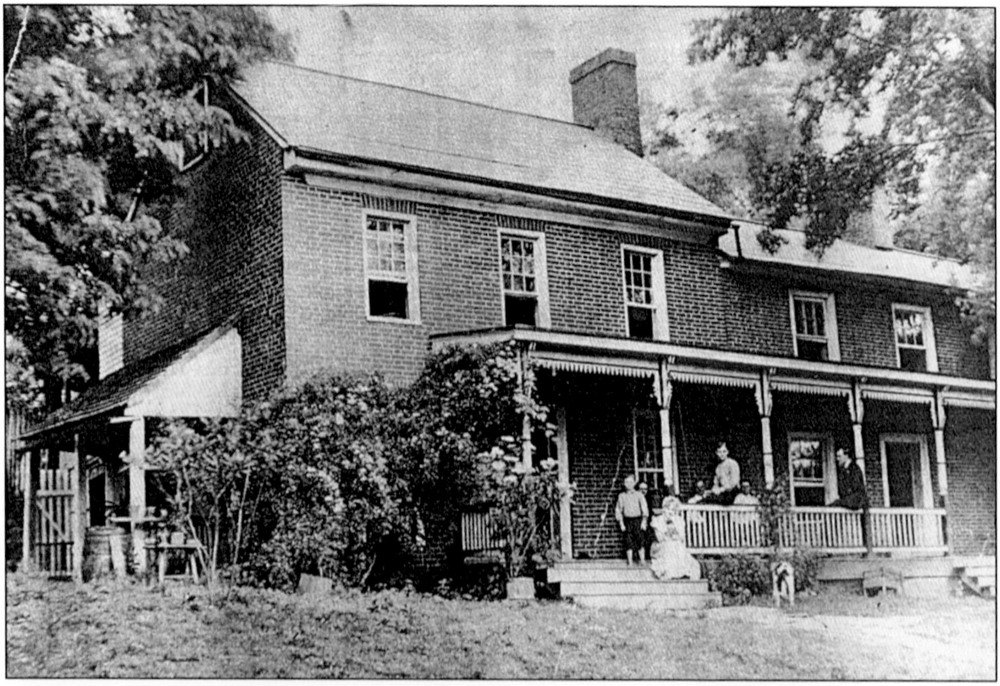

Greensburg Academy, c. 1910. Considered to be one of Greensburg's oldest buildings, the Greensburg Academy was constructed about 1817. It was used as a school where classes were taught by Mentor Graham from 1818 to 1823. This historic house, located at 101 South Second Street, was restored in the 1970s as a private home and, more recently, as a bed and breakfast owned by George Gagnon and Dottie Gagnon.

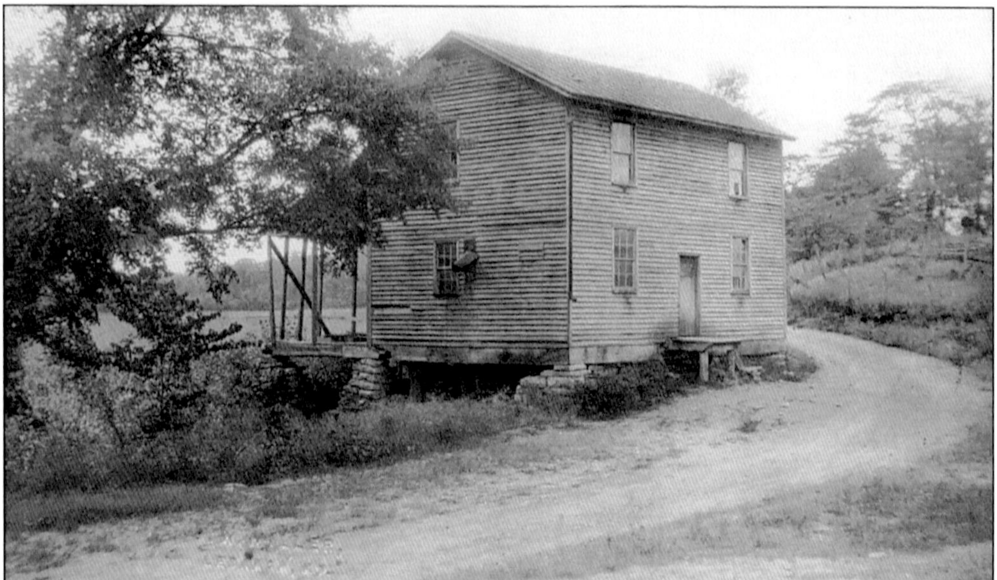

Montgomery's Mill, c. 1915. This mill is located at the narrows of Pitman Creek on land adjoining the original Pitman's Station Tract. A milling operation had originally begun at or near this location in the 1820s. This building was constructed in the late 1800s and ceased operation about 1930.

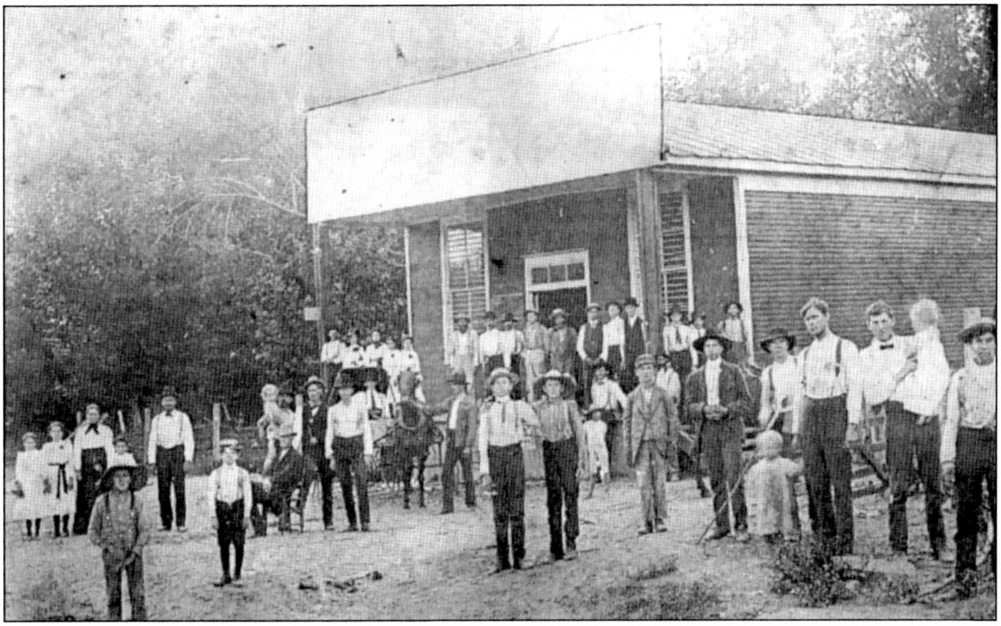

Hubbard and Mitchell Store, c. 1902. This store was located in Liletown, about ten miles south of Greensburg. It was one of the most active little communities during Green County's early years and was one of the first towns in Kentucky to have electricity. A nearby dammed-up stream with a water wheel created the electricity. A local resident owned a large portion of the creek, which included the water wheel, and sold electricity to nearby residents. At a certain time each night he would stop the wheel from turning, effectively turning off the electricity throughout the community and leaving the residents powerless to continue their activities.

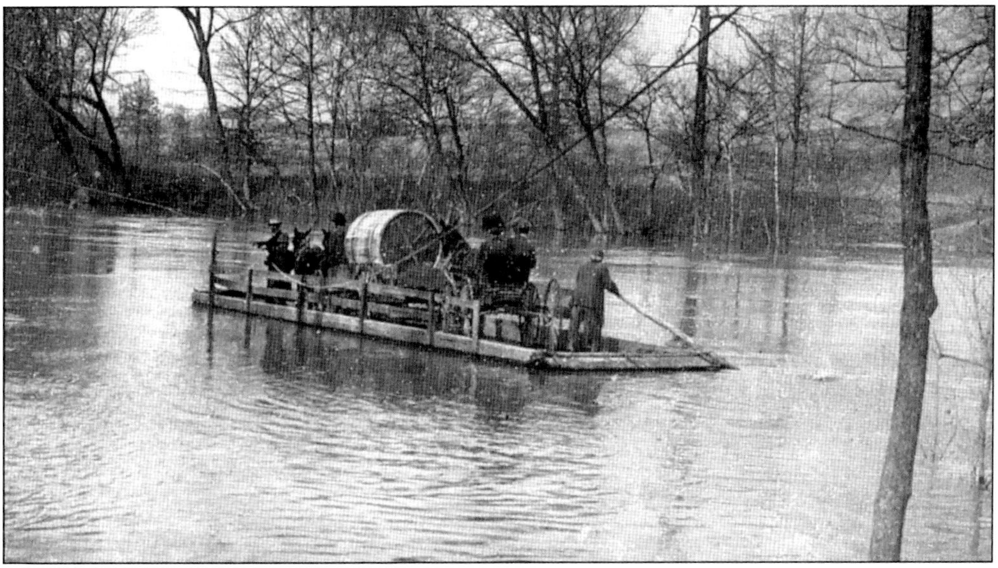

Ferry at Sartin's Ford, c. 1905. This ferry boat, crossing Green River, is typical of those used by many of Kentucky's early settlers before the advent of bridges. Located on the boat are a wagon team with a hogshead of tobacco and a horse and buggy. The construction and operation of ferries was one of the area's earliest businesses.

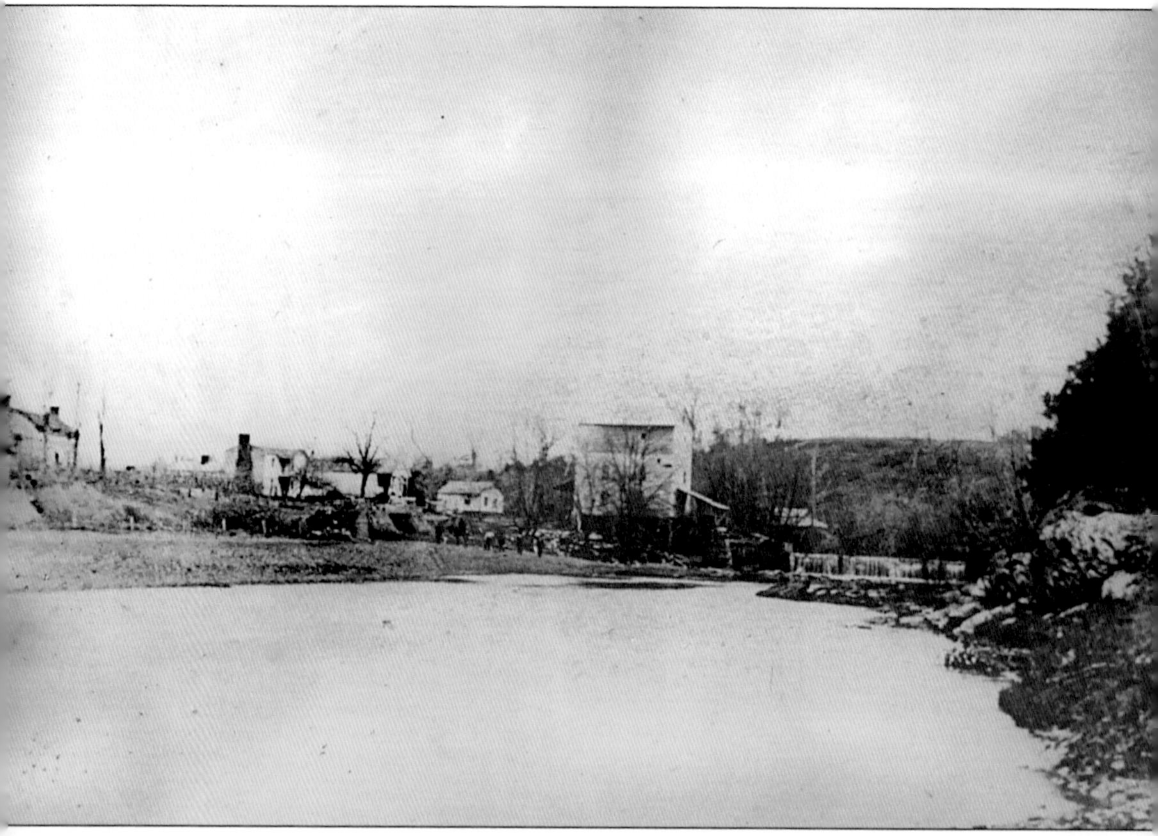

The Lost Town of Oceola, c. 1900. A thriving little village by the name of Oceola was once located on the east side of the Little Barren River in Green County between Greensburg and Horse Cave. Oceola had its beginning about 1860 and existed for only about 45 years. Gooch Mill, the town's grist and rolling mill, is located in the center of the photograph. For many years in the late 1800s, people traveling to and from Oceola would have to cross at a ford located about four or five miles above the mouth of the Little Barren River. Incorporated in 1873, Oceola also had several stores, churches, and blacksmith shops. Abner Gooch was the first and only police judge the town ever had, and Plez Sandidge was the town marshall for many years. Joseph Cunningham built and operated the first store in Oceola; it was located across the road from and nearly opposite the Gooch Mill. This store was later operated by Pleas Chaudoin, J.T. Rhea, and James L. Bale. Bill Pedigo and Bill Defries also operated a store in Oceola for several years. The town was perhaps best known, however, for its many saloons. For a few years there were four saloons in operation at the same time, and the town soon became known as "that wicked little river town" by residents of nearby communities. A church, built in 1874, was used by the Methodists and Cumberland Presbyterians. In addition to church services, political gatherings were frequently held there. About 1898, the church building was dismantled and moved to the small town of Monroe where it was reconstructed and became known as the Monroe Chapel Church. During the 1890s, the river flooded Oceola on several occasions until it was finally abandoned. Like ancient Greek writer Plato's legendary island of Atlantis, which he claimed was "swallowed up by the sea," the once prosperous town was literally consumed by the flooding of Little Barren River. Residents and store owners moved away and Oceola soon ceased to exist. No trace can now be found of the little town of Oceola.

Four

Hart County

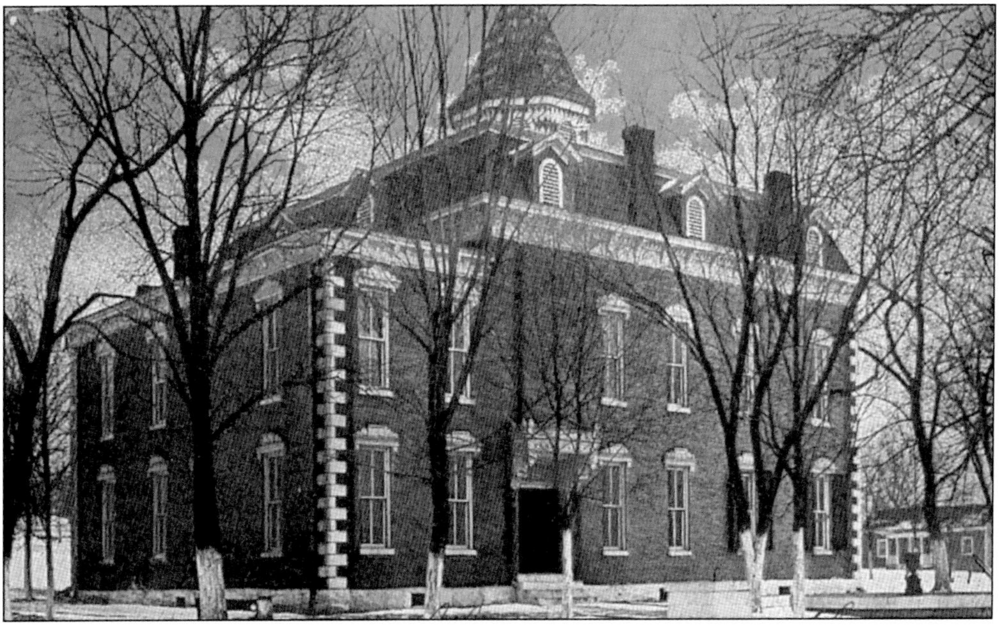

Hart County Court House, *c.* 1915. Kentucky's 61st county was created in 1819 and is named for Capt. Nathaniel G.T. Hart who died at the Battle of the River Raisin. Munfordville, chosen as the county seat, was first known as Big Buffalo Crossing. Later it was renamed for Richard J. Munford who donated 100 acres of land for the town. This is the second courthouse, which was constructed in 1893 at a cost of $15,000. It had eight large rooms and a circuit courtroom. The clerks' offices, constructed of brick, metal, and sand, were designed to be fireproof, but the building burned on January 3, 1928.

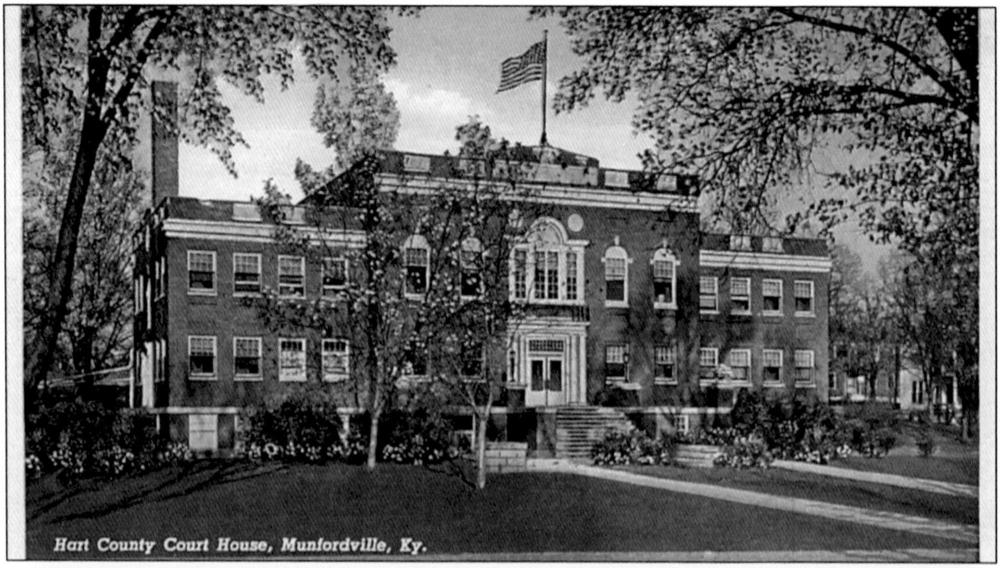

Hart County Court House, c. 1929. This is the third courthouse, and it was built in 1928 after the previous one burned. The Hart Fiscal Court proposed a special tax to pay for the construction. The uproar over the tax brought a proposal from the citizens of Horse Cave that they would construct and give the county a new courthouse if the fiscal court would move the county seat there. After much review, the fiscal court determined that the present tax structure would finance the new building and the county seat stayed in Munfordville. Architect Thomas J. Nolan of Louisville designed it, and Jenkins Construction & Supply of Elizabethtown built the three-story structure in less than a year. It was placed on the National Register of Historic Places in 1980 and is still in use.

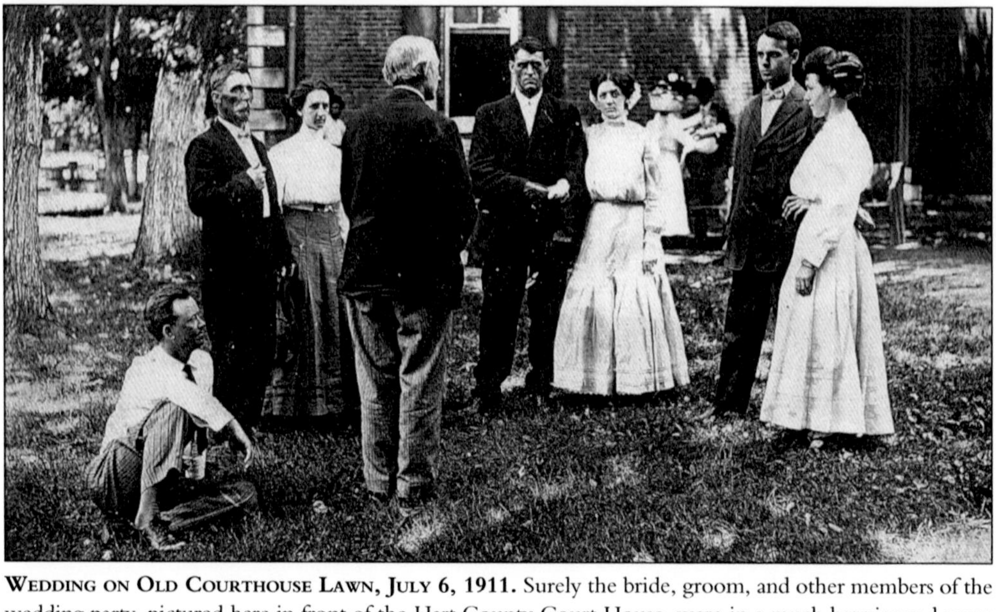

Wedding on Old Courthouse Lawn, July 6, 1911. Surely the bride, groom, and other members of the wedding party, pictured here in front of the Hart County Court House, were in a much happier and more festive mood than it appears. The man seated on the ground is unidentified. The members of the wedding party, from left to right, are Owen Short and his wife, Almedia Short, Judge S.B. Crump, groom John Holt, bride Becky O'Banion, Cecil O'Banion, and Lois O'Banion.

Walton Hotel, c. 1910. Located on the corner of South and Main Streets, this historic building burned in 1930. Many tales are told of visitors, both the famous and infamous, who partook of its hospitality. It was first known as Green River Inn about 1832. Twenty years later it was called Kerr's Inn & Tavern. It is claimed that Jenny Lind stayed here on her 1850s American tour when she traveled from Nashville to Louisville. A local story concerns the killing of local farmer, David Maxey, by Civil War guerrillas in 1861. He was killed in front of his family, when his home was raided. After the war, Dr. C.J. Walton and his wife were operating the hotel when a man entered looking for a meal. Mrs. Walton identified him as the man who "killed my father." Dr. Walton picked up a chair and started after him, but he was able to make his escape.

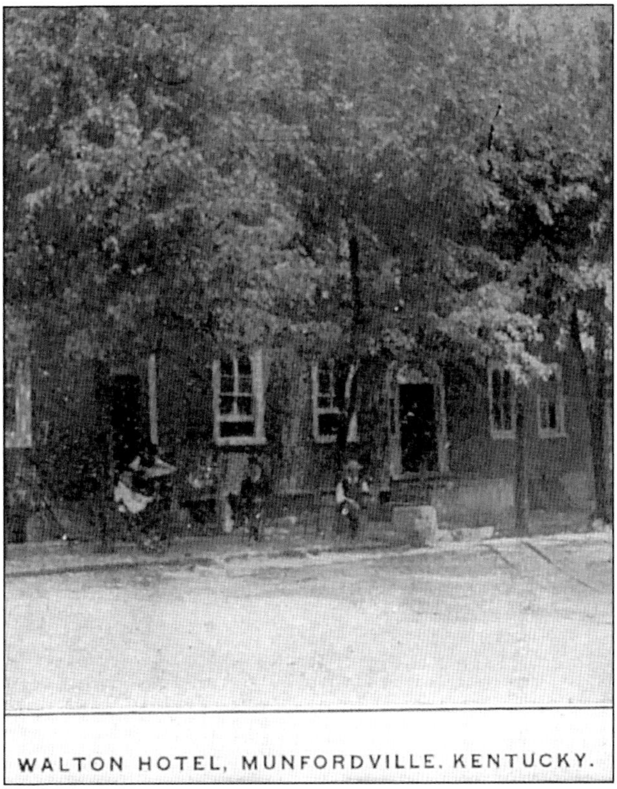

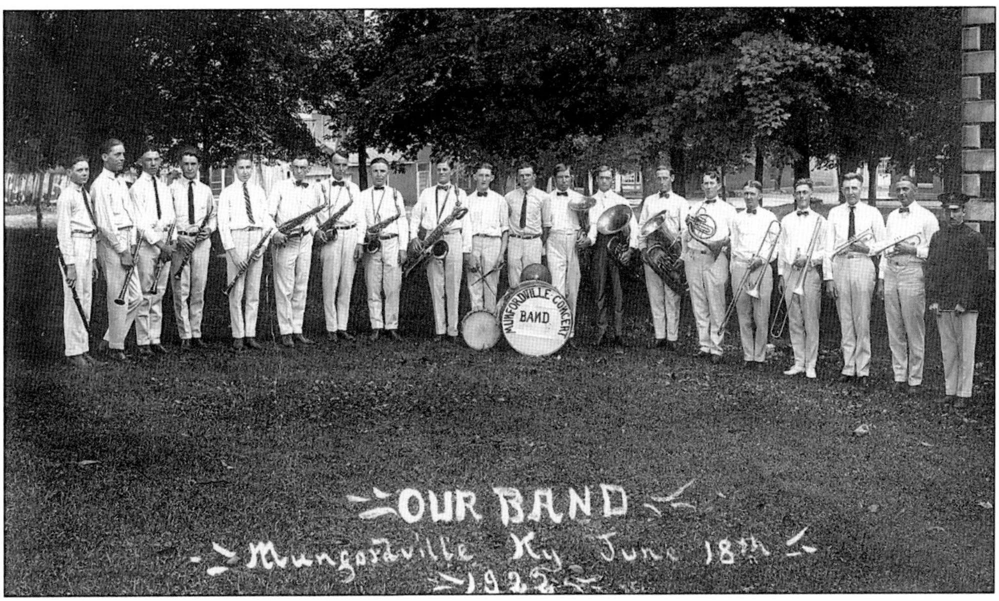

Munfordville Concert Band, June 18, 1925. The talented members of this band are, from left to right, Jack Hubbard, Garland Hubbard, Paul Houston Mansfield, Edgar Craddock, David McCandless, H.Q. Kennady, Logan Brownlee, W.E. (Shorty) Owen, C.B. Larimore, Ed Wheeler, Cecil Gardner, S.E. Williams, C.E. Nichols, Imon Spencer, Charlie Terry, Jack Crutcher, A.E. Harper, Guy Thornbury, William Crutcher, and instructor A.J. Giancola.

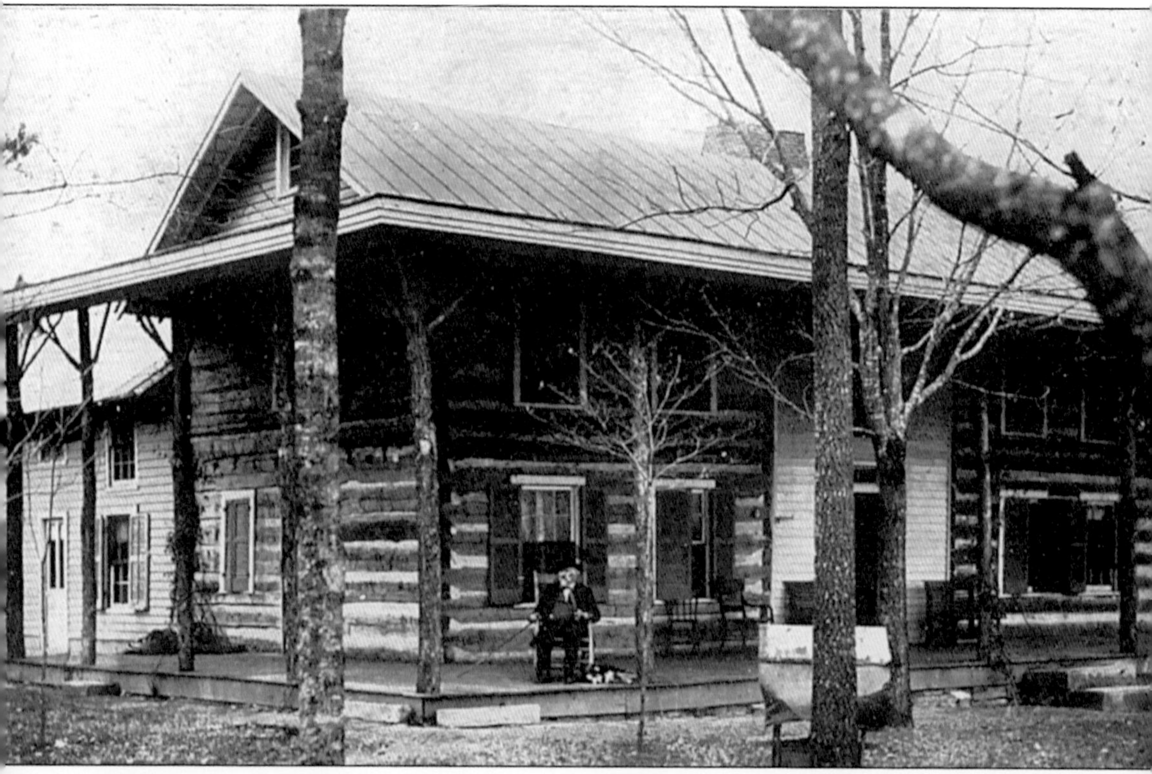

Glen Lily, c. 1910. This two-story log house, located about seven miles east of Munfordville and two miles off Kentucky Highway 357, was built in 1819–1822 by Col. Aylett Harswell Buckner who began construction of this hand-hewn, 10-room house after his marriage to Elizabeth Ann Morehead. This house was located on a 3,000-acre tract of virgin forest. Due to his interest in iron ore and his desire to become an ironmaster, Buckner established the Henry Clay Iron Furnace in the early 1820s but it went out of blast in 1837 due to a shortage of timber for charcoal. At Glen Lily on April 1, 1823 the third child of Col. and Mrs. Buckner was born and named Simon Bolivar Buckner for the great South American patriot and statesman. A graduate of West Point, Simon Buckner served in the Mexican War and in the Civil War as a general in the Confederate Army. He later served as governor of Kentucky (1887–1891), and in 1896 he was nominated for the vice-presidency of the United States. He and his family resided at Glen Lily until his death on January 8, 1914. Lt. Gen. Simon Bolivar Buckner Jr., the highest-ranking American officer killed in World War II, was also born here. Named for Governor Buckner's daughter, Glen Lily burned in 1961 after having been unoccupied for about 15 years.

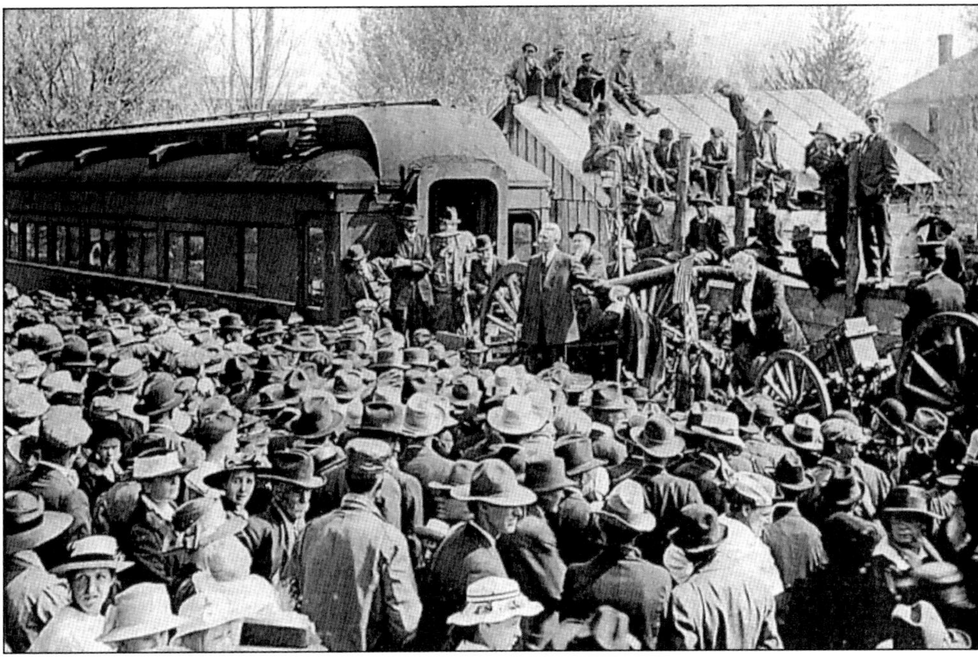

REV. W.A. GANFIELD AT MUNFORDVILLE DEPOT, APRIL 15, 1918. A large crowd has gathered at the Munfordville depot to see and hear Rev. W.A. Ganfield speak from the War Relic Train. On special occasions, famous attorneys, politicians, and preachers often enthralled audiences when their trains stopped at local depots. Note the attire of the people and the small American flag attached to the cannon behind the speaker.

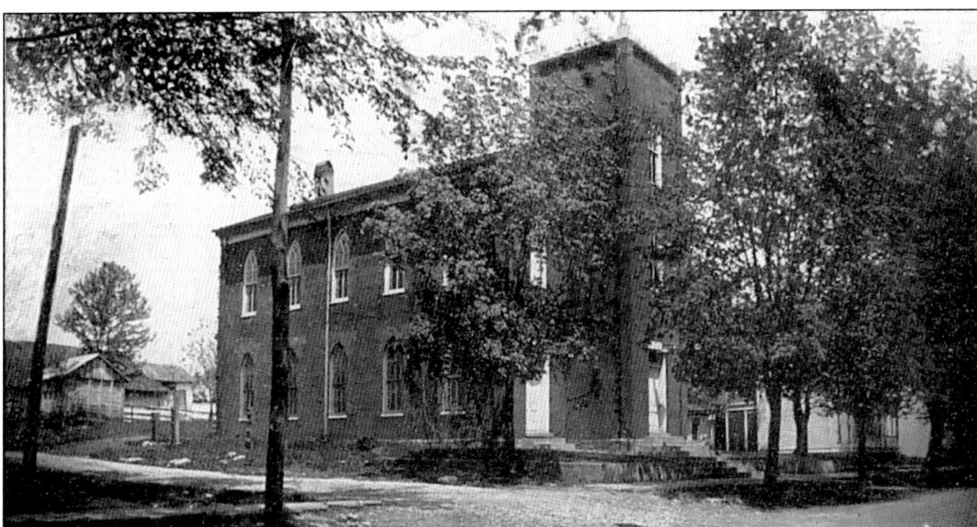

OLD PRESBYTERIAN CHURCH, *c.* 1920. The church was founded in 1829, and this building on the corner of Union and Washington Streets was constructed in the 1830s. During the winter of 1861–1862, Union troops garrisoned to protect the railroad bridge became ill with rheumatism, pneumonia, measles, mumps, and dysentery. The Union army commandeered this three-story church for use as a hospital until the fall of 1865 when the last medical personnel left. The nurses' quarters were in a house at left.

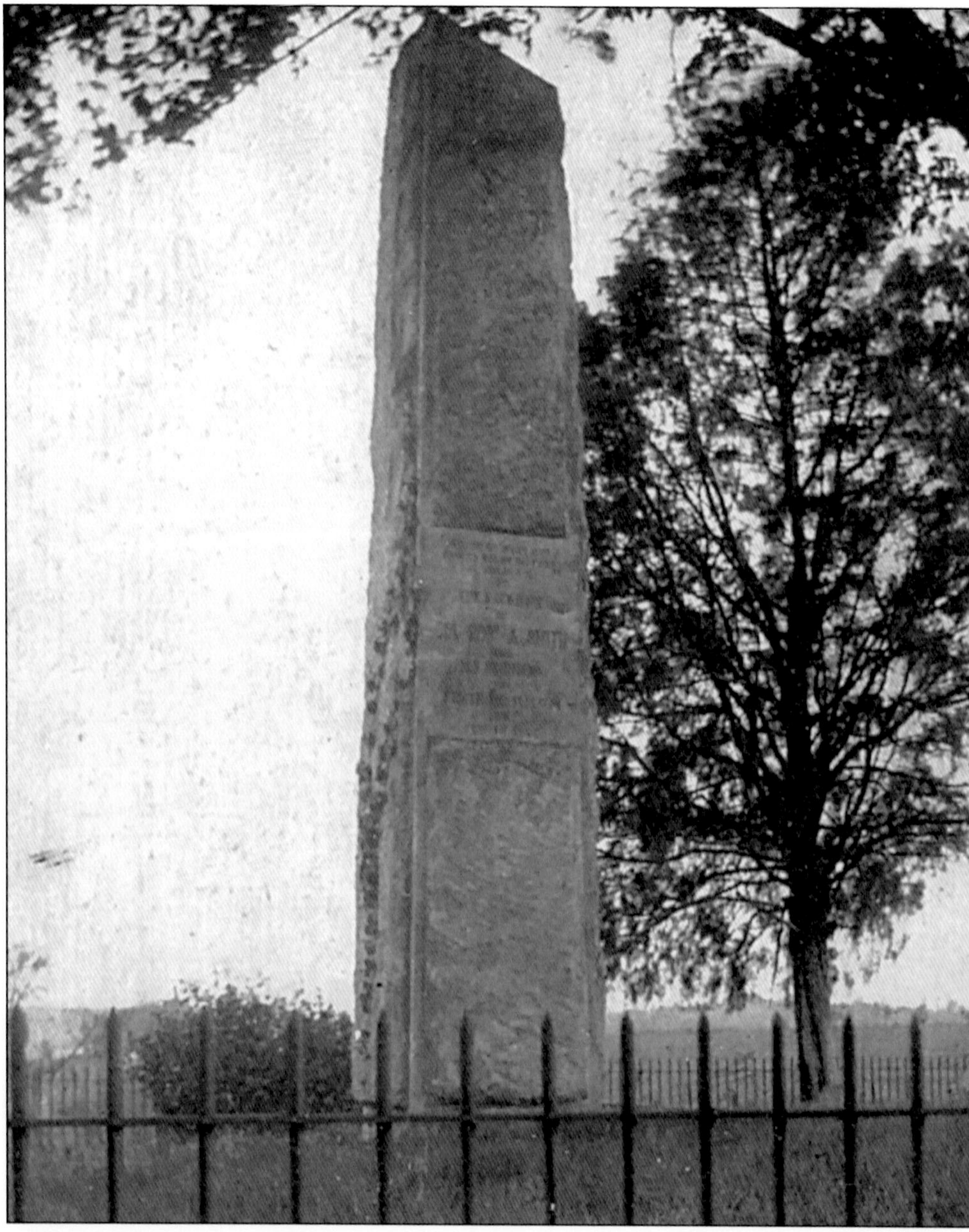

Mississippi Memorial, c. 1920. Col. Robert A. Smith was born in Scotland and came to Mississippi at the urging of his brother James who was a successful businessman in Jackson. Robert Smith organized a volunteer military company and was soon promoted to colonel in the 10th Mississippi Regiment. At the Battle of Munfordville on September 14, 1862, Smith was mortally wounded. He was buried nearby but in the spring of 1863, his sister Mrs. Charles Dudley came from Jackson and took his body back for burial in that city. On September 14, 1884, James Smith and members of the family from Scotland dedicated this monument to his memory. James Smith paid $4,000 for the monument, believed to be the largest single stone in the United States, except for Cleopatra's Needle in New York. It was transported by two flat cars, but unfortunately, a six-foot section broke from the top during the journey, which delayed its arrival.

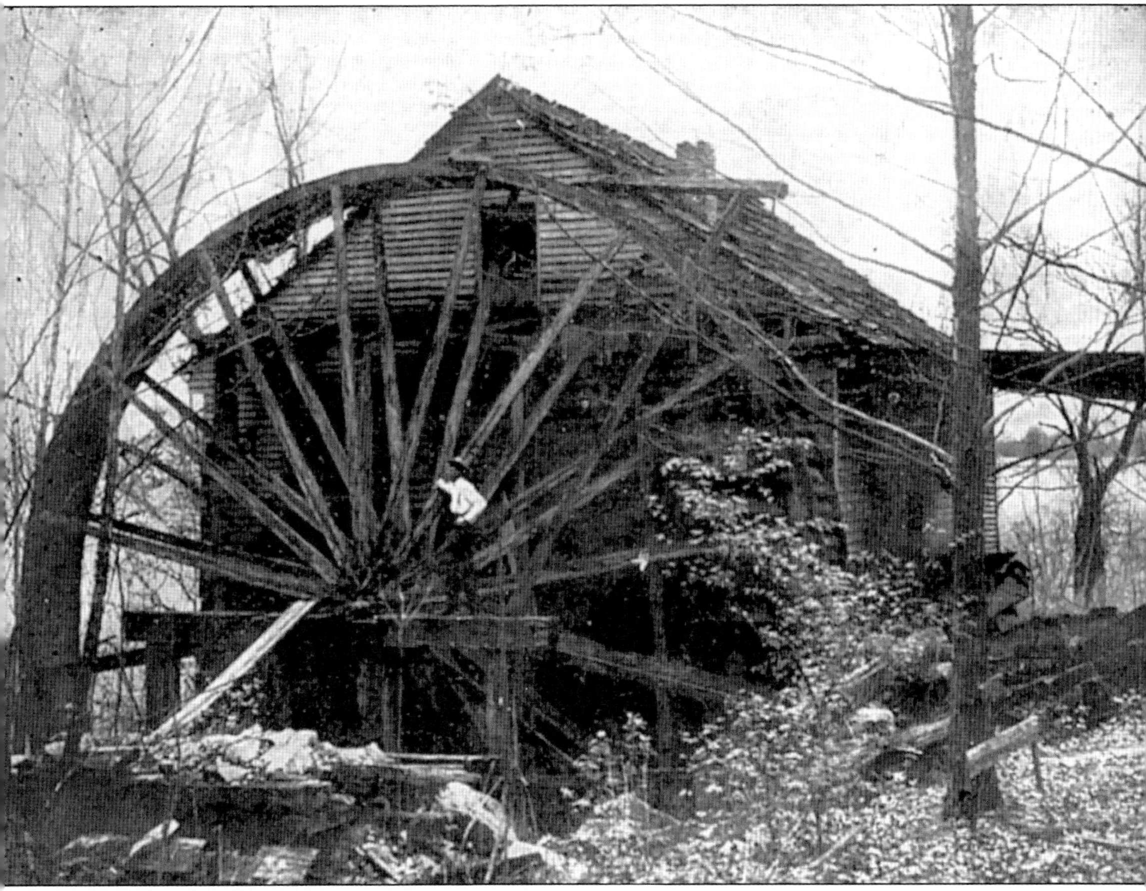

THREE HUNDRED SPRINGS MILL, *C.* 1907. This mill served all of Hart County and much of Green and LaRue Counties during the early 1800s and, for many years, was the only mill south of Green River. Large loads of wheat and corn were hauled by ox team to this mill from both neighboring and distant communities. The mill produced flour and meal that were sold in Cave City, Glasgow, Greensburg, and other nearby towns and communities. Built of hewn logs, it took 12 months to construct the mill and install the machinery; later, the mill was covered with whipsawed boards. The mill was first run by a single undershot water wheel. This was later changed to an overshot wheel that was connected by a wire rope to a second lower overshot wheel, which used the water that had already passed over the first wheel and increased the available power. On one occasion, an attempt was made to install a turbine but this was not successful. Thus, the overshot wheel was put back into service and continued in use as long as the mill was operated. Two burrs were used, with one coarse sectional burr for grinding the wheat and corn. During its operation, several different individuals owned the mill. One of the earliest owners was David Garvin who built the old brick house that stood above the mill for many years. After Garvin's demise, his two sons, Hal Garvin and Dink Garvin, operated the mill. G.W. Blakey purchased the mill about 1875, and he, together with James Bale, his miller, operated it for approximately 25 years. It was then sold to Weeden McInteer who operated it both individually and in partnership with W.R. Wheeler. About 1900 the mill was sold to Henry Deering who ran it with his miller, Charlie Wade, until the competition of roller mills forced him to discontinue its operation. The only other mill in the area with a wooden overshot wheel comparable in size was the Howell Mill, built in 1861, which served portions of LaRue, Taylor, and Green Counties and was located along Otter Creek at Malt in the Ball Hollow section of LaRue County between Hodgenville and Campbellsville.

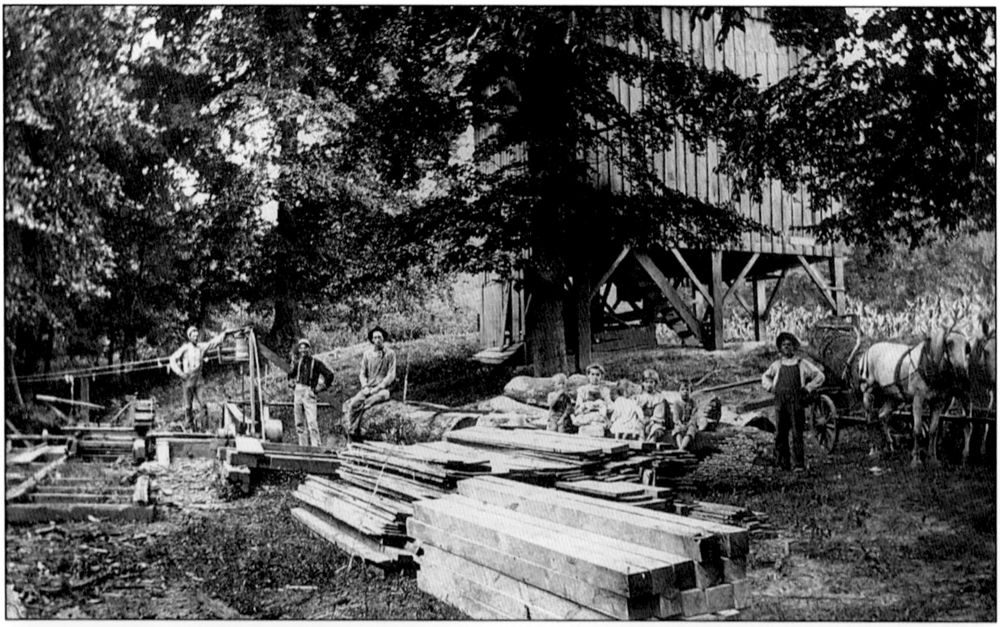

Johnson's Mill, c. 1910. In 1880, L.G. Johnson built this mill located on the north bank of Green River at the mouth of Boiling Springs branch about four miles east of Munfordville. It contained two sets of stone burrs for grinding corn and wheat and had an adjoining sawmill. In 1913, this two-story building was demolished by the highest Green River tide ever known. The first mill located on the site was built about 1862 by Jack Bumgardner. He, and later his heirs, operated it until 1879.

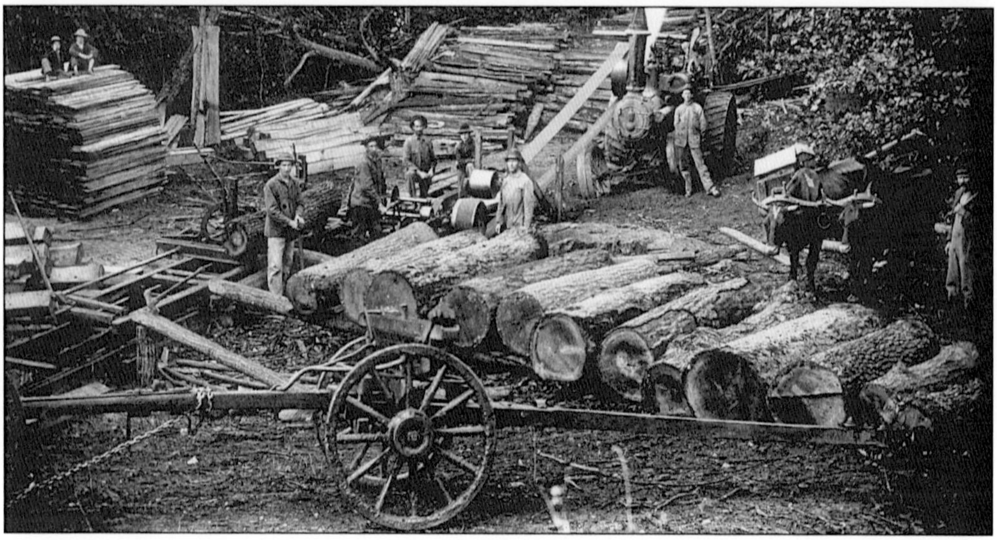

Moss Sawmill, c. 1912. Owned and operated by John H. Moss, this sawmill was located off Highway 88 in Hanyard Hollow. During the late 1800s and early 1900s, virgin forests in Hart and other nearby counties produced trees from six to eight feet in diameter. As the value of timber increased, the lumber industry soon became a major source of income to Kentucky farmers. Portable or "groundhog" sawmill operations such as the one above were routinely moved from one stand of timber to another. For many years it was a familiar sight to see logs floating down Green River to sawmill towns in Kentucky and Tennessee. This image is portrayed in its entirety on the back cover.

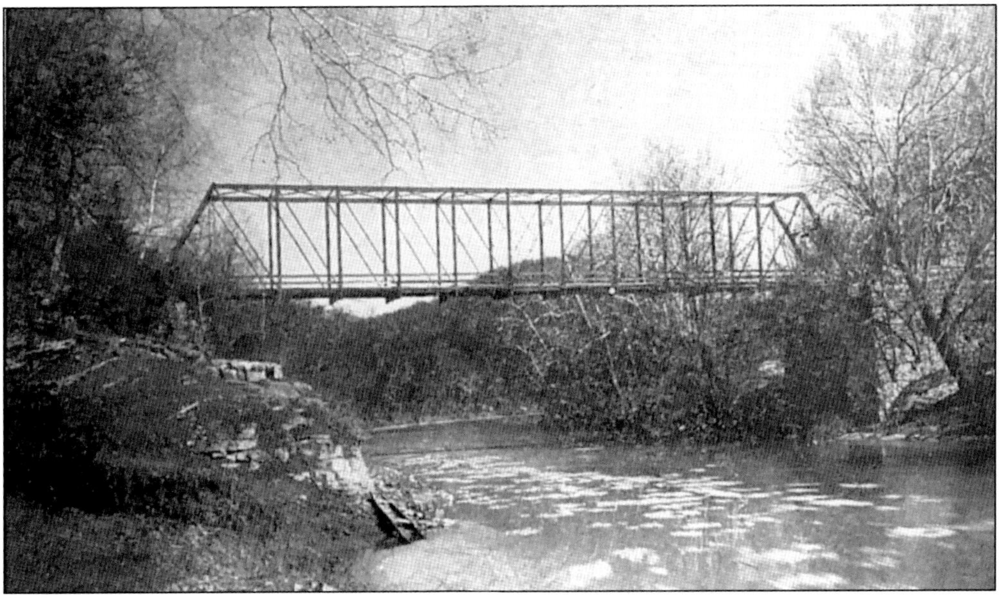

Green River Bridge, Rio, June 12, 1907. This metal bridge was built in 1886 by Henry Bowling Lane. It was ordered from the Monroe Bridge Co. of Cincinnati, Ohio and delivered by L&N Railroad to Rowletts Station. From there it was hauled by mule train teams to the site. It was owned and operated by the Lane family as a toll bridge for many years. The State of Kentucky purchased it in 1928 and discontinued the tolls. The 1917 *AAA Travel Guide* noted the toll on this bridge to be 40¢.

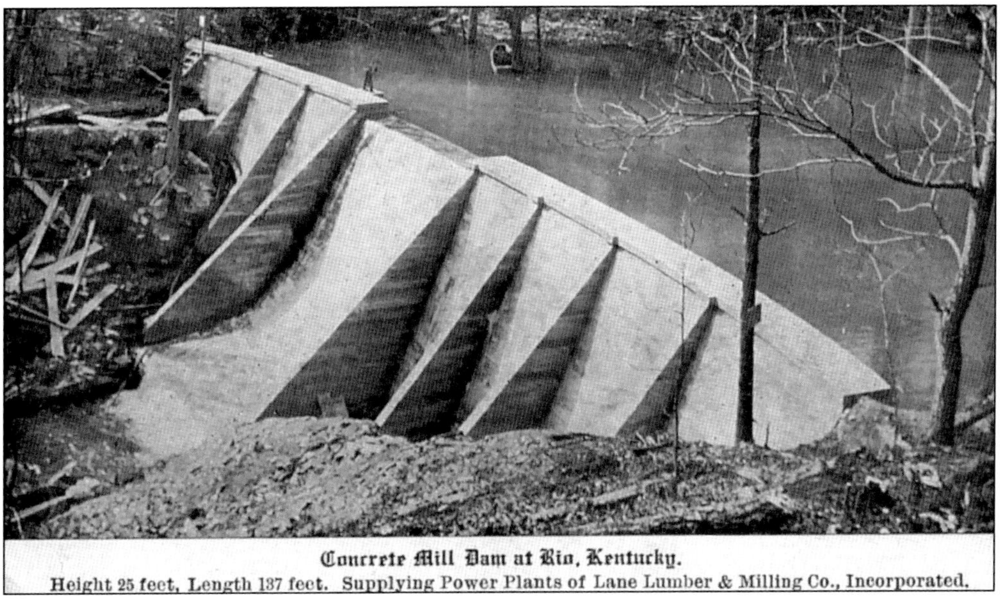

Concrete Mill Dam at Rio, *c.* 1909. H.B. Bowling and his son Rufus Dale Bowling operated the Lane Lumber Co. in this area. Using plans supplied by Kosmos Cement Co. of Louisville, Rufus constructed this 147-foot-long, 27-foot-high, solid concrete structure in 1908. The thickness ranged from 27 feet at the base to 3 feet at the top. It took five railroad cars of cement to build. The impounded water was used to generate electrical power for sawmill operation. Due to the construction of the dam, a light plant became operational in 1916.

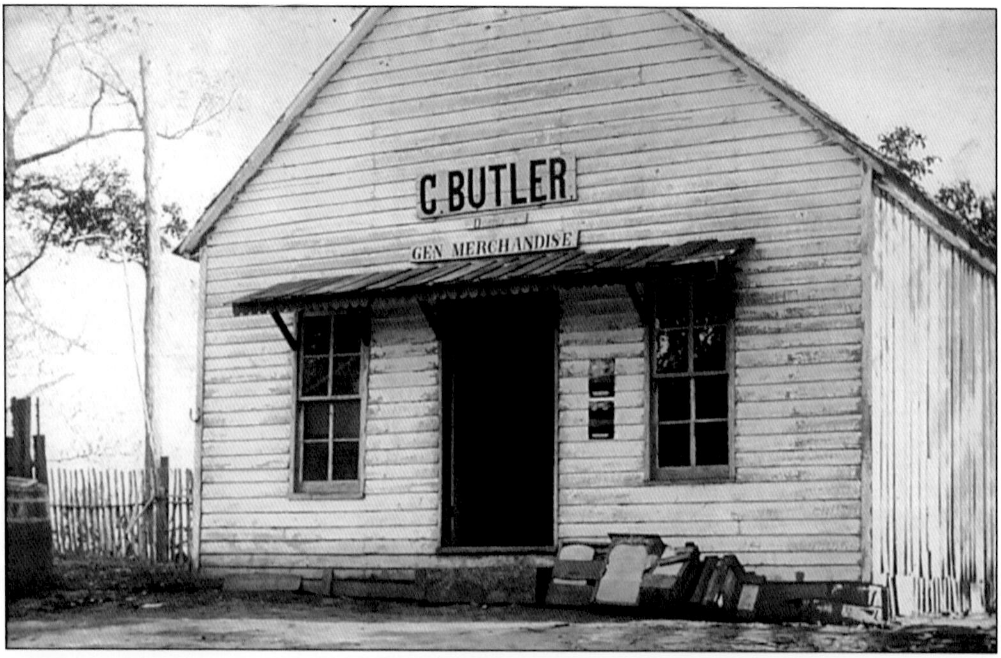

Store and Post Office in Macon, 1910. This general merchandise store and post office building was located in Macon and owned by proprietor C. Butler. On May 24, 1910, Butler made this real photo postcard and mailed it to a resident of Easton Rapid, Michigan. The small town of Macon had a post office from 1904 to 1969.

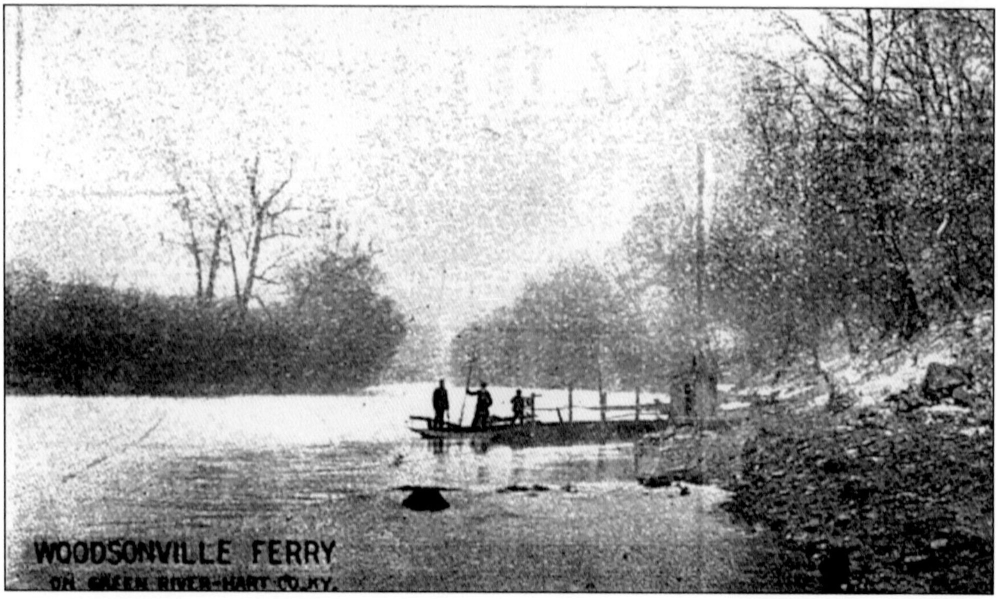

Woodsonville Ferry, *c.* 1907. This ferry, also known as Amos Ferry, was established by James Amos and was located on the south side of Green River in Woodsonville at Big Buffalo Crossing. For many years prior to 1900, people had to use this ferry to cross Green River as no bridge existed in the immediate area. As with Woodsonville, small villages frequently were created and grew in areas where ferries were constructed; some of these later evolved into large towns or cities.

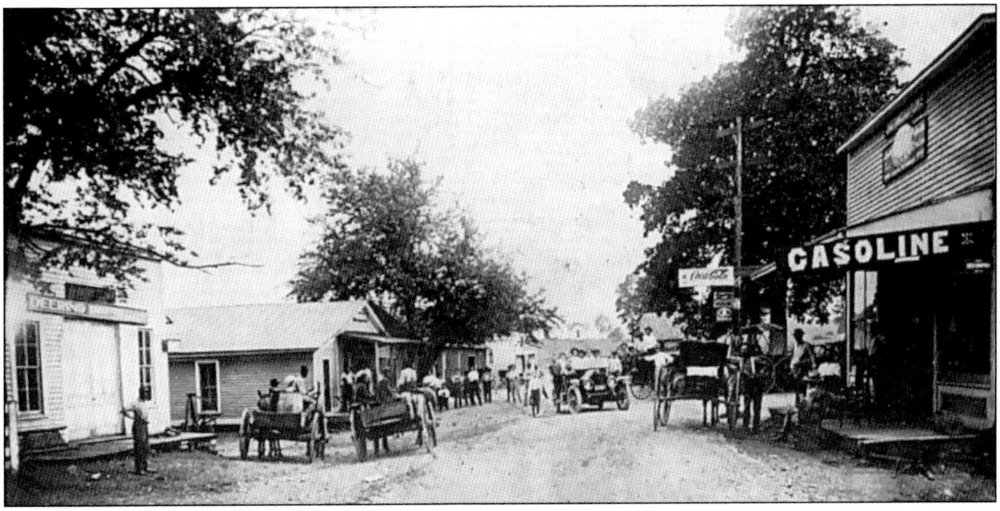

H.W. Smith's Country Store, *c.* 1915. Located at Uno and established in 1906, this store (right) was known far and wide for its delicious hickory-smoked country hams, bacon, and sausage, as well as its sorghum, honey, jams, and jellies. The town of Uno was first known as Clear Point because a man there sold an especially clear brand of moonshine whiskey. According to tradition, one day a slightly inebriated person who desired to acquire additional libations was asked where he was going. He thought for a moment then answered, "You know." This reply ultimately provided the town with the unique name of Uno. Post offices were located in Clear Point from 1843 to 1860 and in Uno from 1887 to 1906.

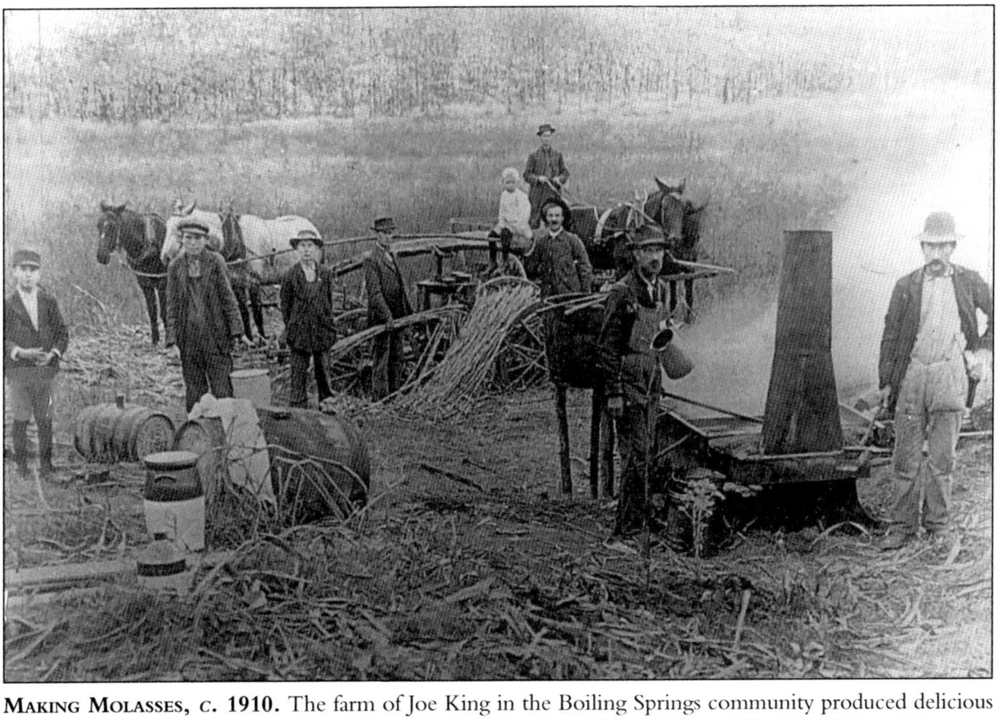

Making Molasses, *c.* 1910. The farm of Joe King in the Boiling Springs community produced delicious molasses for many years. Posing, from left to right, are Rowlett King, Sherman Devore, William Whitman, Ellis King, Judson Johnson (little boy), Lee King (in background), Lawrence Johnson, Jim Whitman, and Joe King.

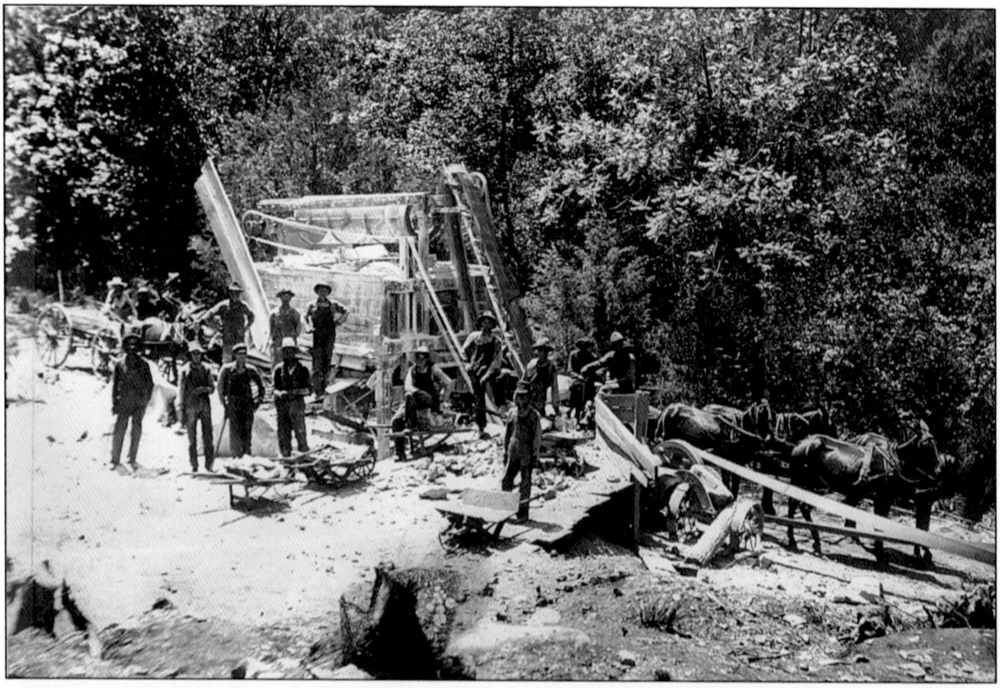

ROCK CRUSHER NEAR PRICEVILLE, c. 1912. This early machine provided crushed stone for many Hart County roads. The quarry site from which the rock was first moved by wheelbarrows was located on land owned by Jeff Craddock. Following the crushing process, the rock was then hauled to nearby roads by horse-pulled wagons. Under the supervision of Judge H.W. Thornbury, workers normally received $1 for a 10-hour workday.

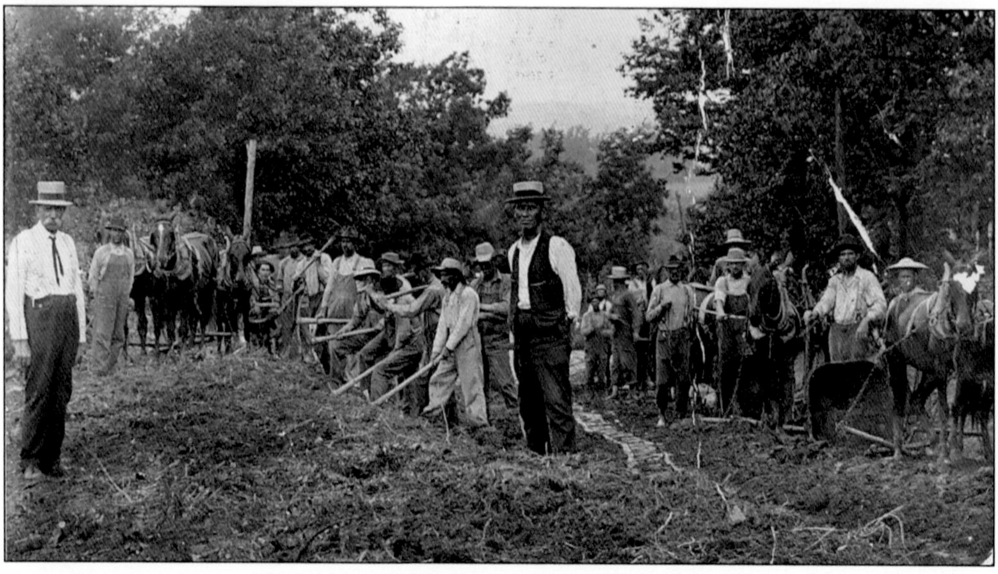

ROAD CONSTRUCTION, c. 1911. Squire Miles Williams, fifth district magistrate, stands at left as he supervises volunteer road construction in his district. Men with picks and grubbing hoes loosen the dirt for the horse-pulled scrapers. During the late 1800s and early 1900s, Hart County citizens were required by law to contribute free roadwork in their communities.

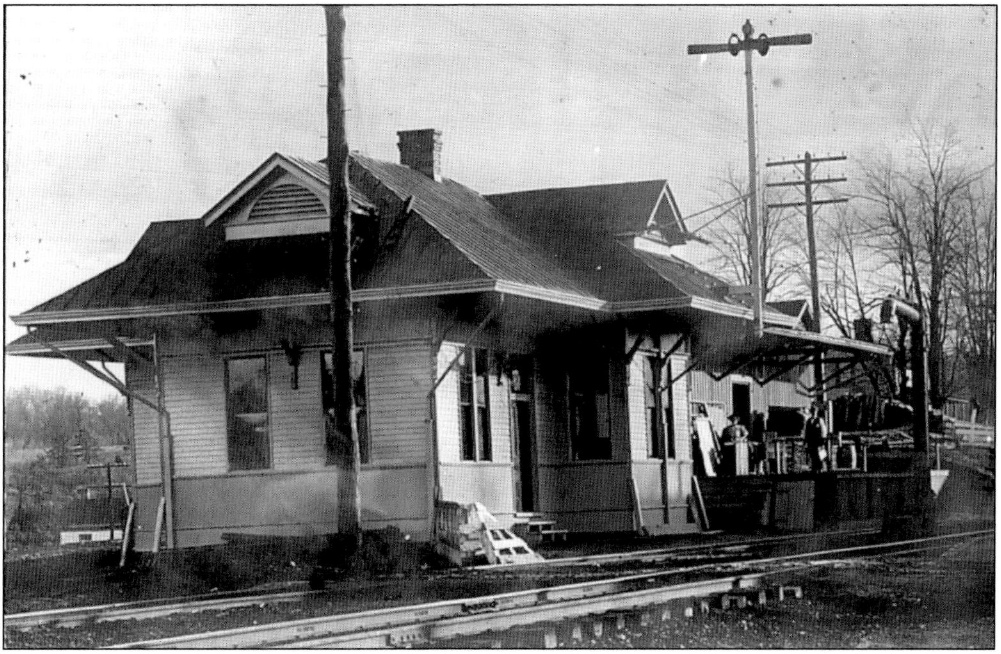

Bonnieville Depot, 1909. This postcard of the L&N depot was mailed from Bonnieville on the 100th anniversary of the birth of Abraham Lincoln, February 12, 1909, to Hodgenville attorney Sam Y. Jones. Serving as the first and second stationmasters were Judge Jameson and William Kendrick, respectively. After the Civil War, depots similar in style to this one were established at nearly every small town and village along the newly built railroad lines. Over 3,500 miles of track had been laid in Kentucky by the 1920s. Following the decline of the railroads, many depots such as this one were abandoned or used as offices and freight stations.

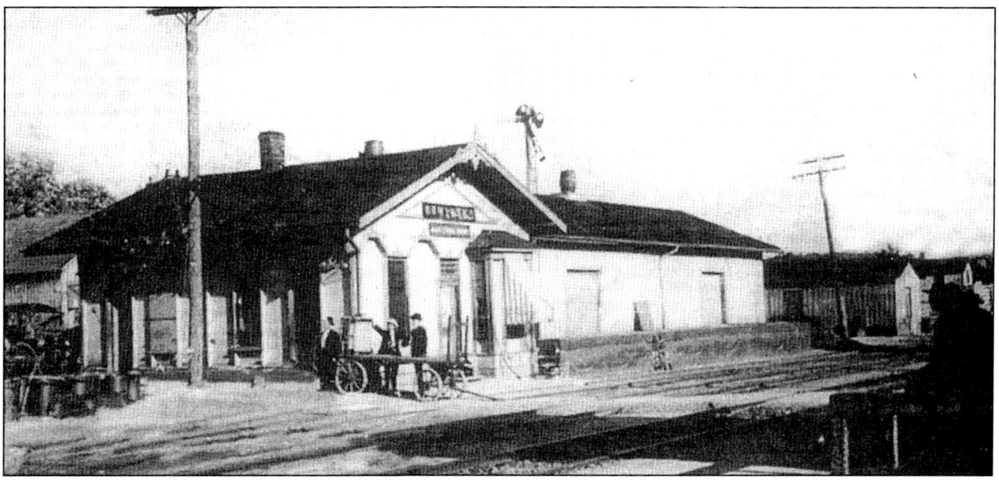

Rowletts L&N Railroad Station, *c.* 1900. From left to right are Curt Leach (merchant), Wilburn Cates (station telegraph operator), and James Logsdon (station agent). This commercially active station provided one of the most important supply lines to Union forces during the Civil War. The Civil War battle at Rowletts Station was one of the earliest skirmishes in central Kentucky and occurred on December 17, 1861. For many years, this depot handled hundreds of tons of freight and livestock that were shipped on a daily basis.

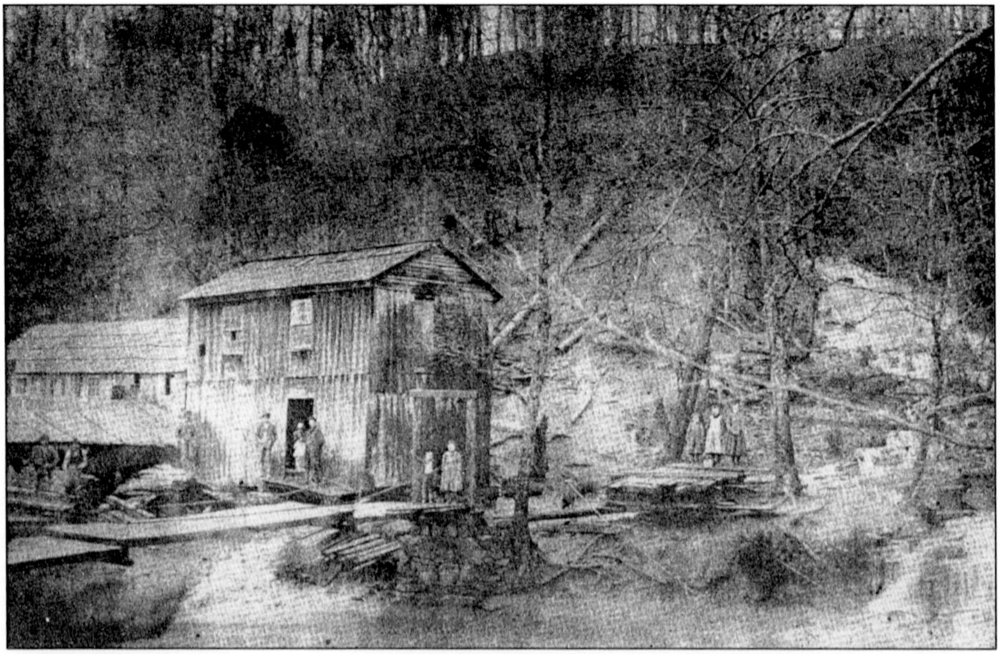

Powder Mills, c. 1900. Located on Lynn Camp Creek near the Green County line, Powder Mills was the site of an important industry—the manufacture of gunpowder—even before Hart County was formed in 1819. Gunpowder made at this mill was shipped by flat boats down the Green, Ohio, and Mississippi Rivers to New Orleans and was used by Gen. Andrew Jackson at the Battle of New Orleans on January 8, 1815. After the gunpowder mill ceased to exist in the mid-1800s, a lumber mill was operated where it stood from 1874 to 1900. During this time, the once-thriving Powder Mills community included the lumber mill, a flour mill, a general store, a carding machine business, a telephone exchange, a post office, and a doctor's office.

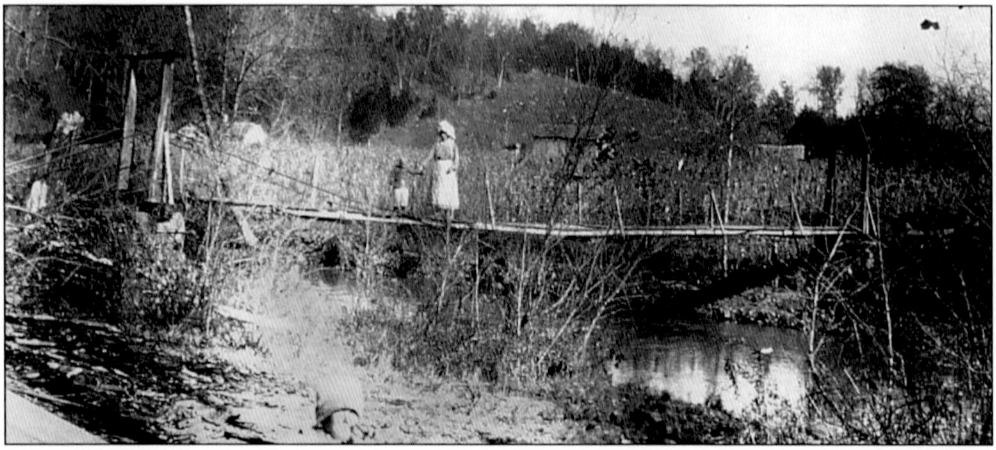

"Swinging" Bridge at Powder Mills, c. 1916. In many rural areas where homes had been built on alternating sides of a creek, the creek bed itself had to be used as a walkway or road in order to permit ingress and egress. In some cases, a simple wooden bridge with supporting anchor posts was required when the creek was high or the terrain steep. This "swinging" wooden bridge with metal cables over Lynn Camp Creek permitted pedestrian crossing only and is typical of those built many years ago throughout the state. The Powder Mills community is to the right but not visible in this image.

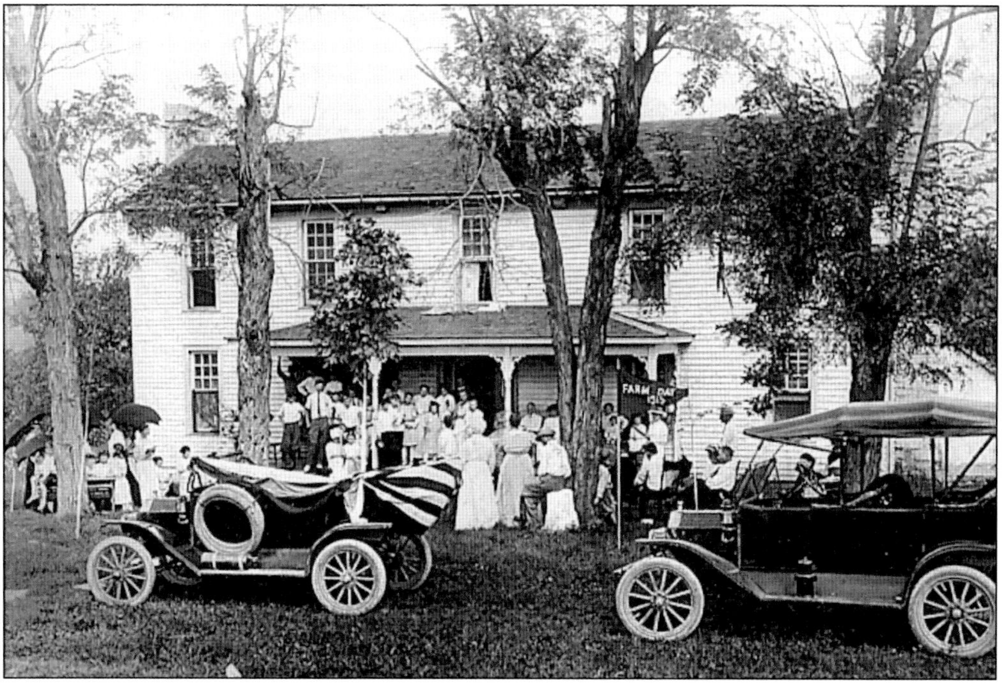

Farm Day, c. 1915. Farm Day was originated to promote agriculture in Hart County during the early 1900s and soon became an annual event. In 1915, Farm Day was celebrated with organ music and singing at the Rob Owens residence in Rowletts. Livestock, produce, and canned goods were on display and students and faculty from all nearby Hart County schools were in attendance.

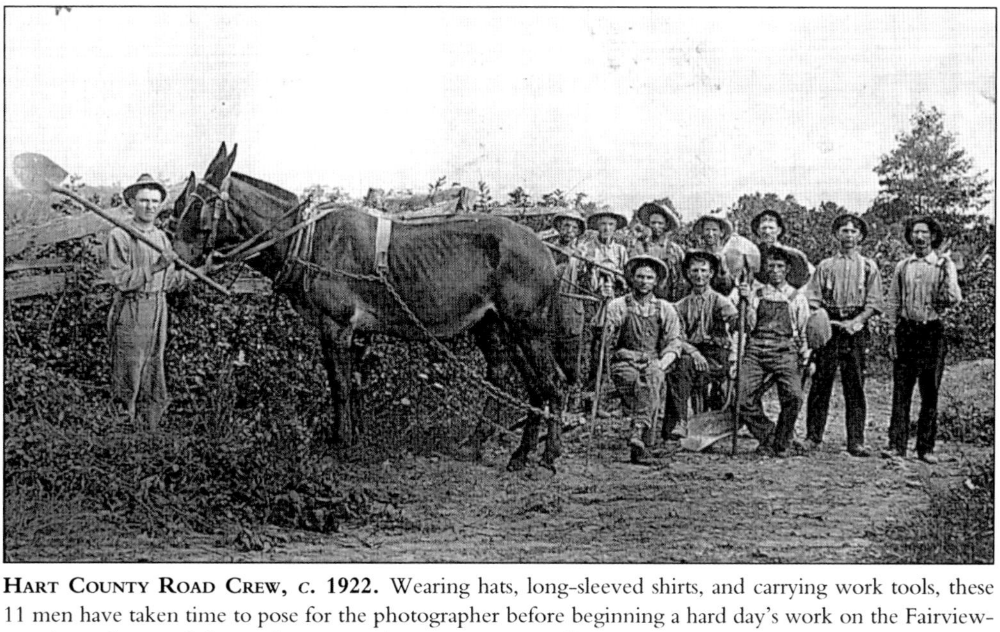

Hart County Road Crew, c. 1922. Wearing hats, long-sleeved shirts, and carrying work tools, these 11 men have taken time to pose for the photographer before beginning a hard day's work on the Fairview-Pascal Road. From left to right are (standing) Damon Russell (holding reins), Porter Lysle, Lee O'Banion, Ed Meadows, Noah Edwards, Lewis Meadows, Alvin Riordan, and Luke Edwards; (seated) Claude Russell, Clay Edwards, and Lawrence Short.

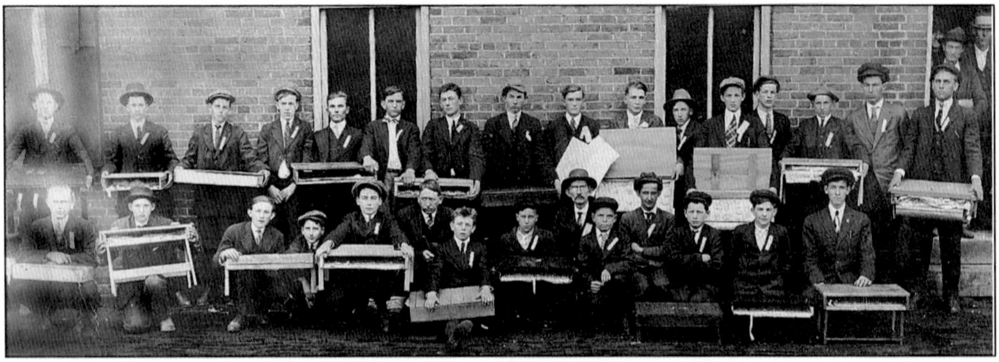

Hart County Hustlers, 1913. The first forum youth organization in Hart County, these young men posed for this picture in May 1913. These students with "lap desks" were known for their hard work and noteworthy accomplishments.

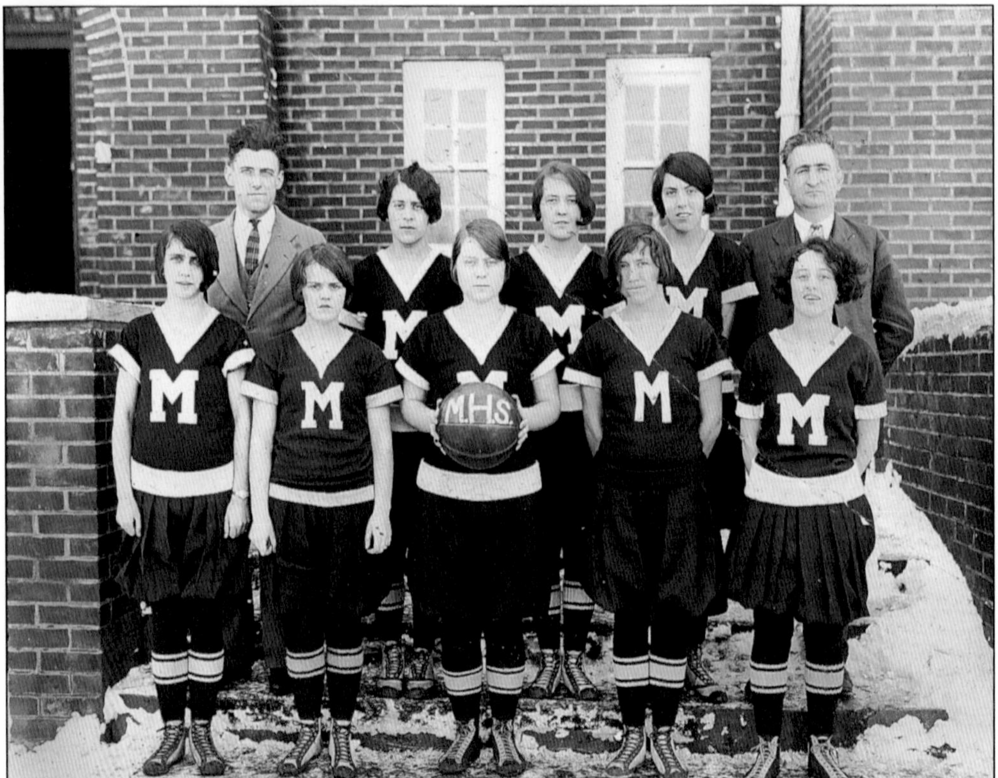

Munfordville Girls Basketball Team, 1926. This stellar group of female athletes comprised one of the best girls high school teams in central Kentucky. They are, from left to right, (front row) Hazel Patterson (Chatten), Ruby McKinney (Galloway), Lucy England, Marquerite Tharp (Stewart), and unidentified; (back row) Coach M.M. Botto, Ruby Storey (Crain), Florence Beville, Jasper Schlinker, and Superintendent H.R. Riley.

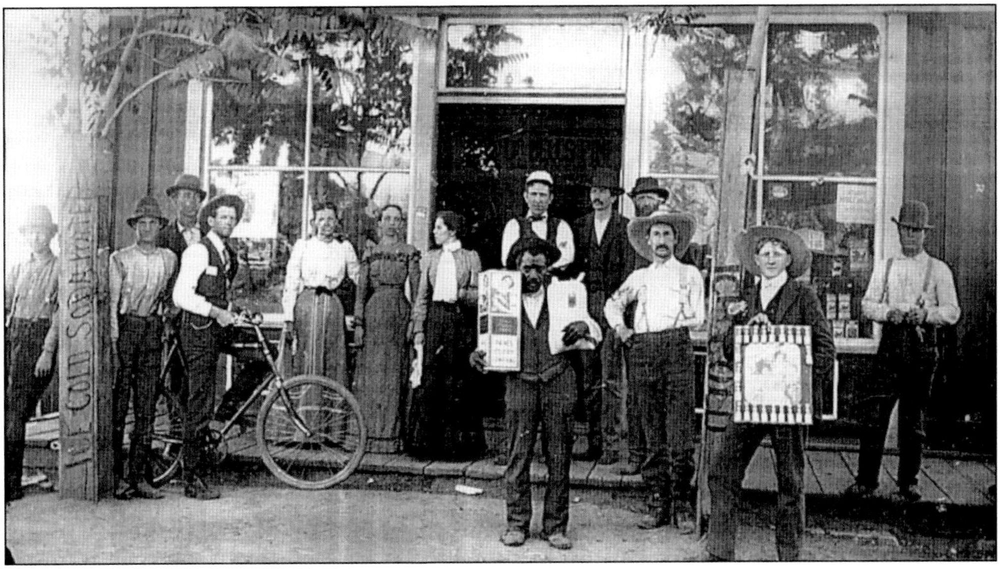

Ed White Grocery and General Store, c. 1905. This store, located in Hardyville, was built in the late 1800s and continued in operation until the early 1900s. Standing in the doorway wearing a light-colored cap is store owner Ed White. The words, "Ice Cold Soda Water," are printed on the wooden casing that serves to protect and straighten the young tree at left. A framed picture with decorative tassels revealing two lovely ladies is proudly displayed by the young man at right.

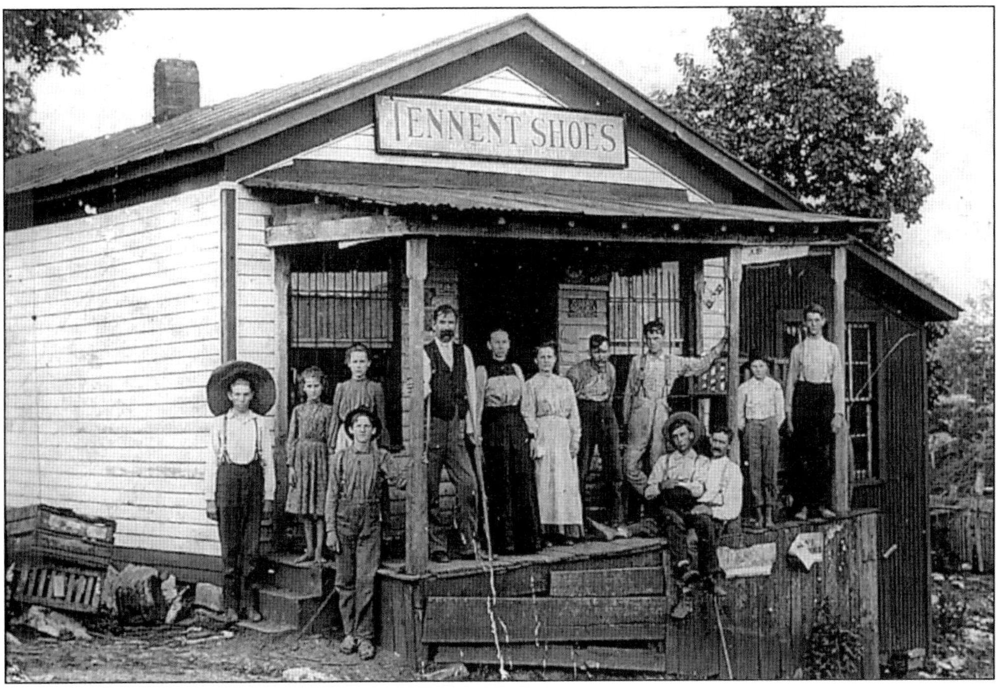

Hinesdale Store, c. 1905. Located near the Boiling Springs Church, this country store was owned and operated for many years by Jim Perkins. He and his wife are standing together below the prominent "Tennent Shoes" sign. Stores such as this were prevalent throughout many of the small communities in Hart County during the late 1800s and early 1900s.

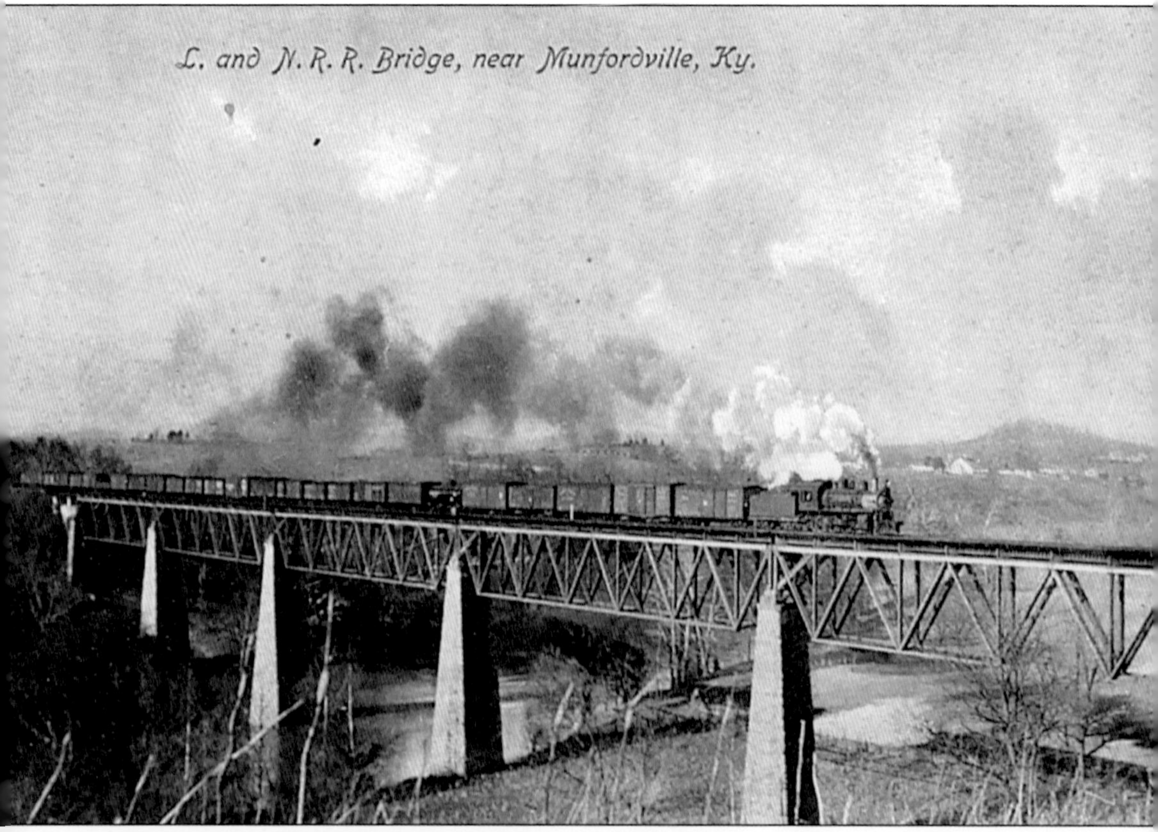

L&N RAILROAD BRIDGE NEAR MUNFORDVILLE, *c.* 1910. When this bridge was opened in 1859, it was the second largest iron bridge on the North American continent. Albert Fink designed and supervised the construction of this engineering marvel. It took 11 months of masonry work to complete the massive piers and abutments and 7 months of ironwork to complete the span. A locomotive slowly ran across the bridge for the first time in July 1859. In September 1861, more than 500 Confederate soldiers occupied Woodsonville in an attempt to seize the railroad crossing. Unable to advance, Hart County native Gen. Simon B. Buckner (CSA) was ordered to destroy the bridge and "fall back" to Cave City. After protesting what he considered an "injudicious" order, he was adamantly ordered to proceed. Holes were drilled in the two southernmost piers for explosives but only the charge in the southernmost one was detonated dropping two spans of bridge to the ground. It was enough to carry out the spirit of the order. On December 17, 1861, Albert Fink arrived with his crew to repair the damages. Time constraints caused the new repairs to be made of a "cobwebby structure of long wood poles," and work was completed in less than a month. It stood intact and in use until September 20, 1862 when the Confederate Army under Gen. Braxton Bragg burned it to prevent its further use by the Union Army. Union soldiers protected the newly rebuilt bridge from November 1862 until the end of the war when permanent repairs were made in 1865. In 1898, the grade of the tracks was raised and pedestals were added on top of the stone piers to create the bridge pictured above.

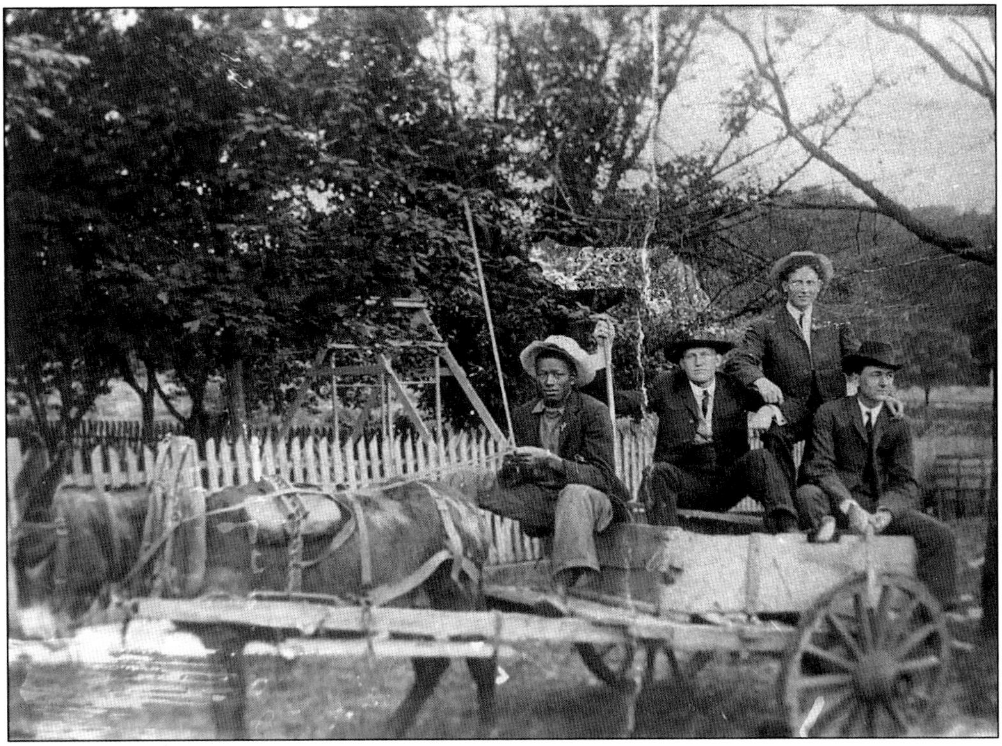

Rapid Transit in Rowletts, c. 1904. Driven by Robert Ballinger, this early 1900s mule cart is winding its way down Water Street in Horse Cave. Posing behind Ballinger, from left to right, are Rowletts residents James Blakey, Willard Cates, and Ben Patterson.

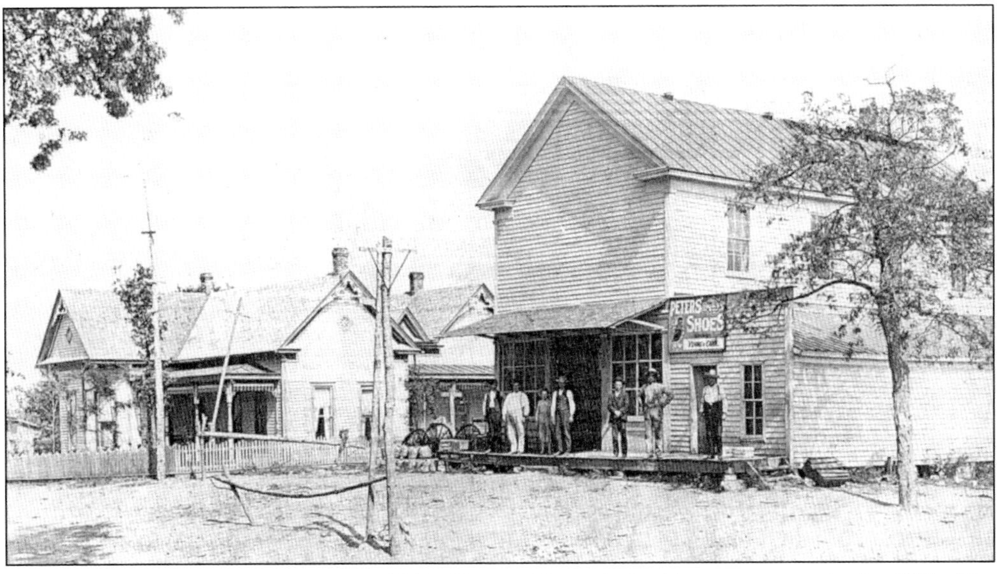

W.T. Young Store In Monroe, c. 1910. Thomas Young built this country store in the 1860s. The "Peters' Shoes" sign in this early 1900s image reveals the proprietors to be "Young and Cann." Posing on the store porch, from left to right, are Webb Brewer, W.T. Young, Coy Cann, Will Dishman, Wilbern Kidd, John Rodgers, and J.W. Cann.

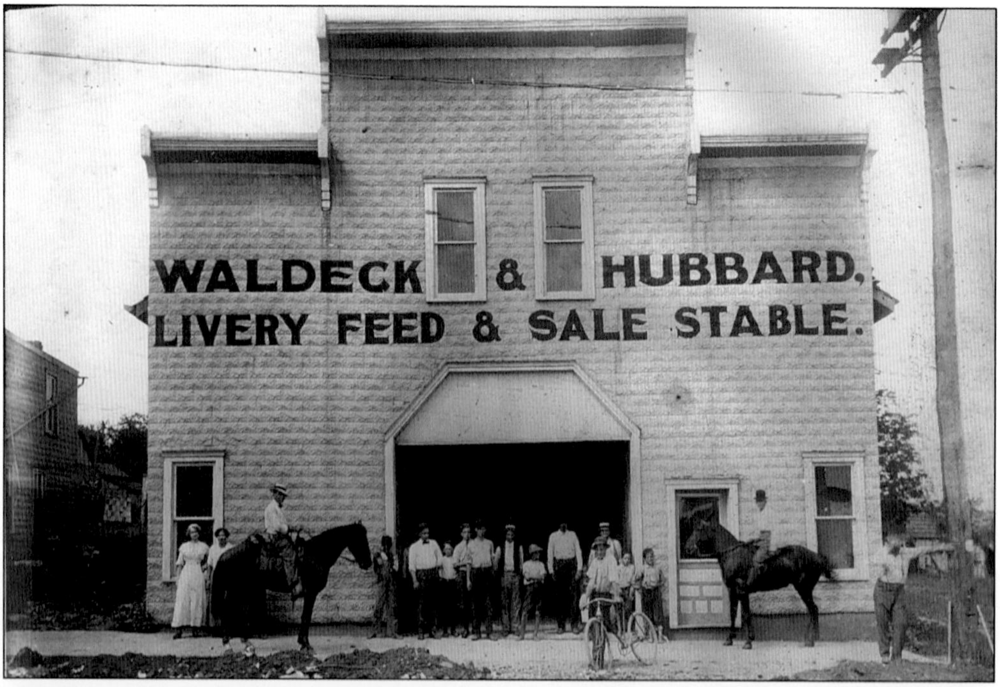

Waldeck & Hubbard Livery Feed & Sale Stable, c. 1904. This building was located on First and Main Streets in Munfordville. The business was owned and operated by W.E. Waldeck and John Hubbard.

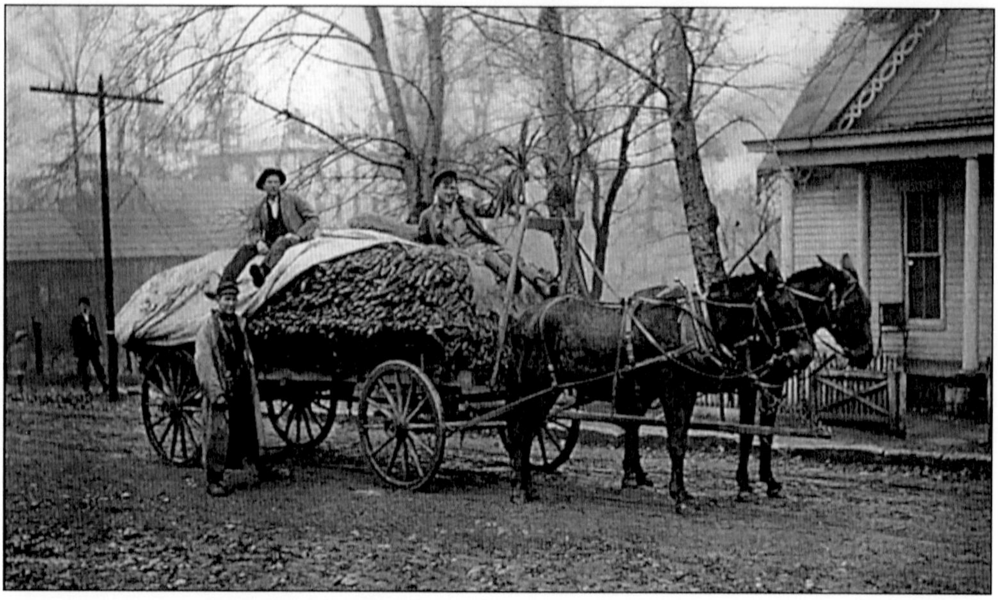

Hauling Tobacco to Market, c. 1918. Showing Highway 31E in Canmer, this scene depicts, from left to right, J.W. Hedgepeth, John Atherton, and James Clinton Hedgepeth hauling a load of tobacco to a tobacco warehouse. The building at left is the Russell Blacksmith Shop and the large two-story building, barely visible behind it, is the Canmer School. The house at right is the residence of Ab Russell and Zack Russell.

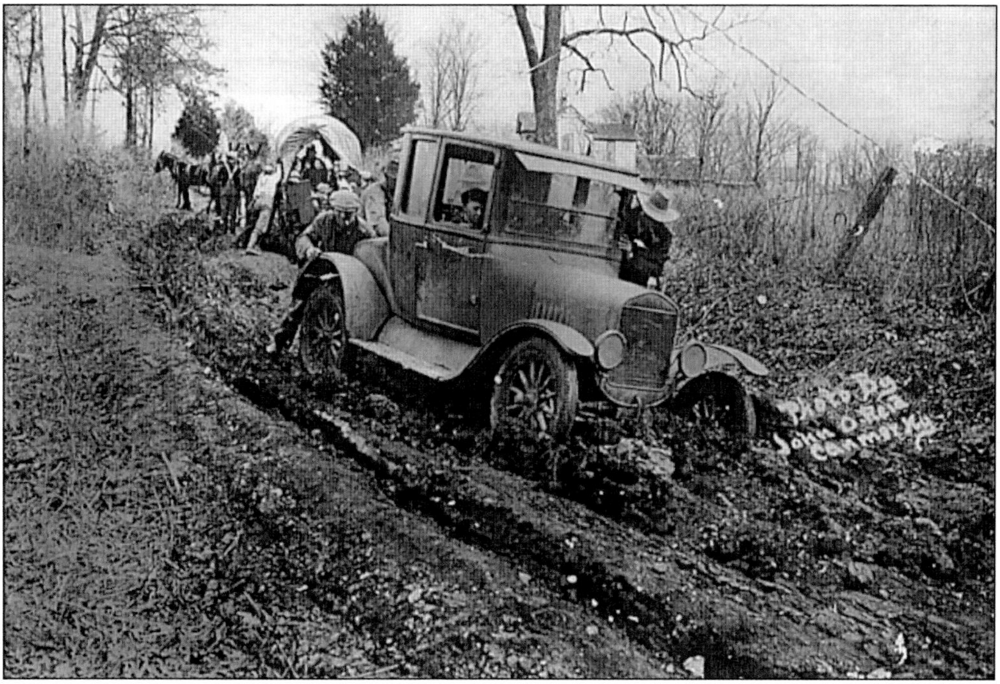

STUCK IN THE MUD, *c.* 1918. This real photo postcard was made by noted photographer John O. Reid of Canmer. Prior to the advent of school buses, children traveled from their homes to Hart Memorial School by a covered wagon pulled by two teams of mules. Both the covered wagon full of students and the Model T Ford in the foreground are stuck in the mud. The house in the background is the J.W. Sherfey home on Sherfey's Hill near Canmer.

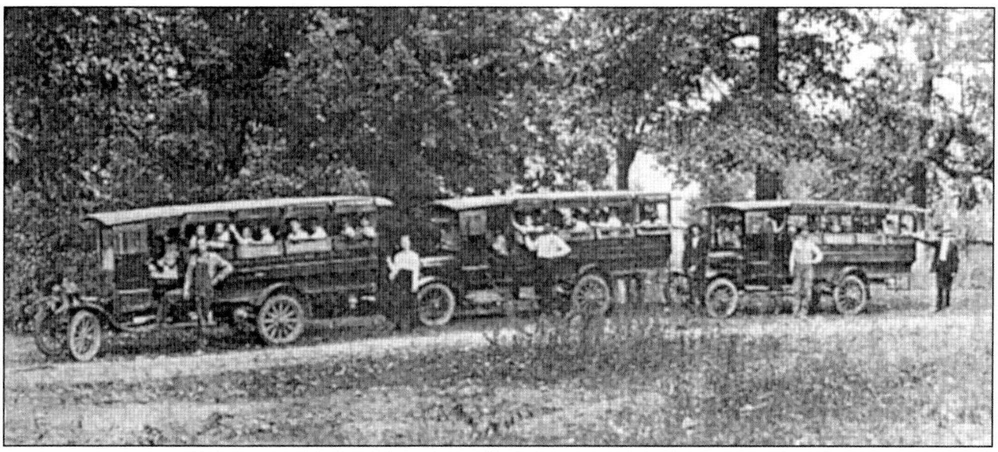

NEW SCHOOL BUSES, *c.* 1920. The opening of the new Memorial Consolidated School occurred on September 12, 1920. Rather than covered wagons, motorized vehicles designed to transport children from their homes to school were first used this year. Monty Bunnell, Mrs. Stanley Pulliam, Jesse McInteer, L.C. Curry, and bus driver Jack Reid stand by the buses as they and the children proudly pose for the photographer. Reid, Harry Bryant, and Clyde Locke were among the first school bus drivers in Hart County.

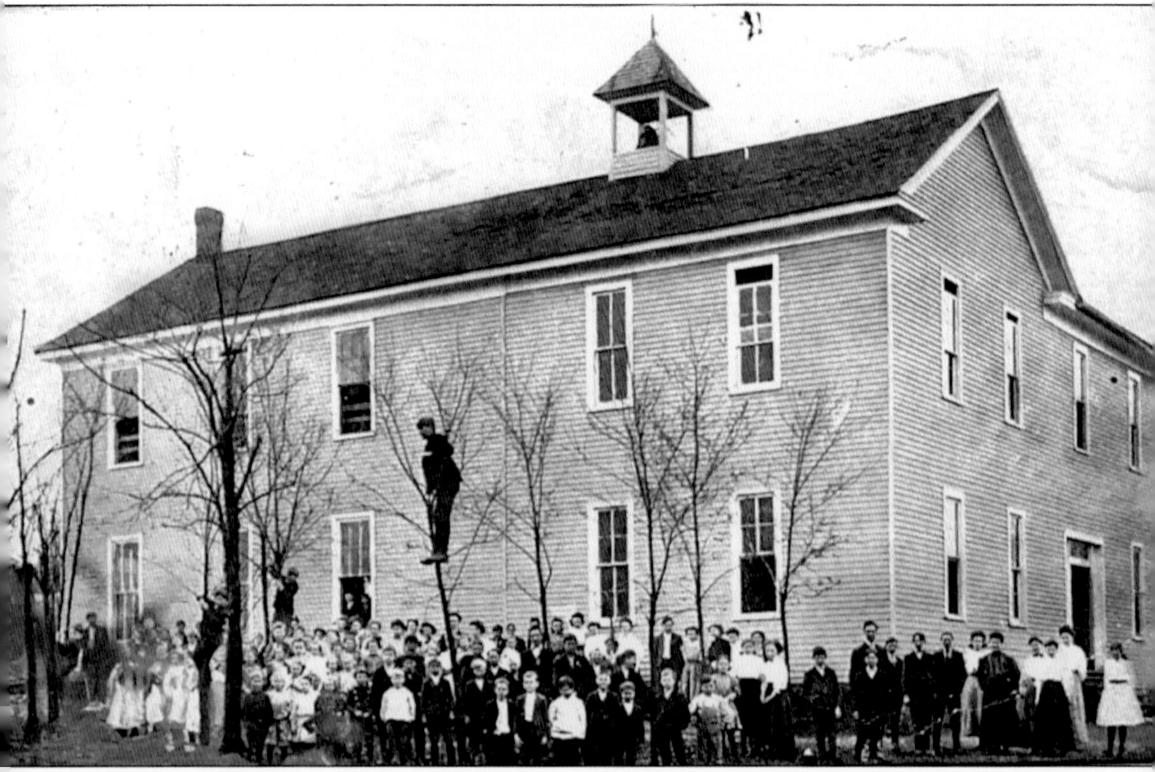

SCHOOL HOUSE, HORSE CAVE, C. 1910. This frame building on Cave Street in Horse Cave was the Horse Cave Graded Common School organized in 1898 by Prof. Moses E. Wood and his wife. It offered high school and "Normal" courses, which were for teachers. It was the only high school in Hart County until 1910, when another one was established at Munfordville. In 1903, newspaper advertising proclaimed that it would be "Opening Sept. 21-May 1 . . . an eight-months, free school for Bona-Fide Resident Children." This card was sent by a female teacher requesting more clothing be sent to her in her trunk. She marked with an "X" the room in which she taught her nine pupils who planned to give a recital. It was the last second-story window on the right.

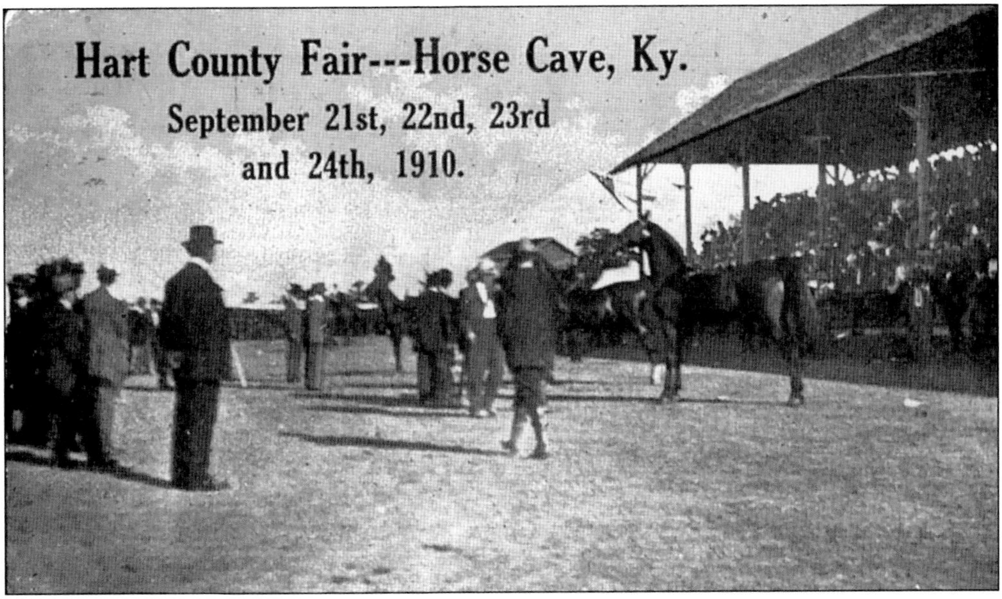

Showing Kentucky Thoroughbreds, 1910. Most county fairs in central Kentucky had their beginnings between 1905 and 1915. Contests to determine the best among various breeds of horses, cattle, mules, and other livestock were always one of the highlights of this annual event.

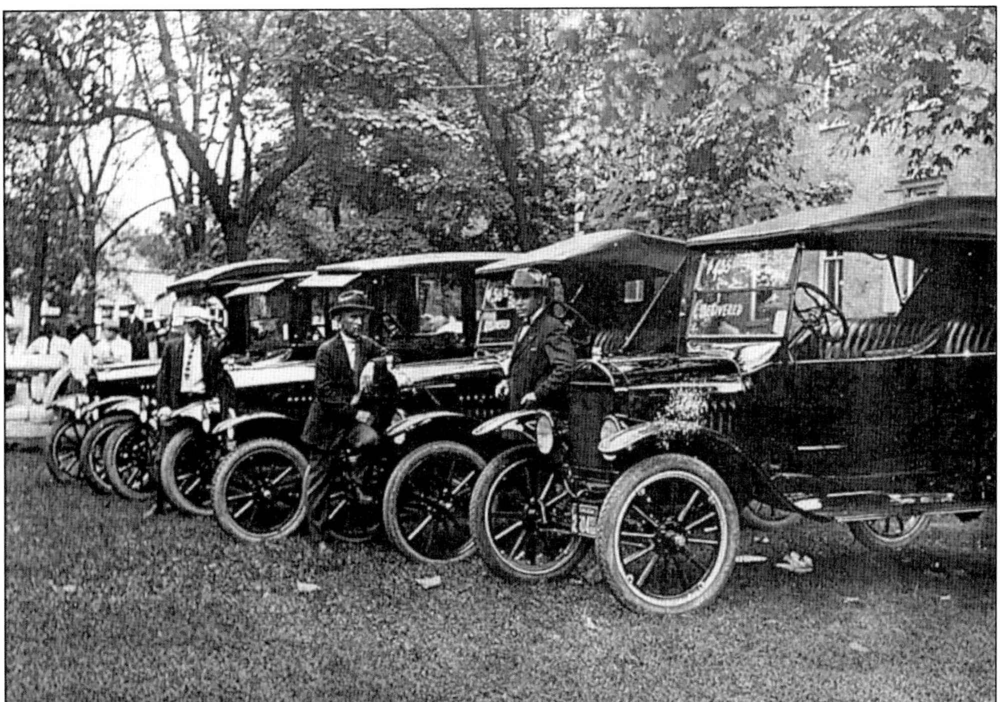

Model Ts at Hart County Fair, 1924. These five Model Ts at the Hart County fair have prices displayed on the top portion of their front windshields. The sale price on the windshield of the Model T at right is "$455 Delivered," and the Model T next to it is priced at "$316 Delivered."

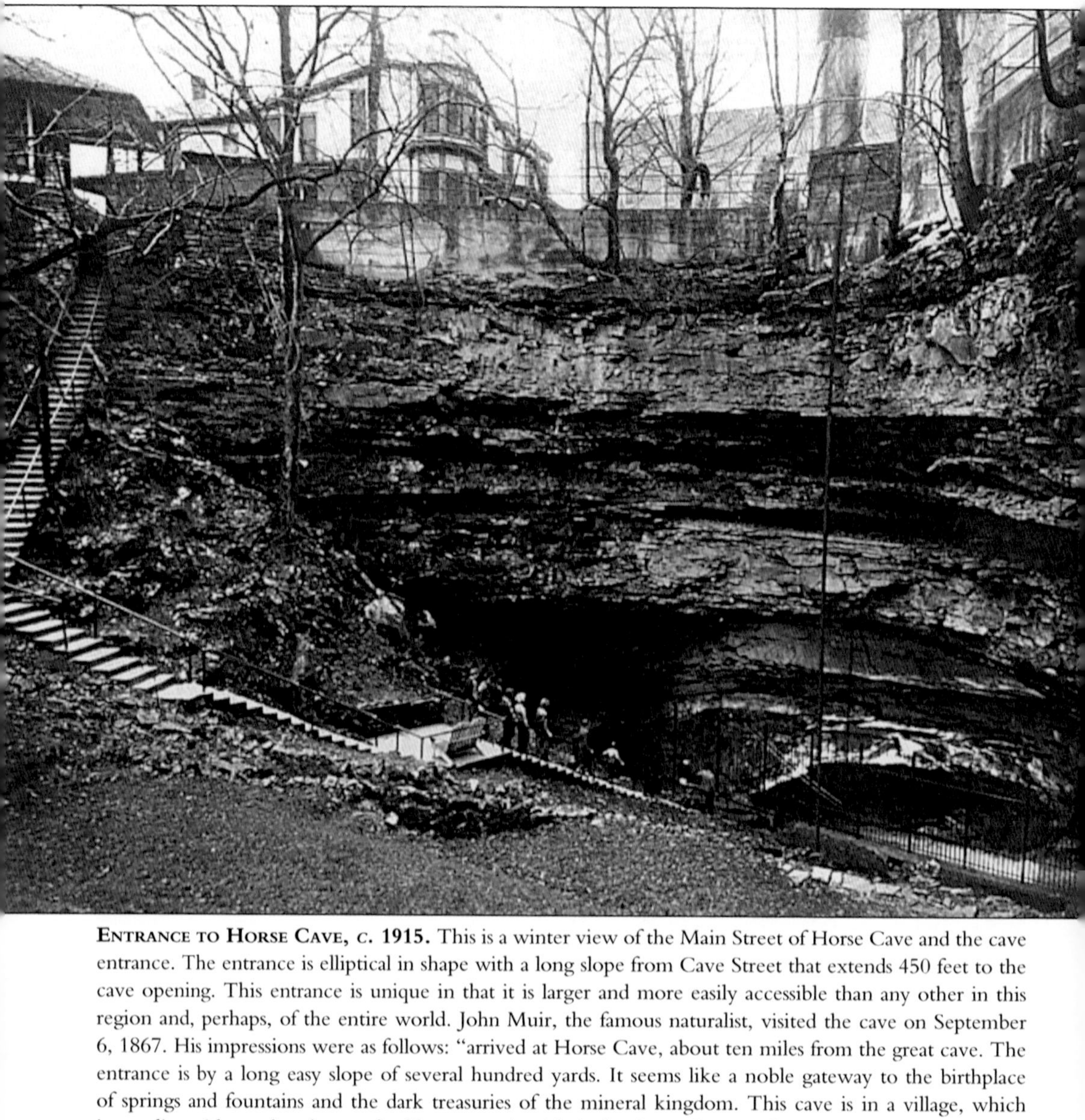

Entrance to Horse Cave, c. 1915. This is a winter view of the Main Street of Horse Cave and the cave entrance. The entrance is elliptical in shape with a long slope from Cave Street that extends 450 feet to the cave opening. This entrance is unique in that it is larger and more easily accessible than any other in this region and, perhaps, of the entire world. John Muir, the famous naturalist, visited the cave on September 6, 1867. His impressions were as follows: "arrived at Horse Cave, about ten miles from the great cave. The entrance is by a long easy slope of several hundred yards. It seems like a noble gateway to the birthplace of springs and fountains and the dark treasuries of the mineral kingdom. This cave is in a village, which it supplies with an abundance of cold water and cold air that issues from its fern-clad lips. In hot weather crowds of people sit about it in the shade of the trees that guard it. This magnificent fan is capable of cooling everybody in town at once."

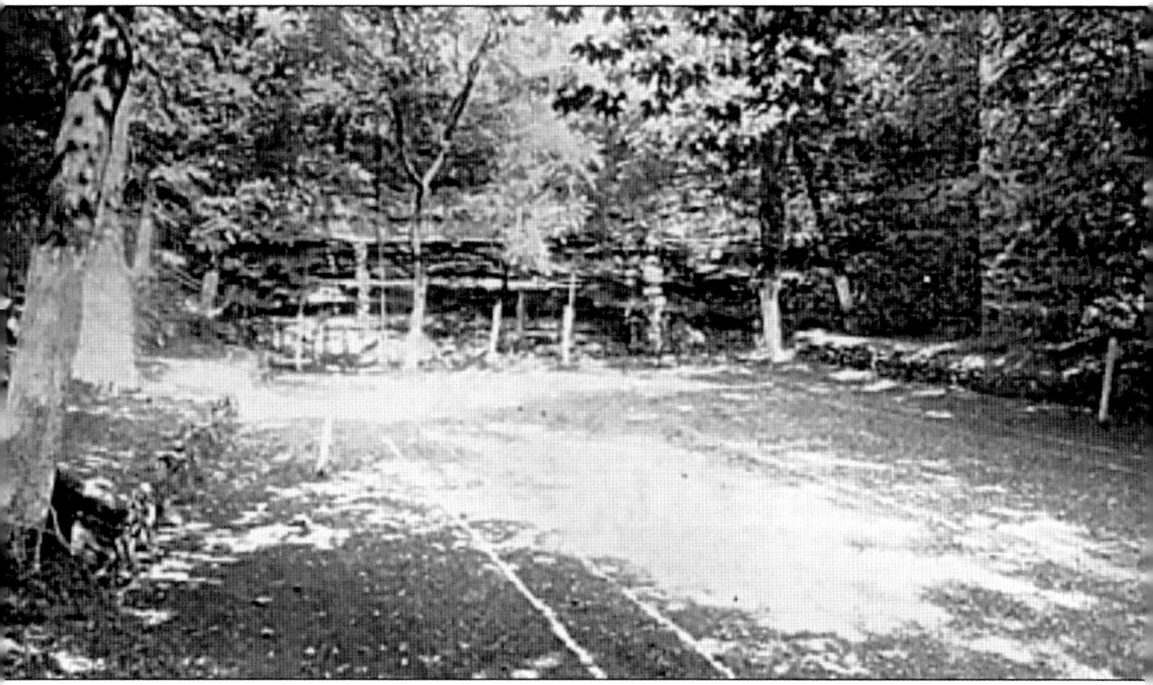

Tennis Courts at Hidden River Cave, c. 1917. In 1889, Dr. B.A. Thomas bought this cave, and in 1890, he built a dam and installed a hydraulic ram. Pumps were added to furnish water to the town. The waterworks served the town well until the 1930s. In 1895, a dynamo was put in and electricity was made available to the town. In 1908, Dr. H.B. Thomas bought out the other heirs of his deceased father and, by 1916, was ready to show the cave to tourists. He built a long flight of concrete steps with iron railings from the ground level to the cave entrance and river. He terraced the grounds and constructed a tennis court at the entrance. Footbridges were built across the river 225 feet below the ground. Electric lights were installed, making it the only cave to have electric lighting at its opening. Dr. Thomas held a contest to name the new attraction and offered the winner a prize of $2.50 in gold. Dr. D.C. Donan of Three Springs, Hart County, was the winner with the name "Hidden River Cave." In the 1940s, problems with pollution caused the cave's popularity to wane. These concerns were resolved, and the cave continues to be a natural wonder for viewers.

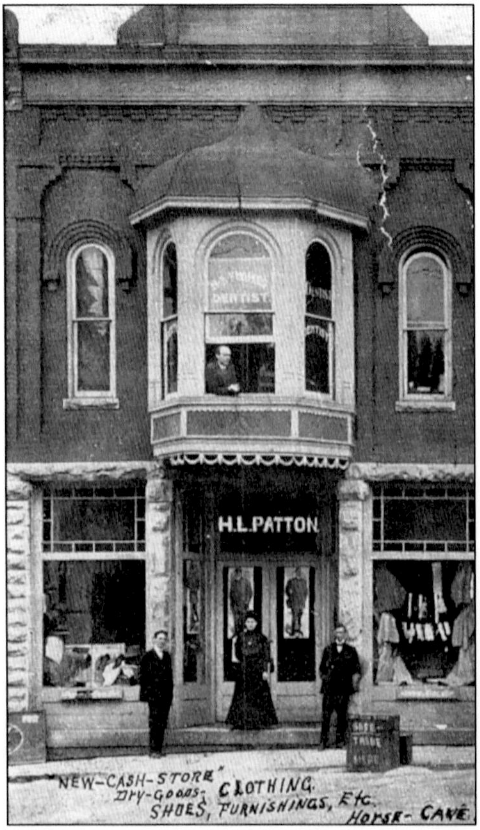

NEW CASH STORE-H.L. PATTON, HORSE CAVE, c. 1906. Horse Cave was established in the 1840s and incorporated in 1864. Residents of the town voted in 1869 to change the name to Caverna, but public confusion caused the return of the original name. Proprietor H.L. Patton advertises at the bottom of this early Horse Cave postcard that his store has dry goods, clothing, shoes, furnishings, etc. for sale. Dr. Harry Thomas sits in the window of his dentist office. The building housed a vaudeville theater on the second floor. This building burned about 1910 and the structure, which was rebuilt on this site, currently houses the Horse Cave Theater.

BAPTIST CHURCH, HORSE CAVE, c. 1920. The first assemblage of Baptists to organize a church in Horse Cave was in 1868. The Baptists, Methodists, Presbyterians, and Campbellites built and used one church during the early part of 1868. It was located on Church Street, and the Free Masons used the second story. A frame structure was built in 1886 and used by the Baptists until this structure was completed in 1911. The old frame building was sold and moved. The present church at this site was constructed in 1957.

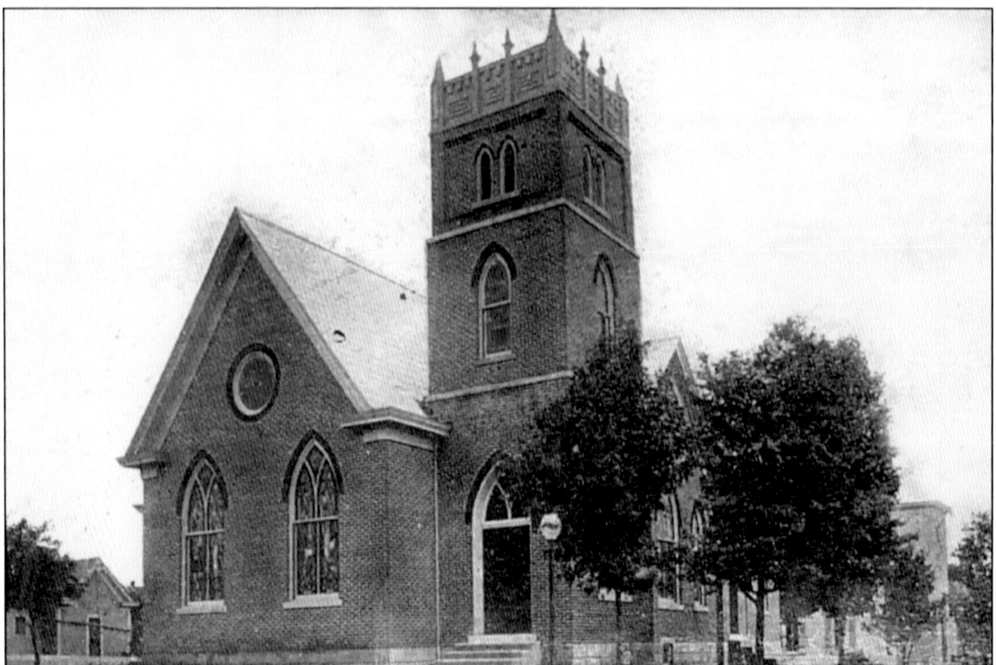

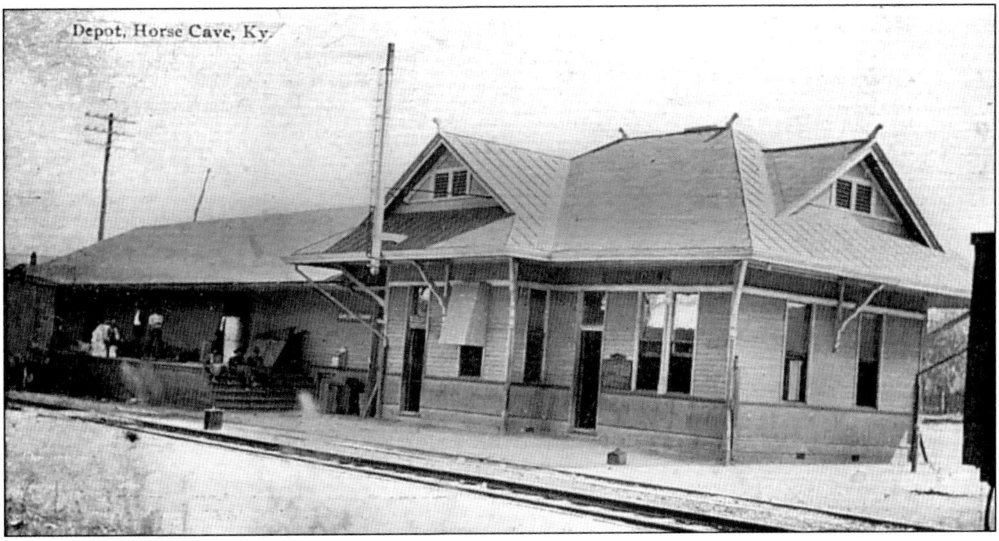

HORSE CAVE DEPOT, *c.* 1915. The first depot was built on land donated to the L&N Railroad by Maj. Albert Anderson, the founder of Horse Cave. Anderson stipulated that the station be called Horse Cave after the nearby cave. The station was burned in 1862, and the building pictured here was constructed a short time afterward on trestles over a sinkhole that was later filled in.

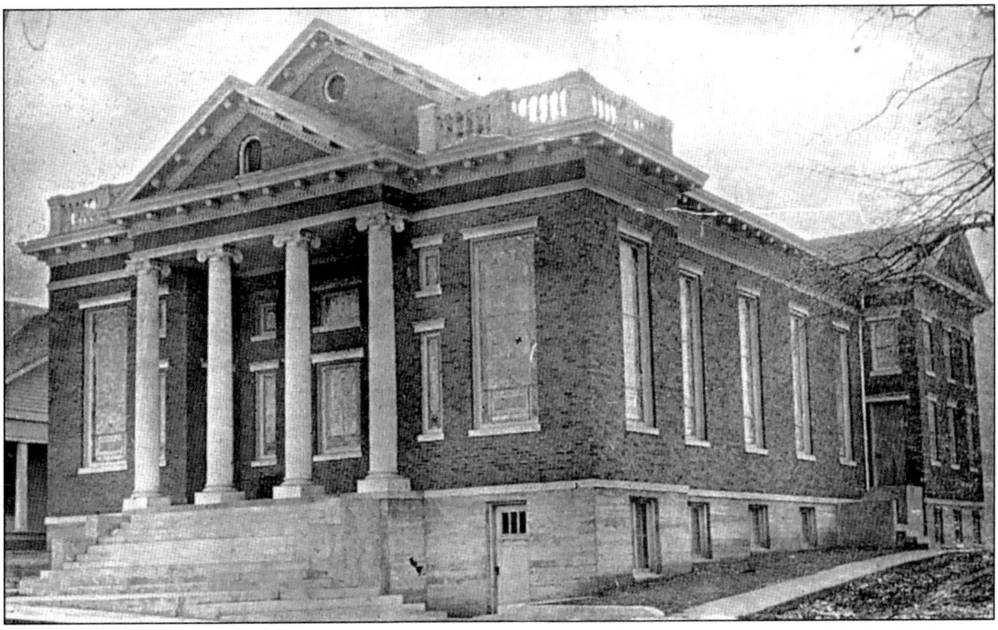

METHODIST CHURCH, HORSE CAVE, *c.* 1924. The Methodist congregation traces their beginnings to 1868. They worshiped in a frame building built in 1880. As early as 1913 they talked of the need for a new building. Local contractor Clarence Owens began building the $40,000 structure in 1922, but a shortage of building supplies held up its completion. Although the brick walls and roof had been constructed for some time, the interior was not completed until 1924. The congregation met in the basement for three years. The first service in the auditorium was held in February 1924, but the official dedication occurred in June 1924, with almost 3,000 people in attendance. Approximately 1,800 people partook of the dinner served in the basement.

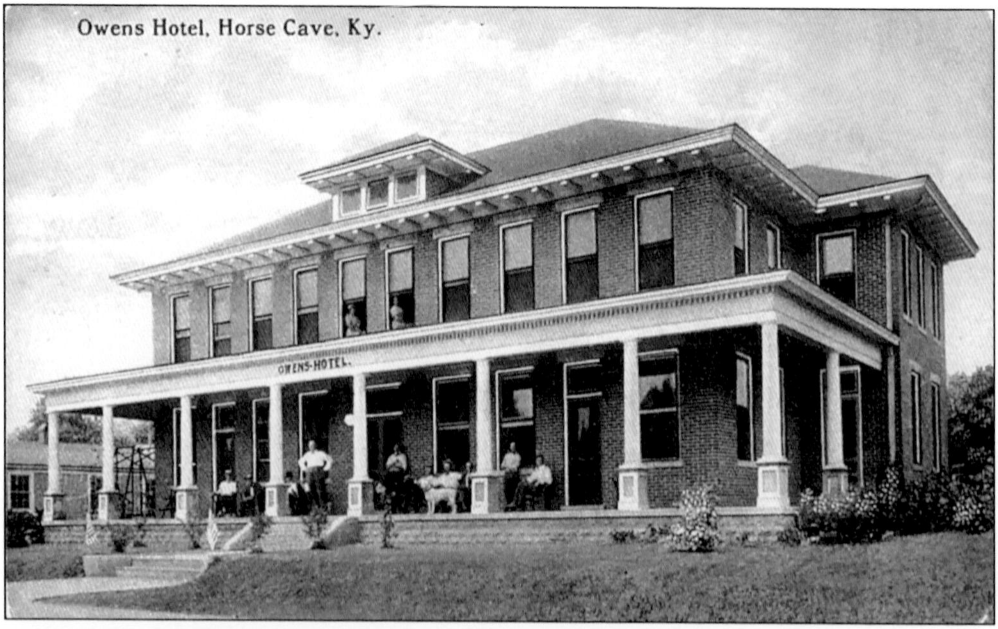

Owens Hotel, Horse Cave, *c.* 1920. This hotel was built in 1908 by Clarence Owens and the annex was added in 1925. The main building was destroyed by fire in 1930 and was later rebuilt.

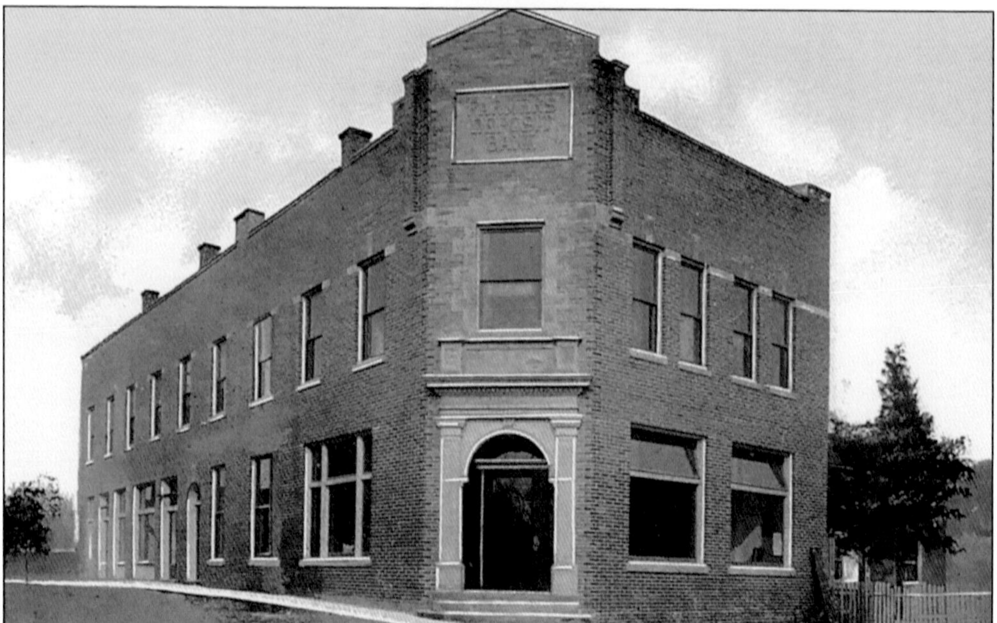

Farmers Deposit Bank, *c.* 1910. This bank was located on the corner of Main Street and Higby Avenue in Horse Cave. It closed in 1926 and was reorganized as Horse Cave State Bank. In the 1930s, the pictured brick exterior was replaced by an art deco facade that exists today.

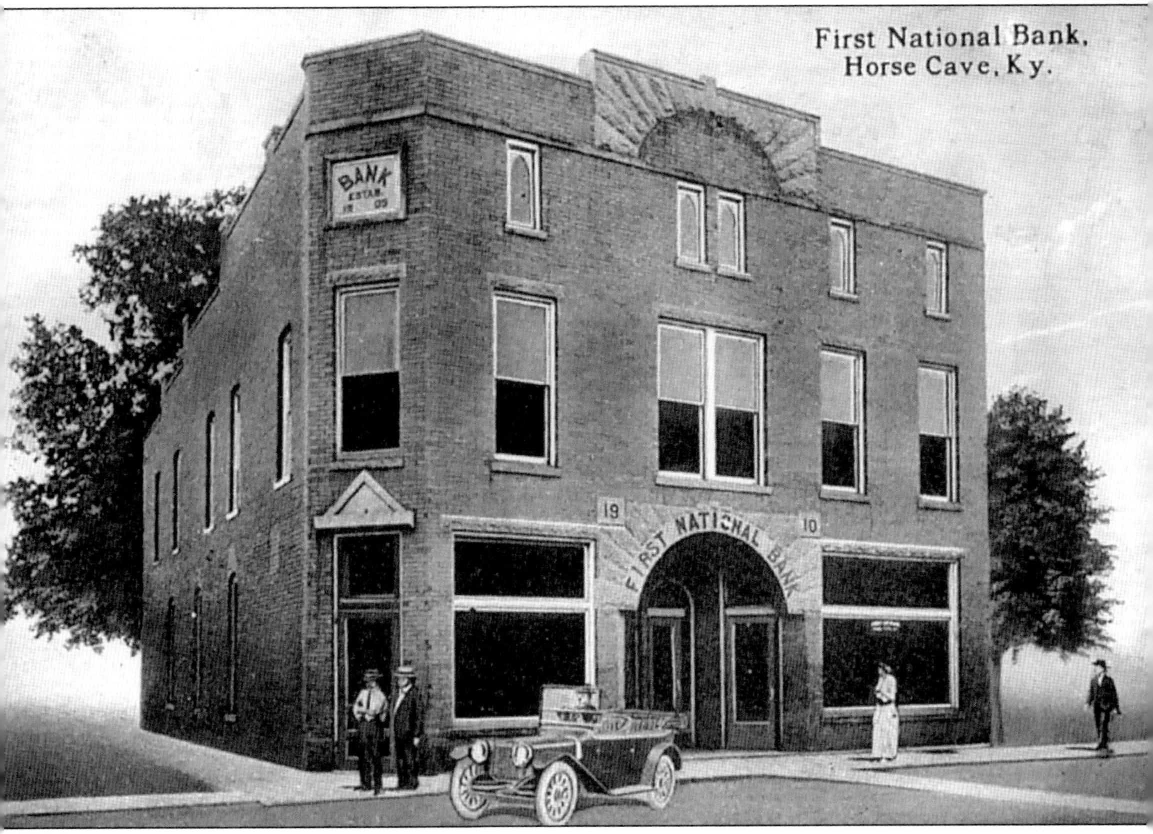

First National Bank, c. 1915. Although the bank was established in 1905, this building, located across the street from Farmer's Deposit Bank, was constructed in 1910. In 1924, Will Bell, the controversial president of First National Bank, was actually tried and acquitted of conspiracy to rob the Canmer Bank. In 1926, when bank examiners visited First National Bank, Coy Cann, vice-president and cashier, left the bank and drove his Buick down Highway 31W to Richardson Crossing where he parked his car and committed "suicide by locomotive." It was later learned that he had misappropriated the funds that many customers had left with him to be deposited. In 1930, the Bank of Kentucky failed, due in large part to the Great Depression. As First National Bank was one of its correspondent banks, it was forced to close that same year. Shortly thereafter, Will Bell walked to a barn behind his house and hanged himself with a T-Model brake rod.

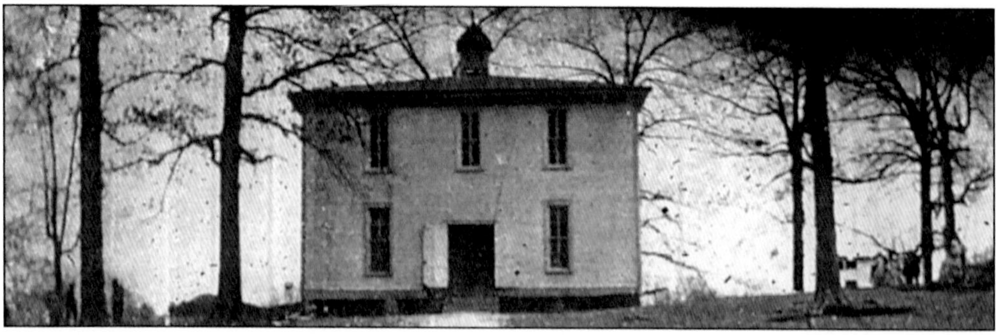

Canmer Graded and High School, c. 1915. The Canmer Graded and High School opened on September 9, 1912. It also was a "Normal School" that educated teachers. After taking courses here, the teacher candidates would take their final tests for certification at Munfordville. It was a boarding school where students from all the surrounding counties attended. They would board in private households. L.L. Hudson was the principal at the time the above picture was taken. After the school closed in 1919, the bell used in the tower was given to Hart Memorial High School.

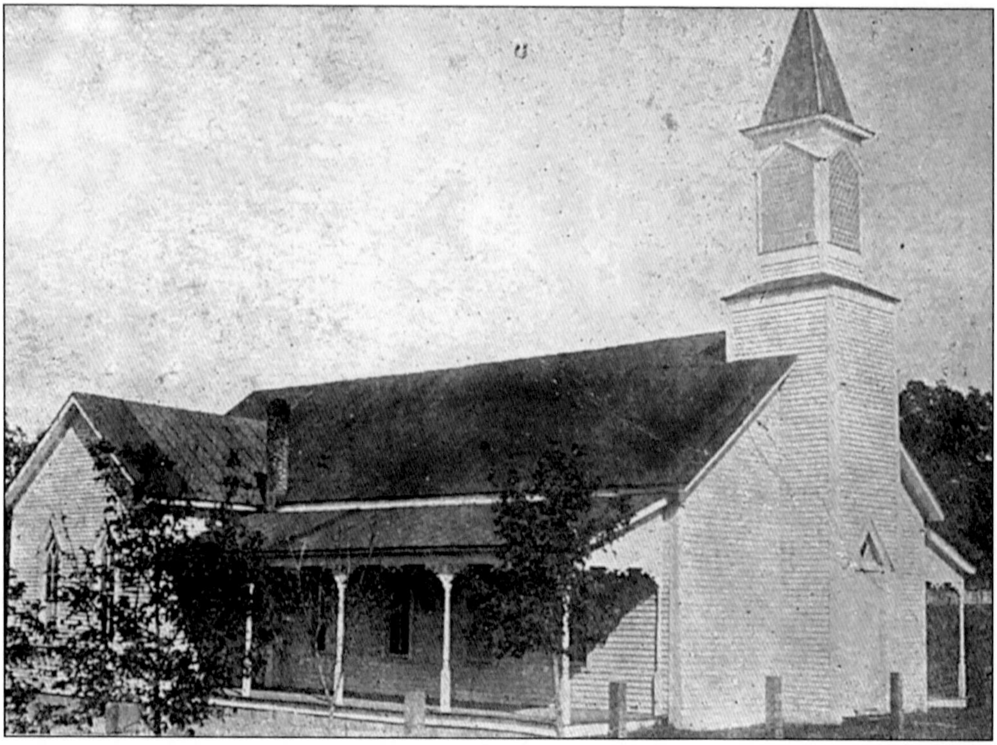

Methodist Church, Canmer, c. 1910. This building was constructed in 1893, one year before the Baptist Church was built behind it. On the first and third Sundays, the Methodist Church hosted services, which the Baptists attended, and on the alternate Sundays the Methodists attended the Baptist services. In the 1920s and 1930s, three-week-long revivals were held with people attending to hear the preaching and join the singing into the wee hours of the evening. The McDowells, a string instrument group from Indiana, provided the music. Emma Walton was the church pianist and community piano teacher in the 1930s. The side porches were put to good use when church dinners were spread after services. Each summer a new No. 2 washtub would be bought just to hold lemonade served from a tin dipper for the "church spreads."

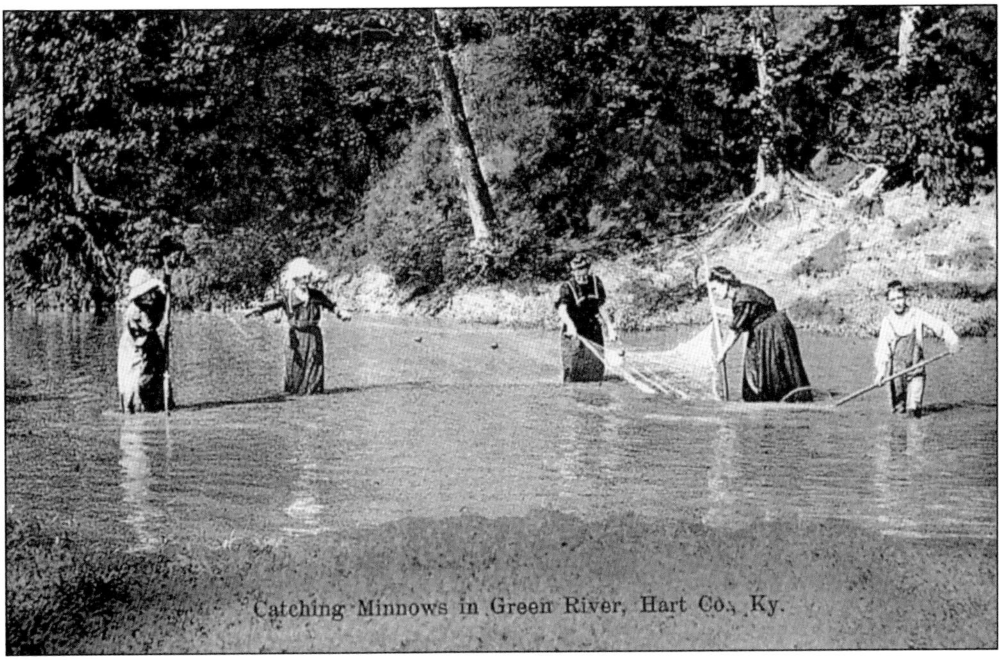

Seining for Minnows, c. 1909. Even seining for minnows in Green River was a time for these Hart County ladies to look pert and wear their Sunday finest, as this image reveals. Perhaps one purpose for the young boy's presence was to assist in carrying the ladies' many forthcoming "catches of the day" that the minnows would doubtless help provide.

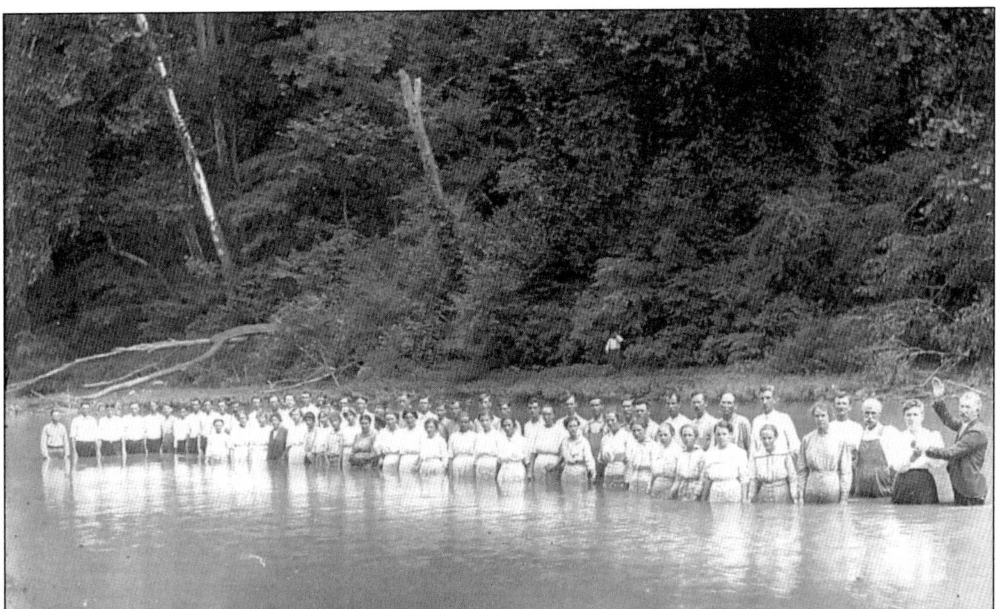

River Baptism, c. 1915. Candidates for baptism and Rev. W.T. Parrish (right) pose for this picture while standing in the river prior to being baptized. This site was used for church baptisms for many decades. The ceremony usually occurred on a Sunday afternoon, following the morning church service and a picnic lunch.

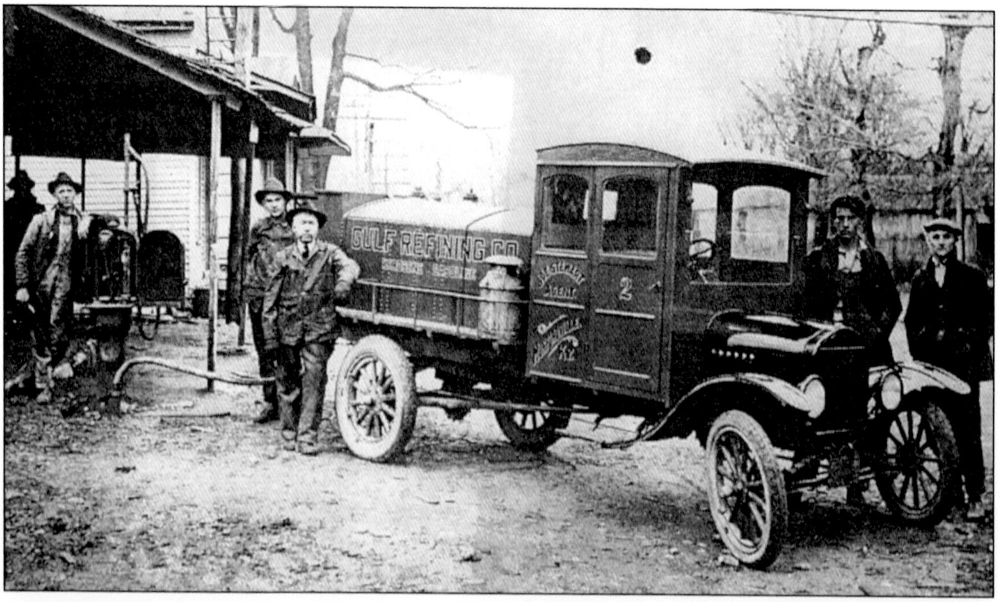

Early Gulf Distributors, c. 1925. The words "Gulf Refining Co." appear on this early 1920s Model TT one-ton truck. Printed below the rear side window is "Joe Stewart-Agent" and beneath his name in fancy angular script is "Hardyville, KY." An underground tank beneath a gas pump is being filled with gasoline from the truck's tank through the hose at left. Gulf distributors Joe Stewart and B.C. Brachey owned this gasoline and coal oil tank delivery truck.

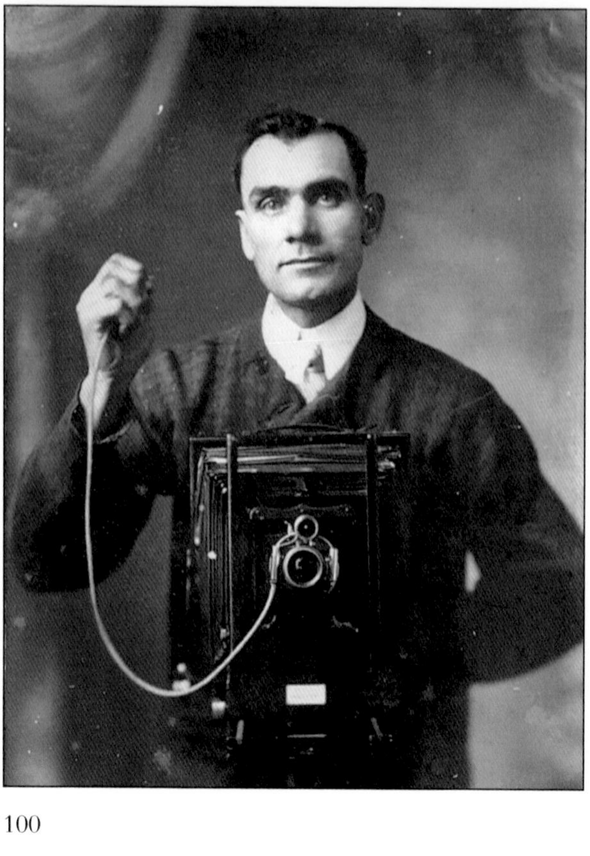

Look Pleasant, Please . . . I Want Your Picture, c. 1920. With these words, noted Hart County photographer John O. Reid has taken another picture that has memorialized for posterity an early 1900s school or church group, a family reunion, a man seated in his first automobile, or a small country store. A resident of Canmer, Reid (1878–1972) became interested in photography at an early age. As word of his talent spread, Reid's services in Hart County as well as in towns and communities throughout adjoining counties became increasingly in demand. Several of the images in this chapter are the result of his work in photography.

Five

TAYLOR COUNTY

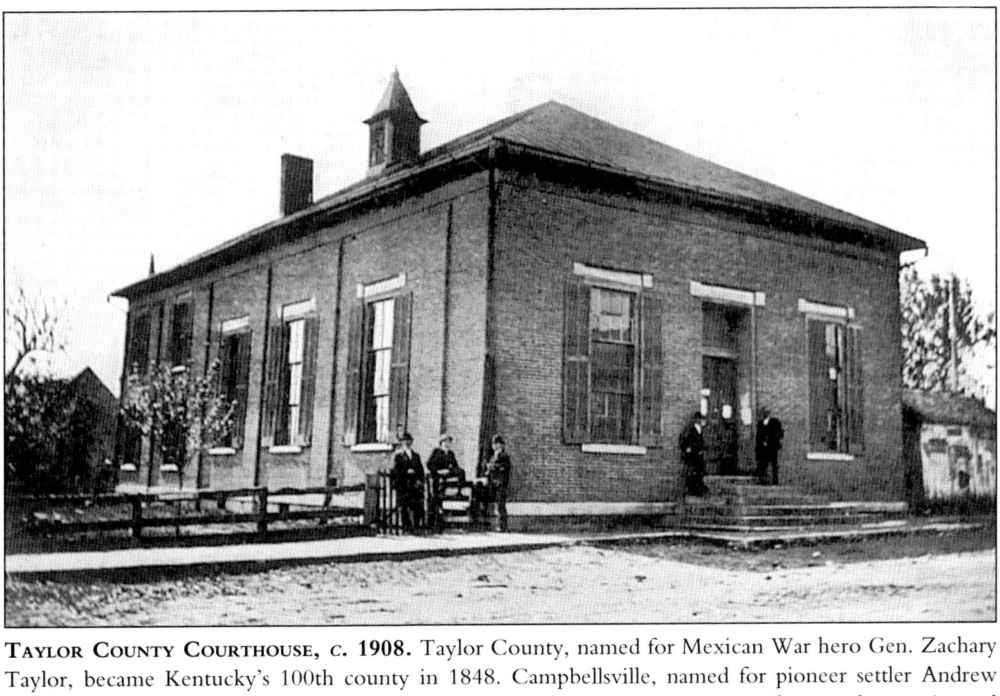

TAYLOR COUNTY COURTHOUSE, *c.* 1908. Taylor County, named for Mexican War hero Gen. Zachary Taylor, became Kentucky's 100th county in 1848. Campbellsville, named for pioneer settler Andrew Campbell who founded the town in 1808, was chosen to be the county seat. The courthouse pictured above was built between 1866 and 1867 to replace the brick structure burned by Confederate general Hylan B. Lyon on Christmas Day in 1864. Lyon had invaded Kentucky with 800 men in December 1864 to enforce CSA draft law and divert Union forces from Nashville. In 23 days he burned seven courthouses used by Union forces. He allowed some local women to save some of the Taylor County records. When he moved out of the state in January his ranks had been reduced to 250 men due to desertions. The clerk's office was built on the square in 1865–1866 and used for the county business until this building was constructed.

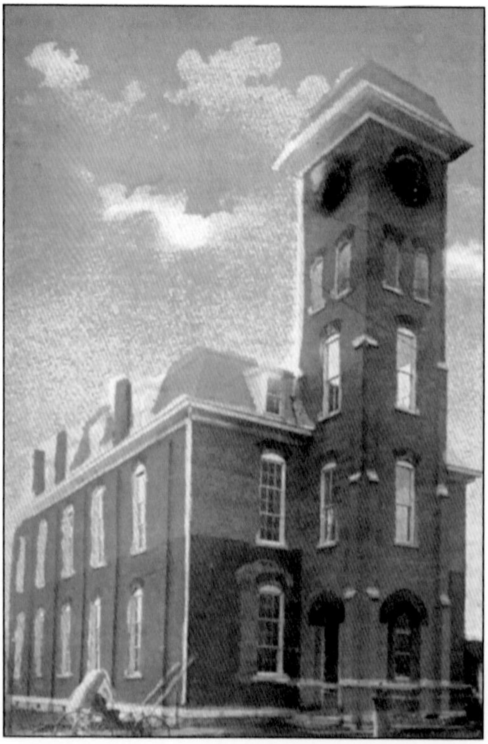

Second Taylor County Courthouse with Clock Tower, *c.* 1915. About 1910 the county court enlarged the 1867 courthouse by adding a second story and a clock tower. In 1965 this building was completely razed and replaced by the present contemporary structure.

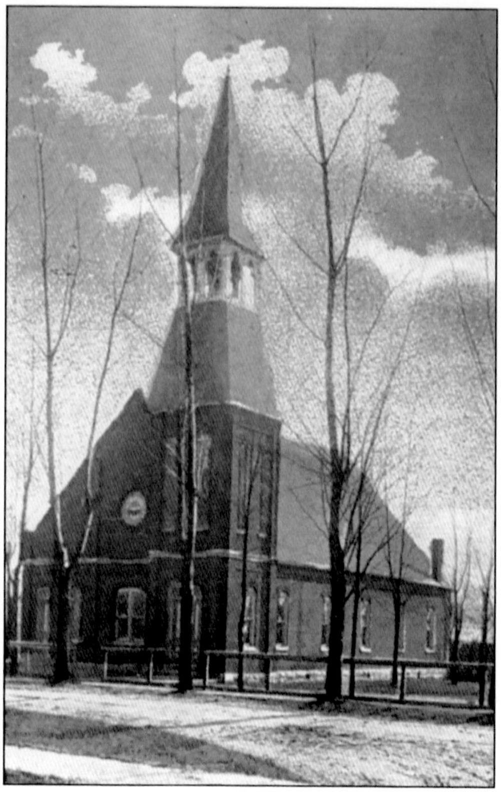

First Presbyterian Church, *c.* 1926. This building was erected in 1892 to replace the first church that was destroyed by fire. The bell was saved and is still in use. In 1924, a new bell tower was constructed and other alterations were made to produce the present edifice. In 1966, this church merged with the Bethel congregation to become the Bethel First Presbyterian Church.

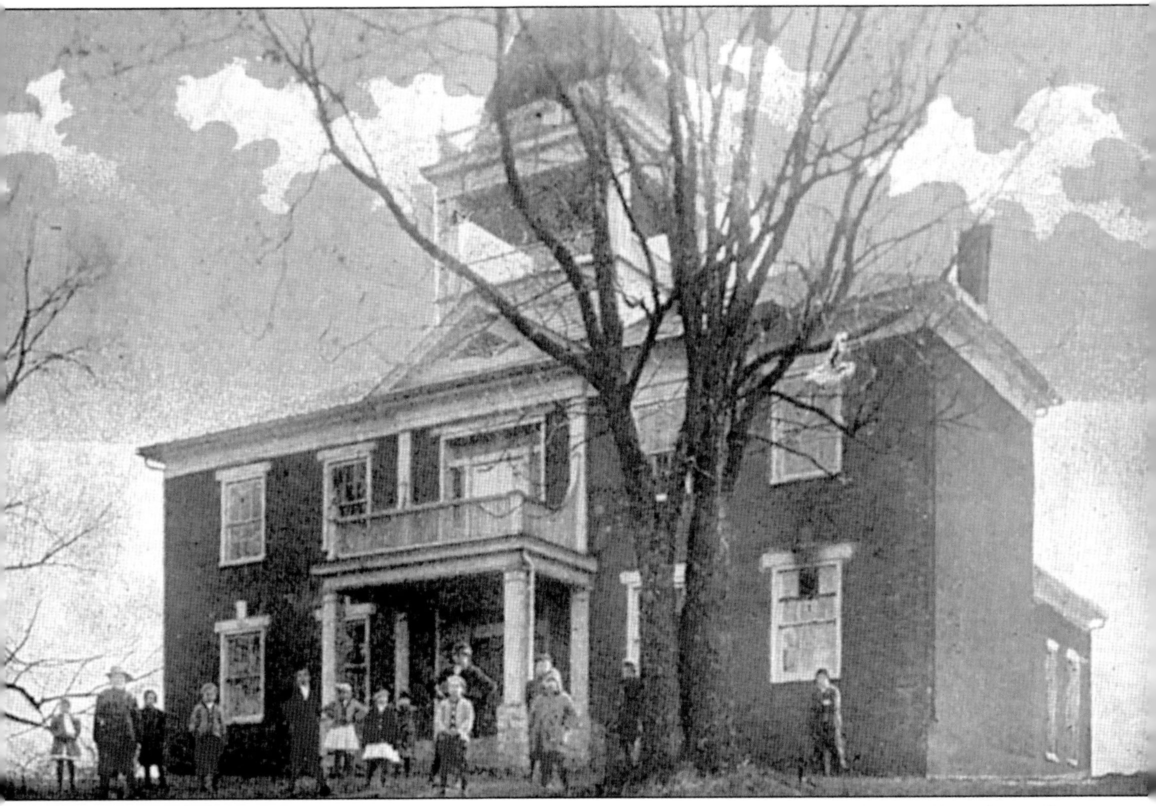

S.W. BUCHANAN COLLEGIATE INSTITUTE, *C.* 1915. Following the fire at the Taylor Academy located on Lebanon Avenue, a group of Presbyterian men purchased the John Bass home, a large residence that stood on the hill overlooking the town spring at the south end of Court Street, and established a private school called the Campbellsville High School. In 1903, the stockholders of Campbellsville High School transferred the property to the joint ownership of the Campbellsville and Bethel Presbyterian Churches with the provision that the school be continued as a high school under Presbyterian control. In 1904, G.H. Buchanan and his wife, S.W. Buchanan, made a donation to the school of $1,500 with the provision that the Bible always be taught in the school as one of the regular courses. The board accepted the donation and by unanimous vote changed the name of the school to S.W. Buchanan Collegiate Institute. The school was discontinued in 1917 and the building torn down.

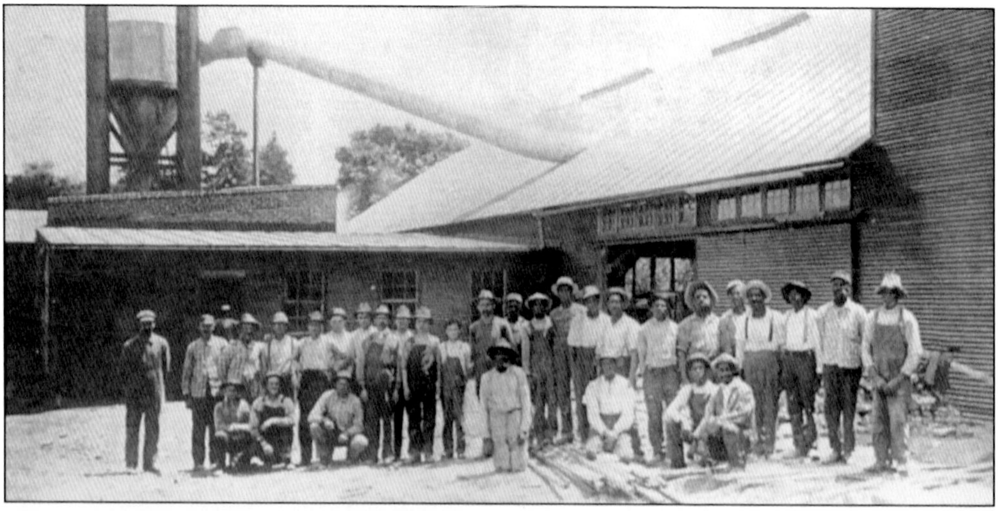

Mill on Jackson Street, c. 1910. During the late 1800s and early 1900s, mills were located on both sides of the railroad tracks near where Houchens grocery is now located. One mill known as "Old Red Mill" was known for its red-painted wooden building. Campbellsville Lumber Company was another milling operation; it was begun by U.P. Walling and later owned and operated by brothers Walter and Ralph Wood about 1900. Henry Parrott and R. Towler Parrott later became partners of the Wood brothers. The mill made lumber, hardwood flooring, and hogsheads for tobacco. On the opposite side of the track were the Gowdy and Parrott Lumber and Stave Mill, which made tobacco hogsheads and staves for the whiskey business.

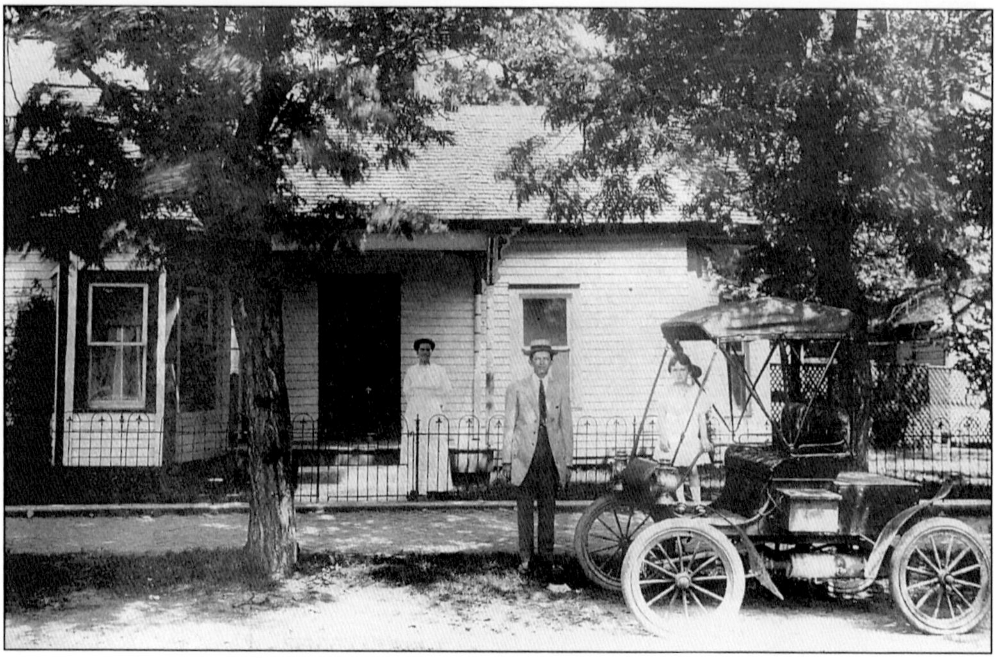

First Car in Campbellsville, c. 1905. Ray Borders and Florence Collins Borders were the proud owners of the first car in Campbellsville. The vehicle was a "curved dash," one-cylinder Oldsmobile with tiller steering, which was used prior to the advent of the steering wheel. The Borders family home was located on Main Street where the Methodist Church stands today.

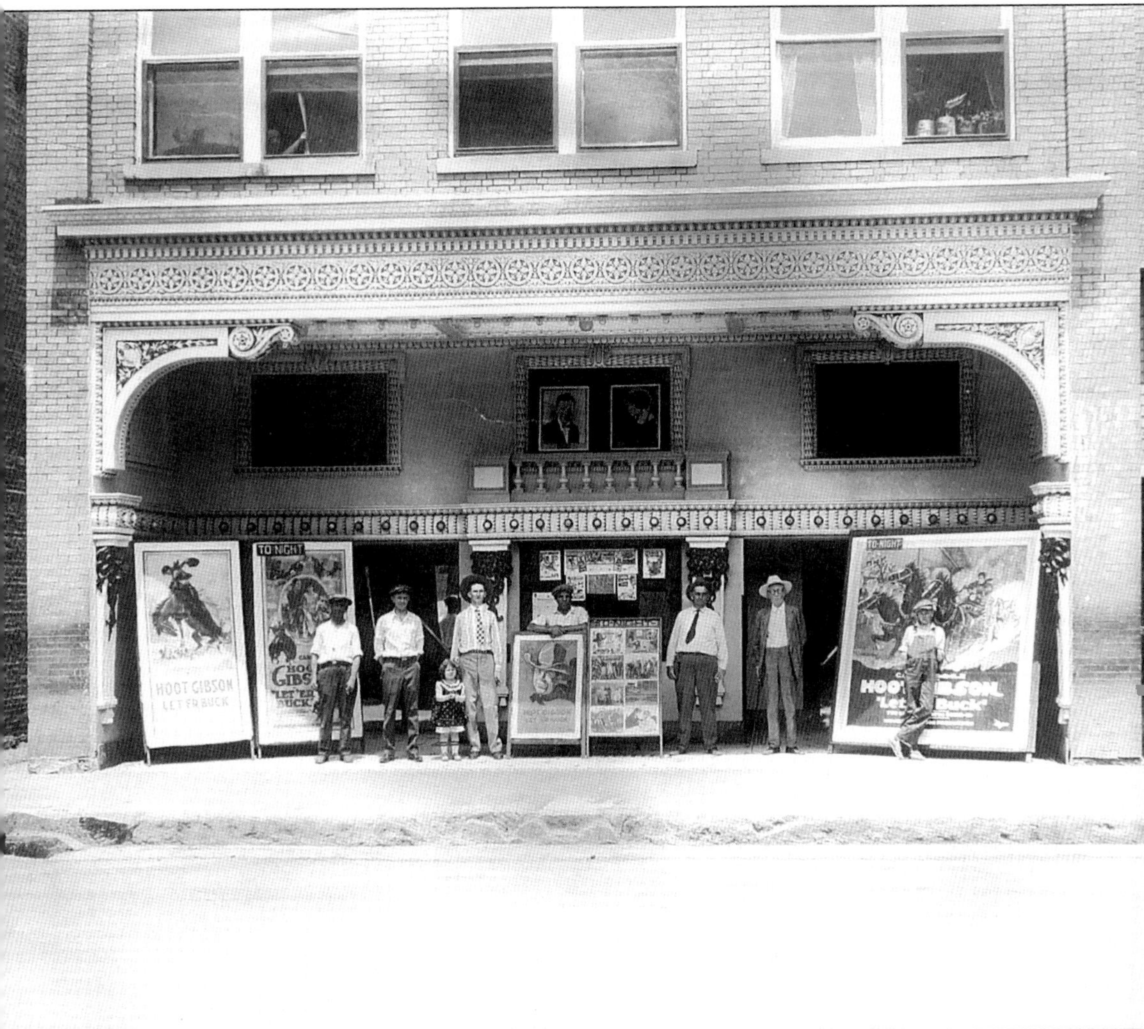

ALHAMBRA THEATER, C. 1924. The Alhambra "Picture" Theater exhibited its first show, a nine-reel special entitled *The Eternal City*, on Thanksgiving Day, November 30, 1916. Located on Main Street, the theater held matinees every Saturday at 1:30 p.m. for the price of 5¢ to 10¢. The numerous signs in the above image left little doubt that the featured attraction that evening was *Let 'Er Buck*, starring Hoot Gibson. Posing in front of the theater are, from left to right, Sam Dix, Owsley Durham, Margaret Mae Sanders, Paul Sanders (theater owner), Jim Meader, Harl Sanders, and an unknown boy.

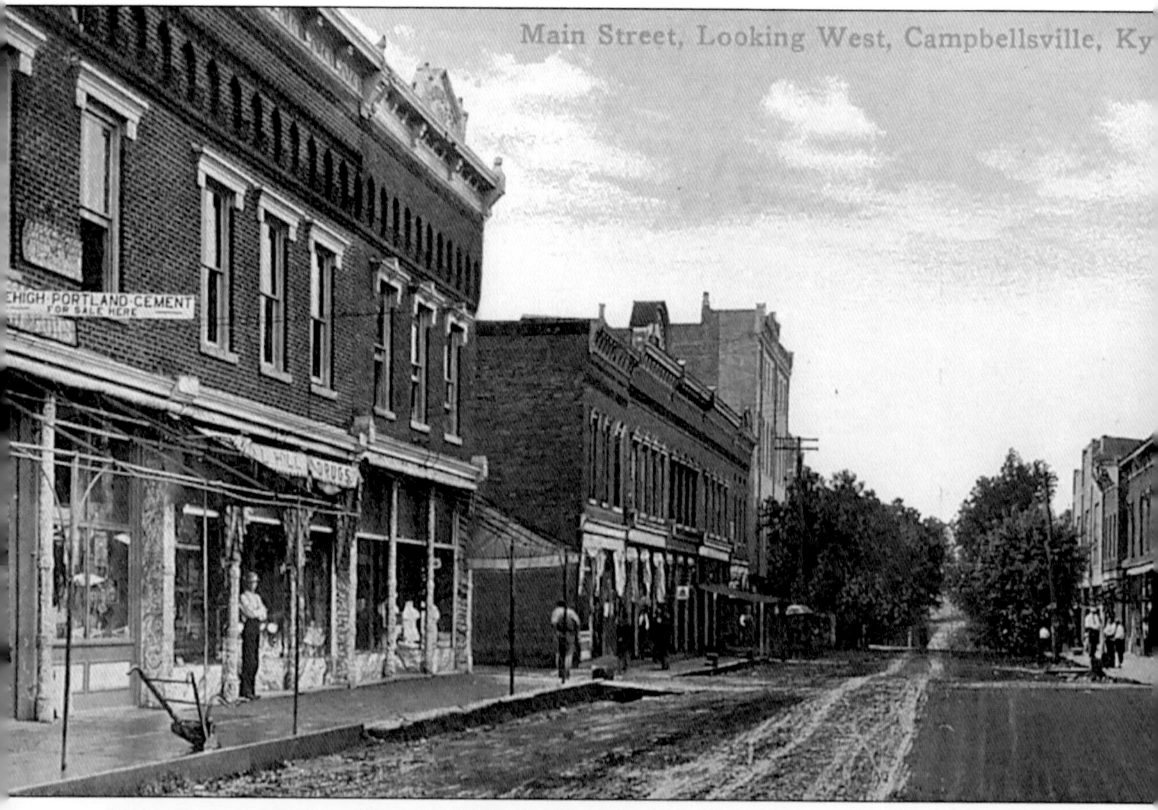

Main Street, Looking West, c. 1908. Looking closely at the signs on the buildings at left one sees Lehigh Portland Cement for sale at a hardware store, then R.L. Hill Drugs and Jewelry Store, where the Campbellsville Circulating Library operated out of a rear room. Next door is Dr. W.T. Chandler's Drug Store, where one could purchase his chicken cholera remedy. Martin Spurling & Co., undertakers since 1896, occupied the third building. Spurling also sold hardware and published postcards. The telephone office was located upstairs in the next establishment. The tallest structure at the end of the row is the Willock Building, which was completed in 1908.

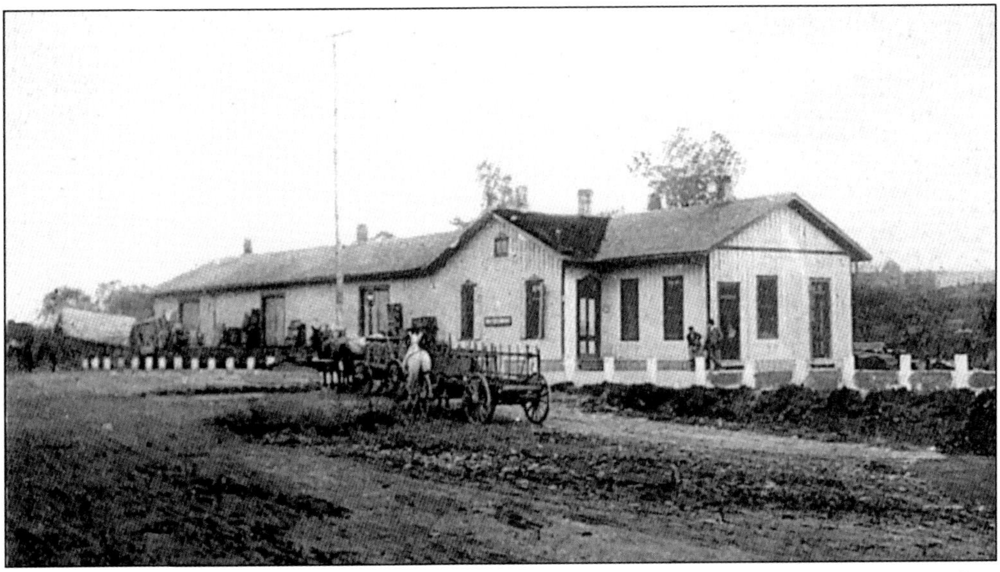

L&N Passenger Depot and Freight Station, c. 1907. This photograph shows the depot located on Depot Street, now called South Central Avenue. After years of bond issues and promises, the Cumberland and Ohio branch of the L&N Railroad was completed to Campbellsville from Lebanon in 1879. In January 1913, the newspaper reported that Taylor Countians agreed to pay the reduced railroad bond of $137,000. This debt hung over the county for 50 years. No one would serve as sheriff because he would have to collect the unpopular railroad tax. This was finally laid to rest in 1919 when each taxpayer in the county paid $53, and Taylor County again had a sheriff.

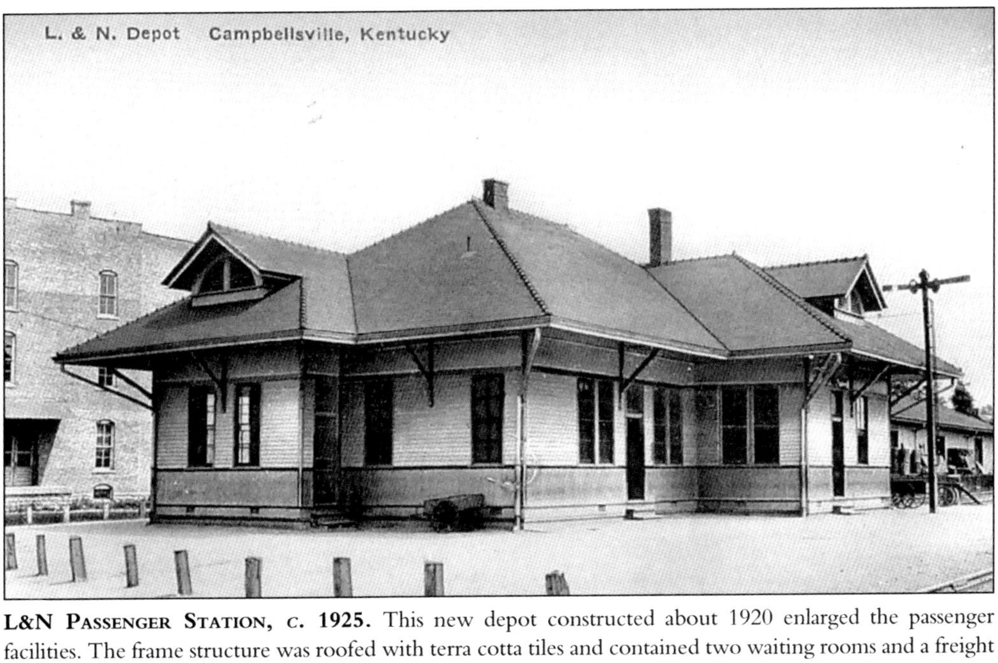

L&N Passenger Station, c. 1925. This new depot constructed about 1920 enlarged the passenger facilities. The frame structure was roofed with terra cotta tiles and contained two waiting rooms and a freight office. The old freight office was still located on the east side of this building. Seven people were employed here. The two-wheeled vehicle shown transported the mail to the post office. The steel-wheeled vehicle on the right transported baggage. White chipped stone surrounded the building.

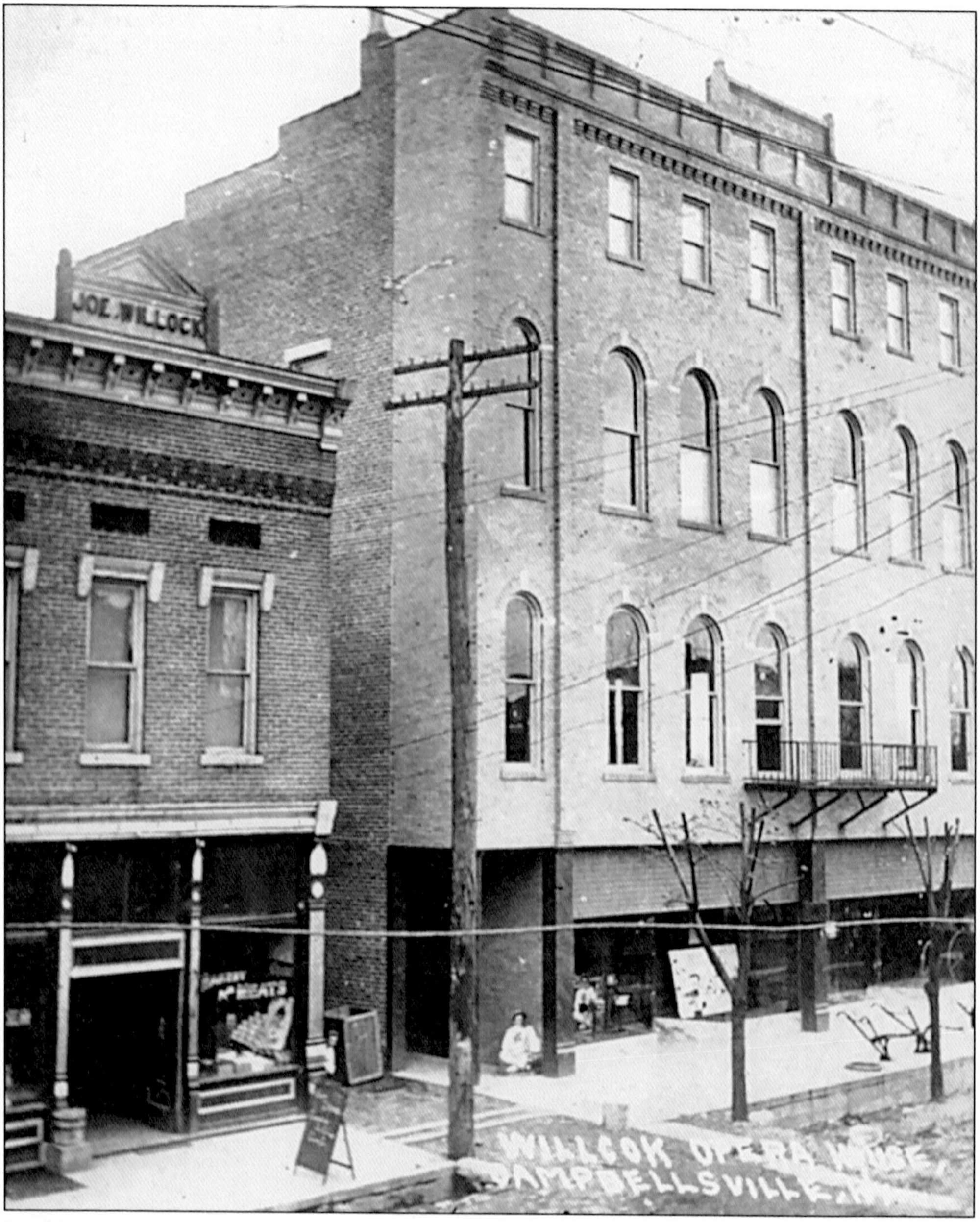

Joe Willock Store, c. 1910. The two-story building seen here was the Joe Willock grocery store. It was told that on fish days he would receive a barrel of fish from the depot, knock out the head of the barrel, spill out the fish, and sell all of them in a short time. He began a Coca-Cola Bottling Co. in the rear basement of this building in 1905 and sold the bottling business to investors from Bowling Green in 1914. In 1908, the four-story Willock Building was constructed. Hatcher-Mitchell Mens Store and Buchanan Lyon Hardware leased the first floor in 1915–1916. On the second floor, an opera house hosted vaudeville acts and a motion picture show. It became a skating rink when the opera house ceased operation in the 1920s. The third floor was the meeting place for the Pitman Masonic Lodge.

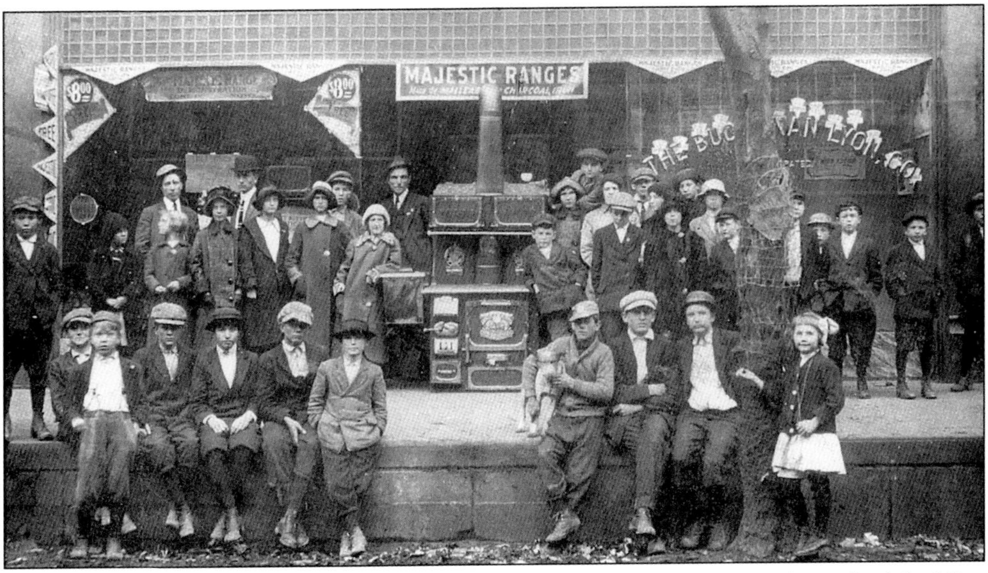

Buchanan-Lyon Company, c. 1915. The owners of this business, located in the Willock building at the lower end of Main Street, are putting on a demonstration and display of Majestic Ranges. Many would-be patrons and children have gathered to pose for the camera on this cold and wintry day in Campbellsville.

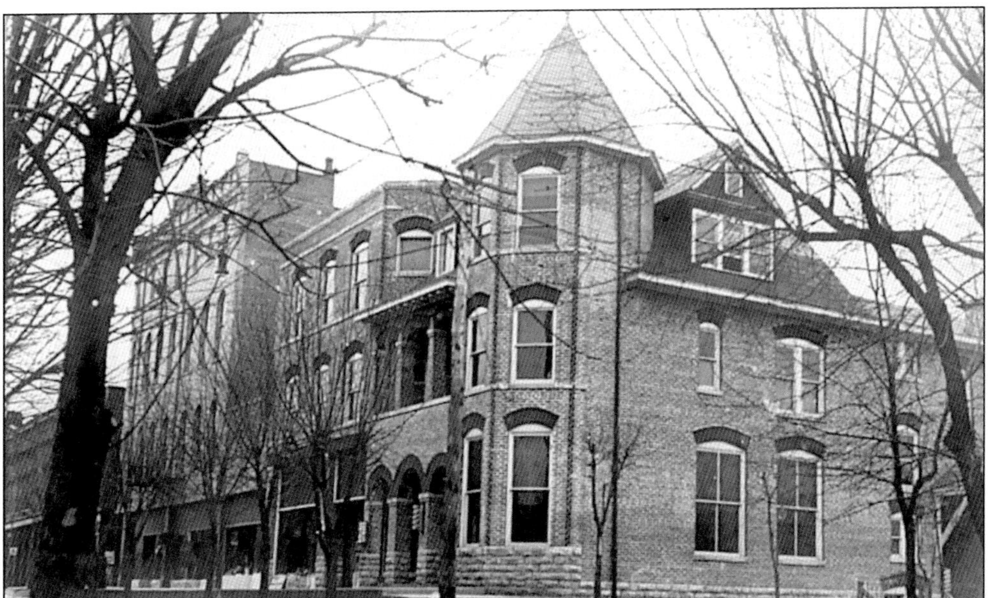

Merchant's Hotel, 1911. This 3-story, 32-room hotel on Main Street in Campbellsville was constructed about 1909. The hotel played an important role in the commercial growth of Campbellsville during the period from 1910 to 1935 when it provided both lodging and meals for traveling salesmen and other visitors to the area. The town's leading hotel during its heyday, it was a social nucleus for many Campbellsville residents. It contained a large dining room and a parlor on the second floor that became a popular recreation spot. It was later operated as a rooming house for several years by a couple affectionately known as "Uncle Walt" and "Aunt Mag" Hoskins.

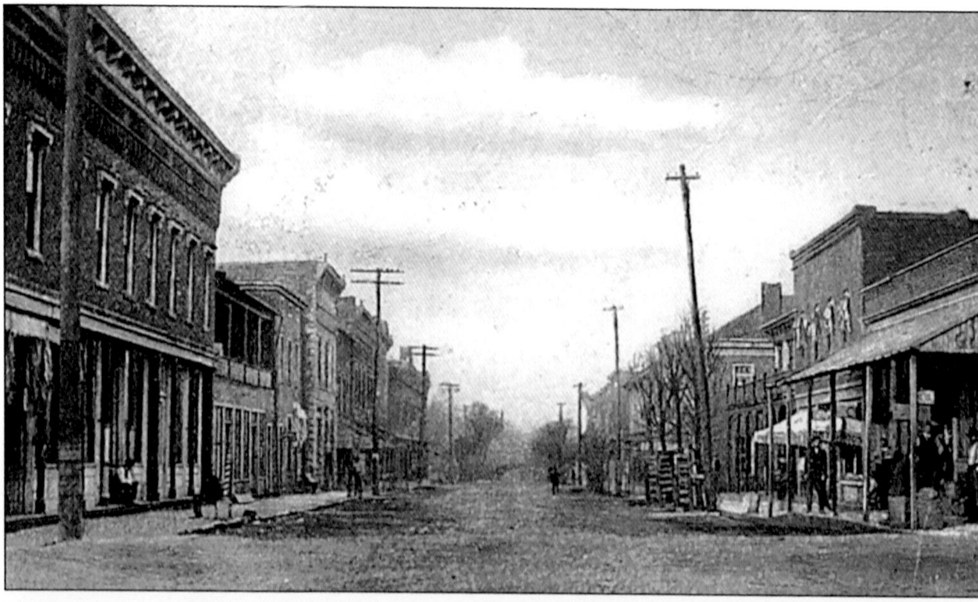

Main Street, c. 1910. Looking west at the intersection of Main Street and Central Avenue, the first building on the right is the grocery store owned by Walter Coakley, next is Norman Hobson's Grocery, then Thomas E. Hoskins' Dry Goods, and just below is the Commercial Hotel. On the left is the Old Post Office Building, the Campbellsvile Hotel, a barber shop complete with a striped pole in front, and the law office of Charles W. Wright. The stone-fronted building across the alley was occupied by Taylor, Pruitt and Jarvis, with the Billy Chandler Novelty Company, established in 1892, next door.

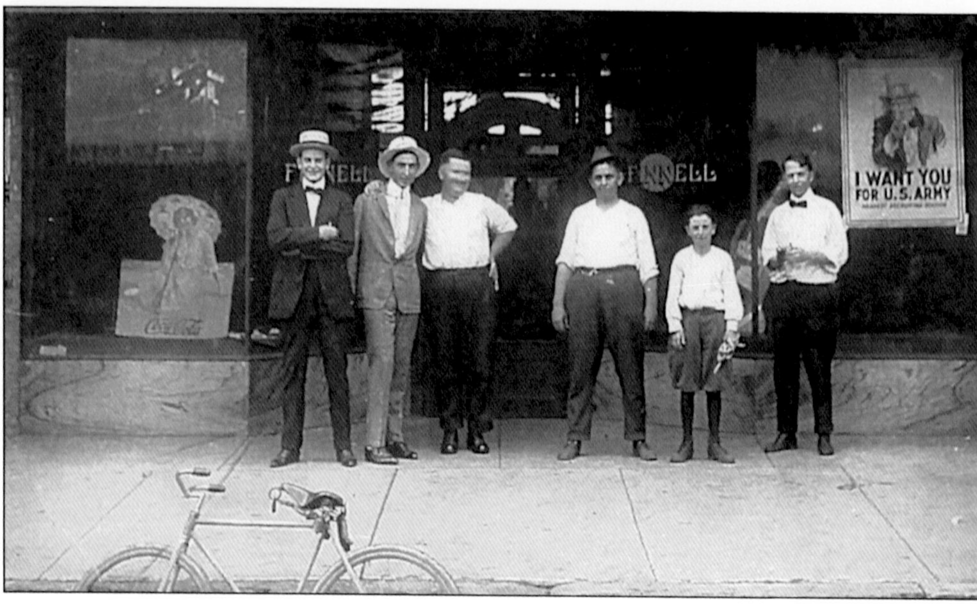

Ricketts and Finnell Confectionery, 1917. This business was located on Main Street in the Davis block. Pictured, from left to right, are George Willson Sr., unidentified, Ray Hobson, Jim Meader, unidentified, and Shirley Finnell. Shirley Finnell sold candy, ice cream, and other confections for many years. A poster of a beautiful lady holding a parasol advertising Coca-Cola is in the left window and the famous "Uncle Sam" recruiting poster for World War I is in the right window.

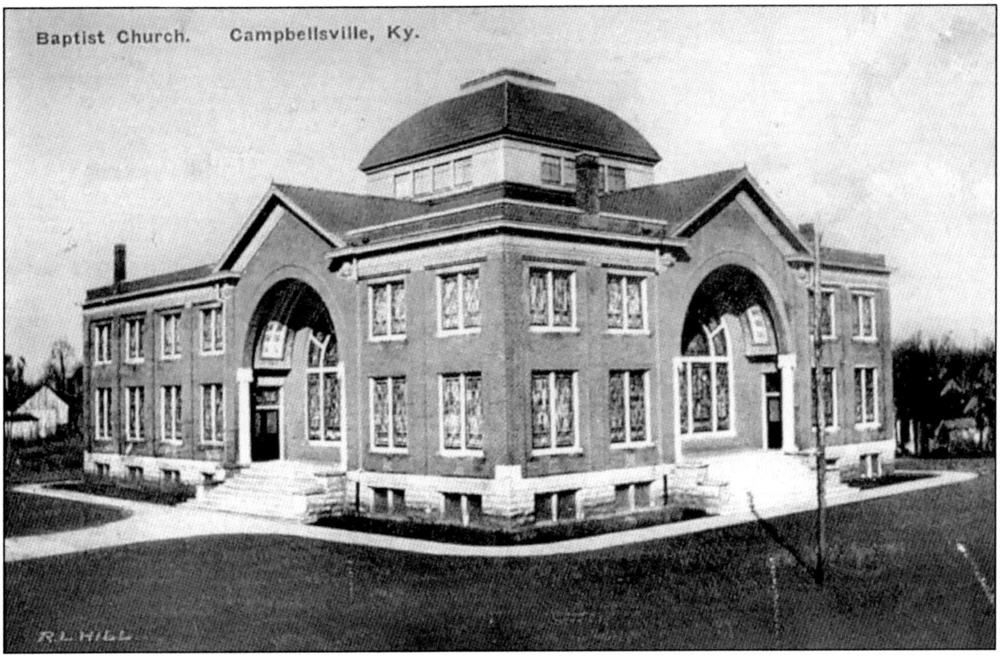

CAMPBELLSVILLE BAPTIST CHURCH, c. 1925. Located on North Central Avenue, the church was constructed in 1915–1916 with some Palladian-style features. A domed ceiling and four walls of arched stained-glass windows added grand architectural details. The church was destroyed by fire in 1962.

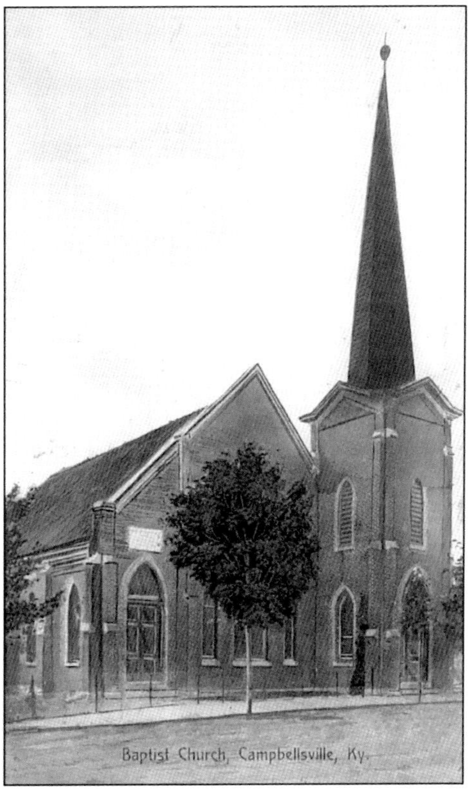

BAPTIST CHURCH, c. 1915. Shuttleworth Memorial Baptist Church was built in 1889. It replaced a frame church where county court was conducted in the 1860s after the Confederate Army burned the courthouse. After building a new church in 1915, this building was sold to the Cumberland Presbyterians two years later. In 1974 it became the home of the Taylor County Library.

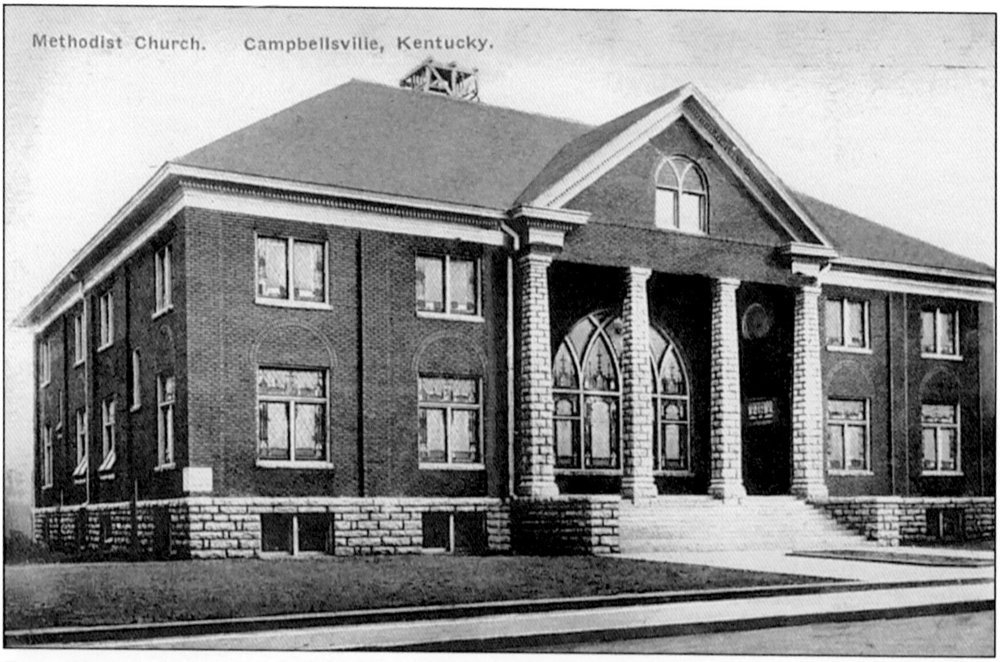

FIRST UNITED METHODIST CHURCH, c. 1925. Located on Main Street, this church was built in 1921. The chief architect and contractor of the congregation's fourth building was J.T. Phillips. It was constructed on a lot donated by W.S. Hill, Edward Hill, and A.C. Hill. The stonework was the handiwork of Buck Mikel. In 1940 a fire damaged the church, but was controlled before it did serious harm.

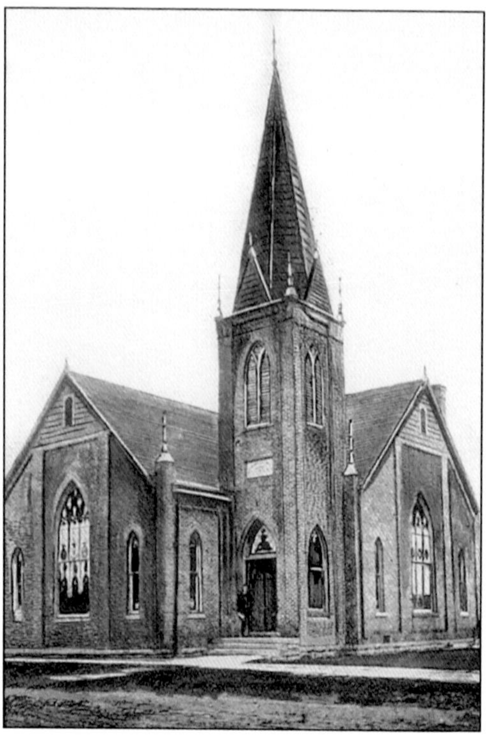

METHODIST CHURCH c. 1918. This third building for Methodist worship was located on Main Street opposite the present Methodist Church. Built in 1901, the main entrance was through the bell tower structure. The building was dismantled in the 1920s, and the old bell was given to Campbellsville College for use in its dining hall.

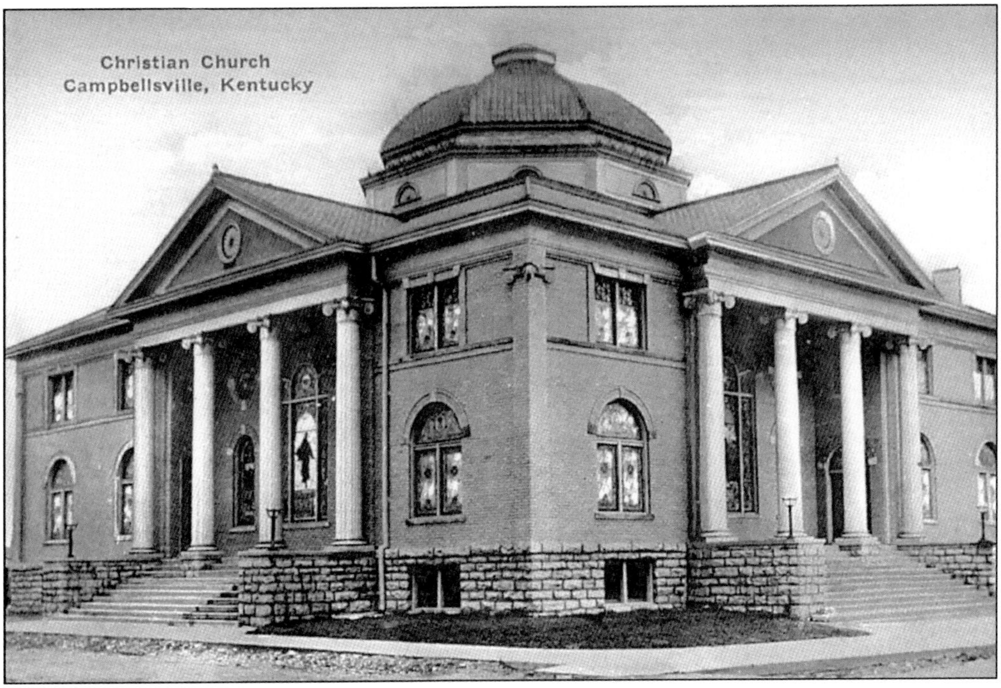

CAMPBELLSVILLE CHRISTIAN CHURCH, c. 1916. A *News Journal* article of May 27, 1915 announced that a new $20,000 church was being built on the Creed Haskins homestead at the corner of Lebanon Avenue and Maple Street. The article read, "J.E. Green, architect of Birmingham, Alabama, is working on the plans and specifications. After the ground breaking of June 1st, the building will be rushed to completion. Their present building is too small." George Gowdy paid for one half of the construction cost. Stone crosswalks connected sidewalks lining the unpaved streets.

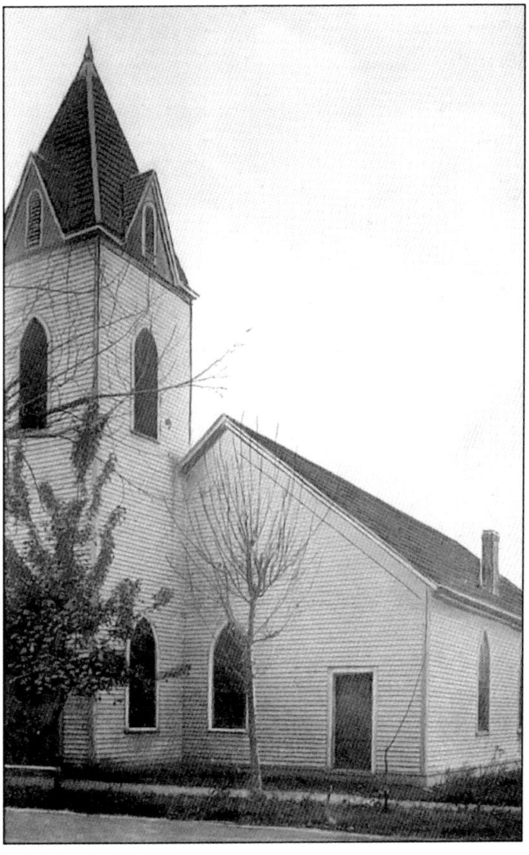

CAMPBELLSVILLE CHRISTIAN CHURCH, c. 1915. This white-frame building built about 1884 was located at 301 Lebanon Avenue.

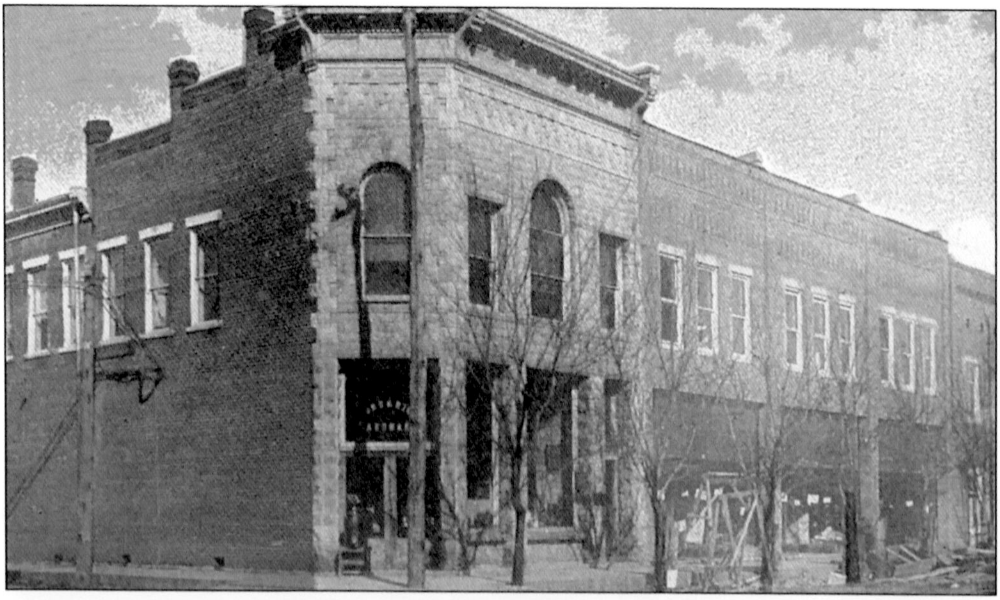

Telephone Exchange over Hord and Hall Hardware, c. 1913. Located on the corner of Main and Depot Streets and built before 1908, this building was occupied by Richard Hord and J.S. Hall as a hardware store. The hardware store was beneath the telephone exchange owned by G.V. Murray. In the daytime, three operators—Mabel Allen Russell, Minnie Ashbrook, and Nina Barbee—handled the calls, while at night one person operated the switchboard. Ben Shapira began a dry goods business in the building north of "Hord and Hall" in 1913.

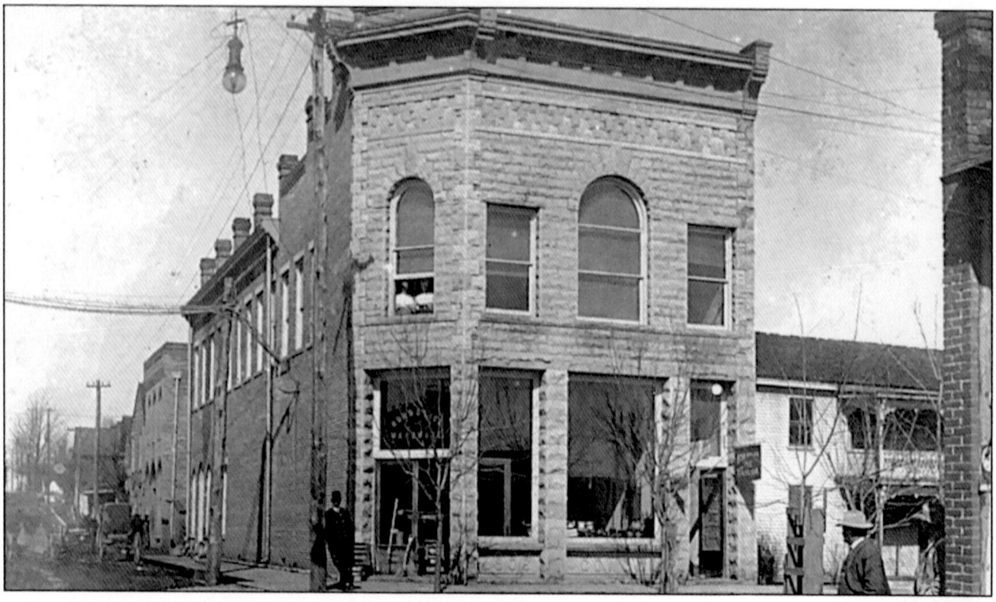

Hord Building, c. 1909. This postcard view of the Hord Building, at the corner of Main Street and Central Avenue, also shows the buildings directly behind it. Bob Hord leans against the post. The brick wall at right was a side of the livery stable that Jim Tom Gowdy operated since 1886. The house at the right of the Hord Building was the home of Dr. and Mrs. S.T. Chandler. Note the early hanging streetlight in this rare image.

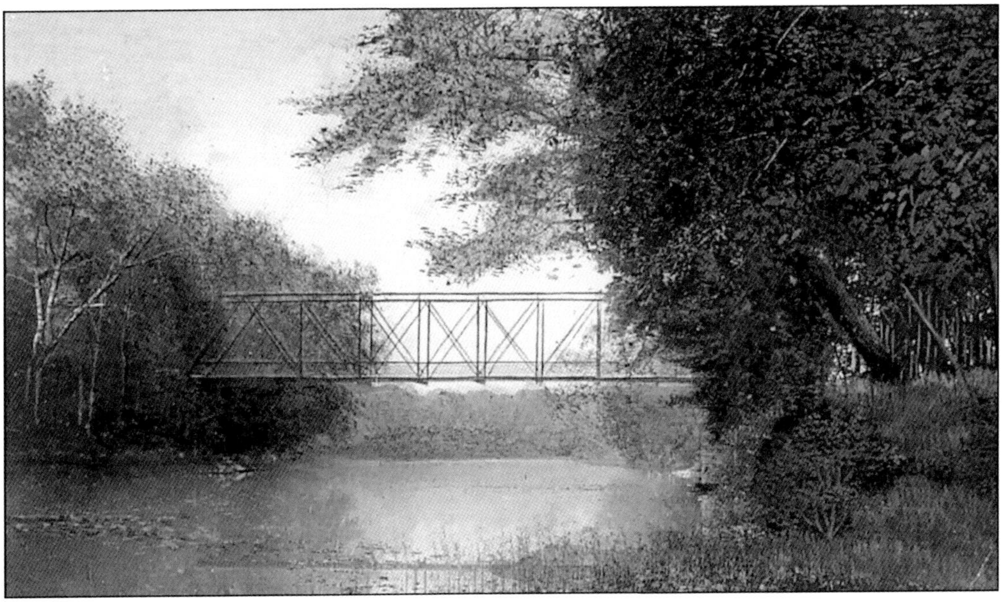

Green River Bridge, c. 1909. This half-truss iron bridge along old Highway 55 was built to replace a wooden bridge that burned on January 1, 1907. Nannie Rice was the first person to drive a horse and buggy over this bridge when it opened four months after the fire. Men from the neighborhood assisted the foreman, Flat Decker, and others who worked for a company from Vincennes, Indiana, that built the bridge. G.H. Gowdy was so anxious to have it completed by March 31,1907, that he offered workmen $100 extra if they could speed up. The area around the bridge has been used for generations by swimmers and picnickers.

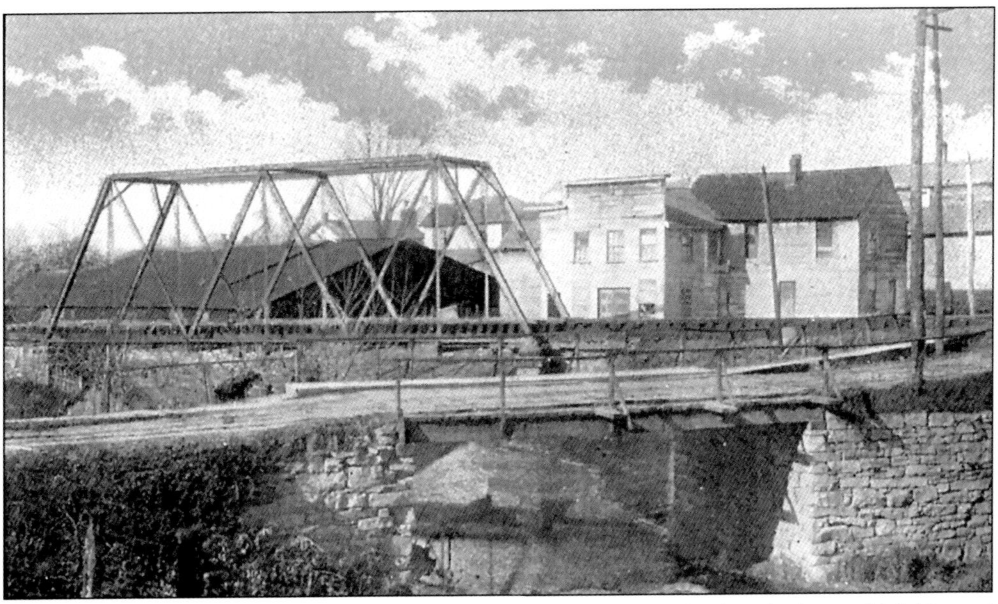

L&N Railroad Bridge over Buckhorn Creek, c. 1910. In 1922, a flood washed away this bridge and several others in the community. Termed a "cloudburst" by the locals, the flood eliminated all the bridges except for one on Columbia Avenue. The community damage was placed at $300,000. During the flood, several feet of water stood in the depot.

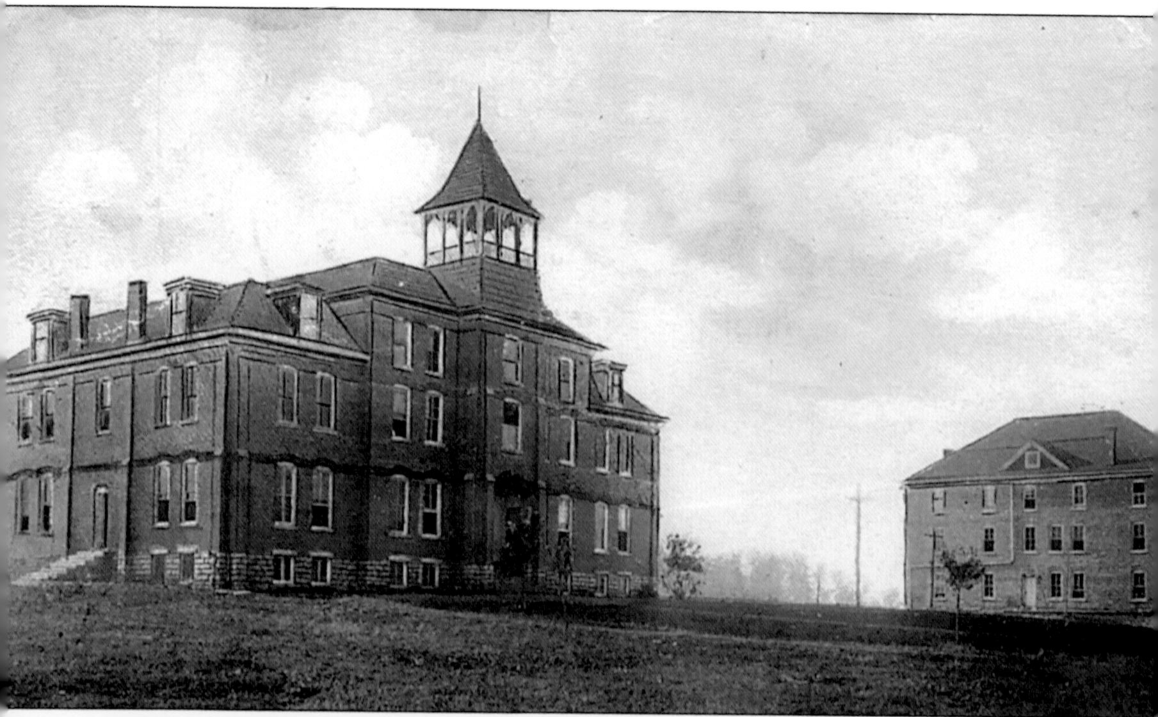

RUSSELL CREEK BAPTIST ACADEMY, C. 1909. The Russell Creek Academy, organized in 1900 and opened six years later, was the forerunner of Campbellsville College. In this 1909 view, the administration building was the largest structure of the school. Its 14 rooms housed most of the classrooms, library, and offices of the school before a fire on April 14, 1939 destroyed the building. The building on the right was the John S. Stapp girls' dormitory that was completed in 1908 at a cost of $3,500. The academy was turned over to the trustees of the public schools in 1911 to be operated by them as a public school until 1913. At that time the Russell Creek Association of Kentucky Baptists decided to take the buildings back from the trustees and control their future use. The academy became Campbellsville Junior College in 1923. This widely respected institution of higher learning has grown considerably and is now known as Cambellsville University.

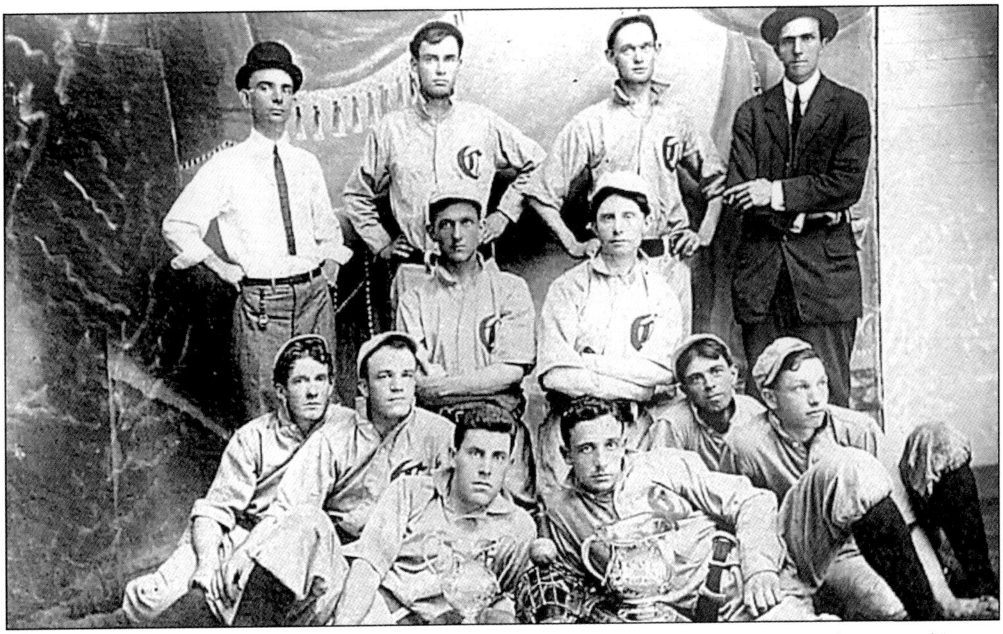

CAMPBELLSVILLE BASEBALL TEAM, C. 1910. Pictured with bats, balls, catching gear, and two trophies are the proud members and coaches of the Campbellsville baseball team. Among those who could be identified are, from left to right, (front row) Brack Sanders, unidentified, unidentified, Lee Williams, Sam Dix, and Merlin Wood; (second row) ? Borders and Jack Sanders; (third row) Oma Goode, Jim Tom Richerson, unidentified, and Dr. E.L. Gowdy. The team's playing field was located on the west end of the present Central Shopping Center off North Broadway.

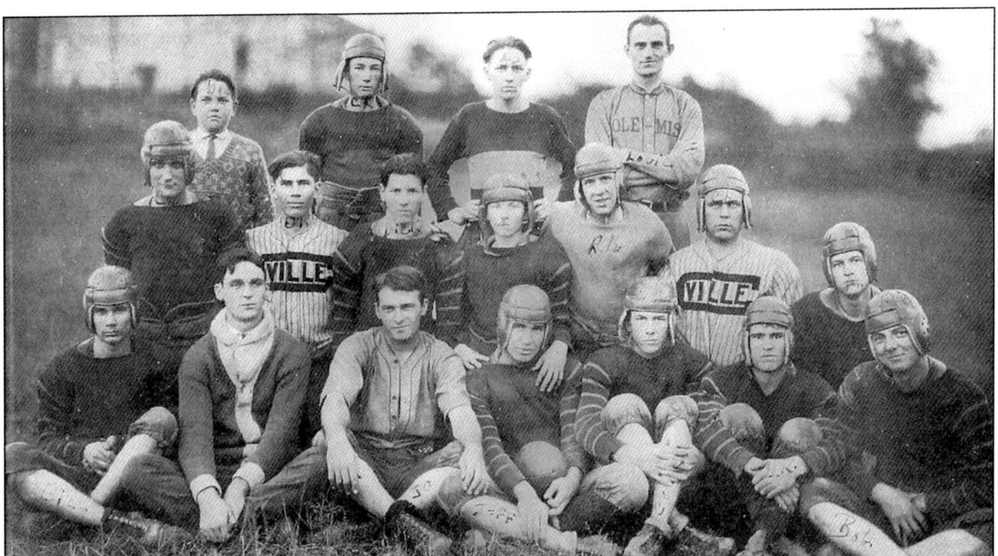

CAMPBELLSVILLE COLLEGE FOOTBALL TEAM, 1927. Team members pictured in various uniforms and attire are, from left to right, (front row) Bill Mitchell, Cameron Wilson, Joe Wilson, Owen Jeffries (captain), unidentified, Gatton Kirtley, and Bob Borders; (second row) Charles Bowen, Auston Kidwell, James Bailey, Gowdy "Rex" Bailey, Crit Harmon, and Henry Turner; (third row) George Lyon, Cecil Risen, Lee Sprowles, and Coach L.C. Henderson.

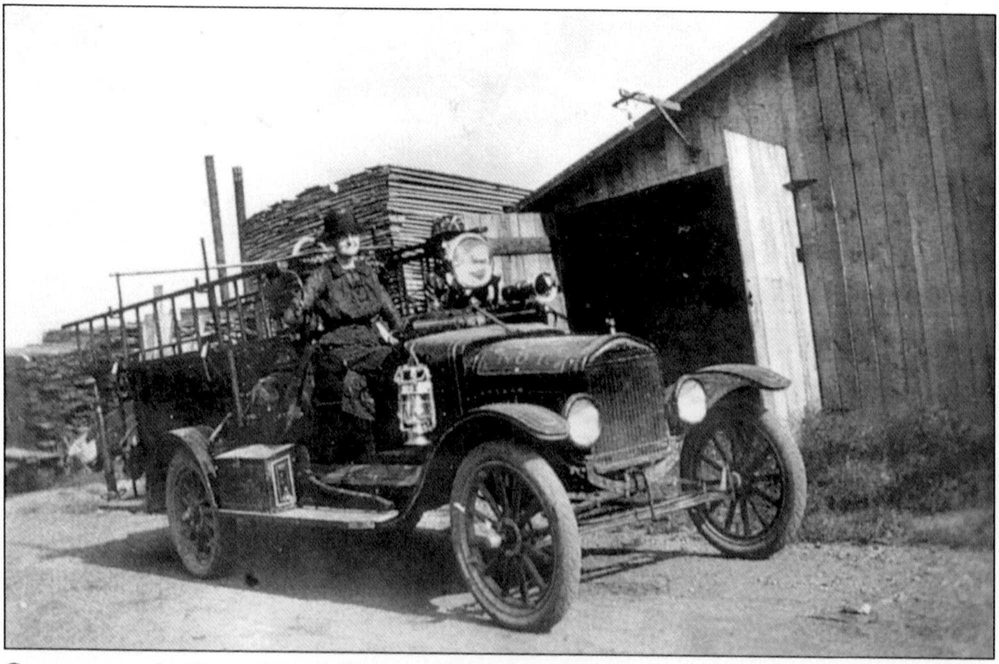

Campbellsville's First Fire Truck, c. 1918. Mrs. W.I. Meader Sr. takes a spin in fire truck No. 1 near the livery stable. The *Campbellsville News-Journal* reported in the August 20, 1914 issue that Mayor J. Hugh Chandler and a committee appointed to investigate the purchasing of a fire apparatus for the city visited fire departments in Lebanon, Springfield, Bardstown, and Louisville. They came home with enough information to secure up-to-date apparatus, which was purchased soon thereafter.

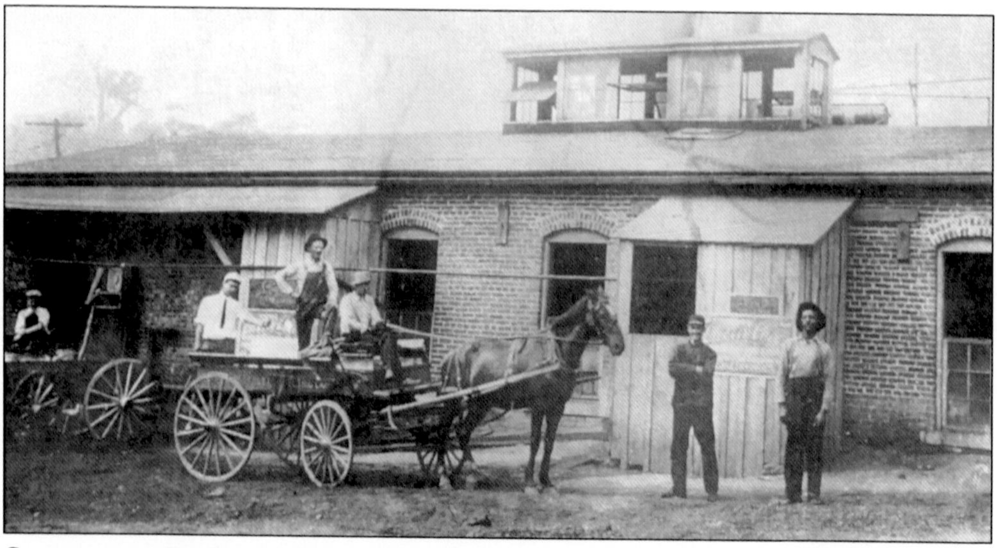

Campbellsville Ice Plant, 1911. A wagon from the Campbellsville Electric Light Company is parked in front of the Campbellsville Ice Plant. The plant was owned by B.S. Kincart and located on Hotchkiss Street. Signs on the building advertise Gay-Ola and Cherry Cheer, drinks produced across the street from the ice plant at the Campbellsville Bottling Works, which was owned by A.J. Arvin and Garland Shipp. According to the signs, Cherry Cheer was the "most delicious drink in the world" and it sold "on ice at soda fountains" for 5¢.

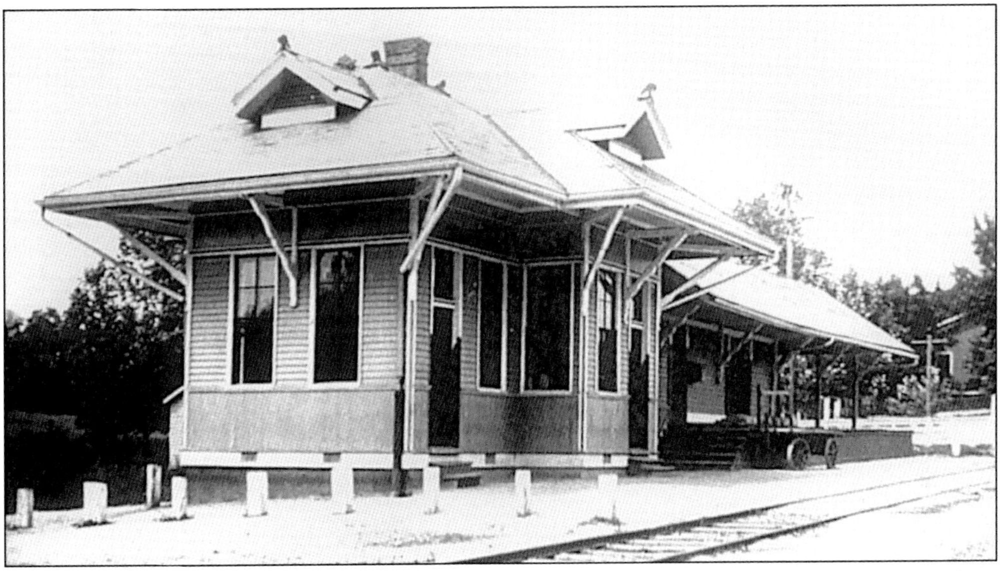

SPURLINGTON DEPOT, C. 1913. During much of the early 1900s, L&N trains regularly traveled a southern route through Marion, Taylor, and Green Counties. In order of arrival after leaving Louisville, the train would stop at Marion County depots in Lebanon, Calvary, and Phillipsburg, then at depots in Spurlington and Campbellsville in Taylor County, and then at Green County depots in Whitewood, Bluff Boom, and Greensburg, the final destination. This rare image of the Spurlington depot is typical of many of the depots constructed along this railroad line and in other small towns and communities throughout Kentucky.

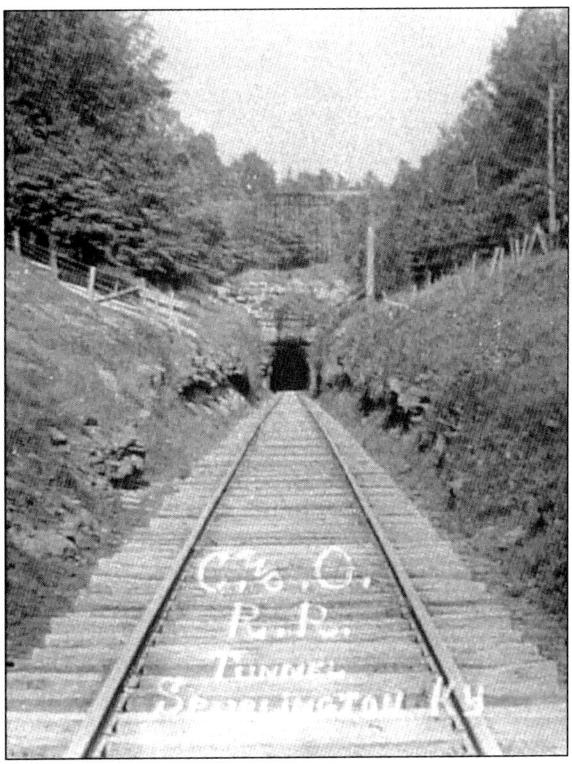

SPURLINGTON RAILROAD TUNNEL, C. 1920. Construction of this tunnel began on February 26, 1872, when John Spurling dug the first shovelful of dirt. Michael Emmett Keegan of Ireland was head of the construction crew. Work actually began at the southern and northern approaches in March 1872. Laborers started the shaft hole that year on July 10 and completed it on September 23. The shaft extended 89 feet through solid rock. The 1,856-foot-long tunnel led from Taylor County into Marion County. The first train ran through the tunnel on October 3, 1879. A Taylor County woman, Nancy Bass, is believed to be buried in the cemetery above the tunnel. Throughout much of her life, she was considered by many to be a witch who performed magic tricks and put spells on people. Some area residents believe she continues to haunt people who travel through the tunnel.

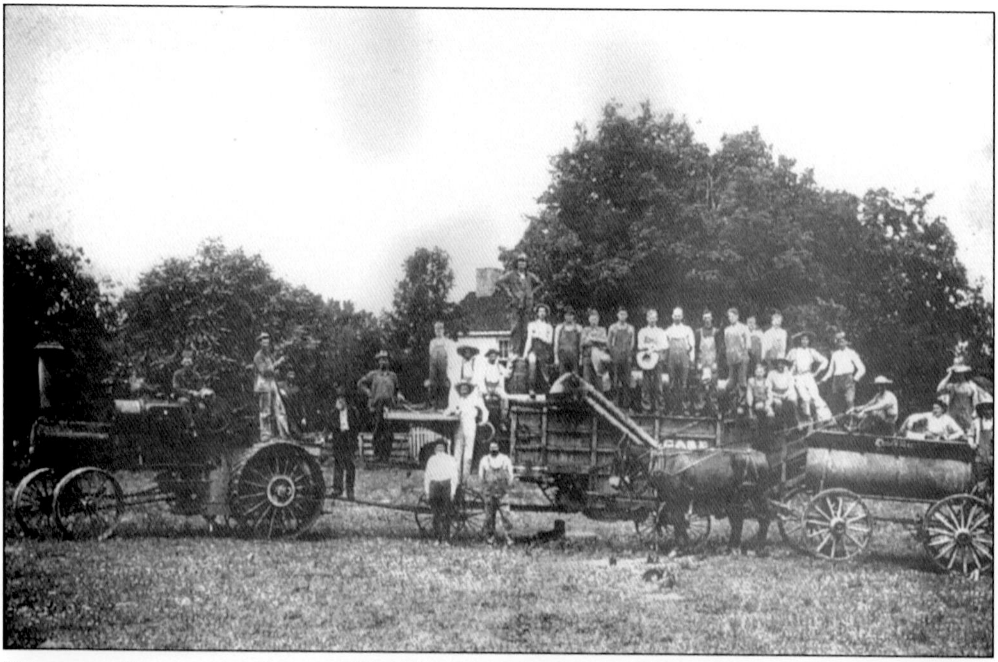

THRESHING CREW AT ROMINE, *c.* 1915. Prior to beginning the threshing process, this 30-man crew poses for the photographer at the Millard Gore farm. A Case traction steam engine can be seen at left. A wooden Case threshing machine is partially obscured by the mule that has been pulling the water wagon at right. The J.I. Case Threshing Machine Co. advertising postcard below reveals a typical farming operation in the early 1900s. The process began as water was poured into the Case steam engine at left. Steam was soon created, which supplied the energy necessary to operate the Case threshing machine at right. The threshing began when bundles of wheat were forked from wagons onto the conveyor and into the machine and ended when the wheat grains were threshed out and the straw was blown into a stack.

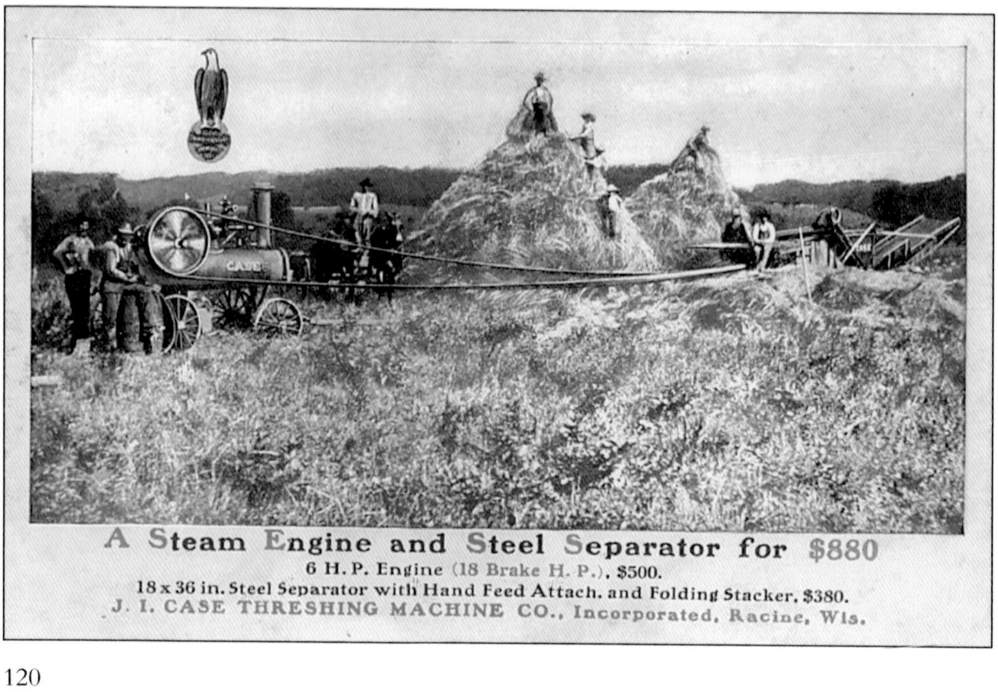

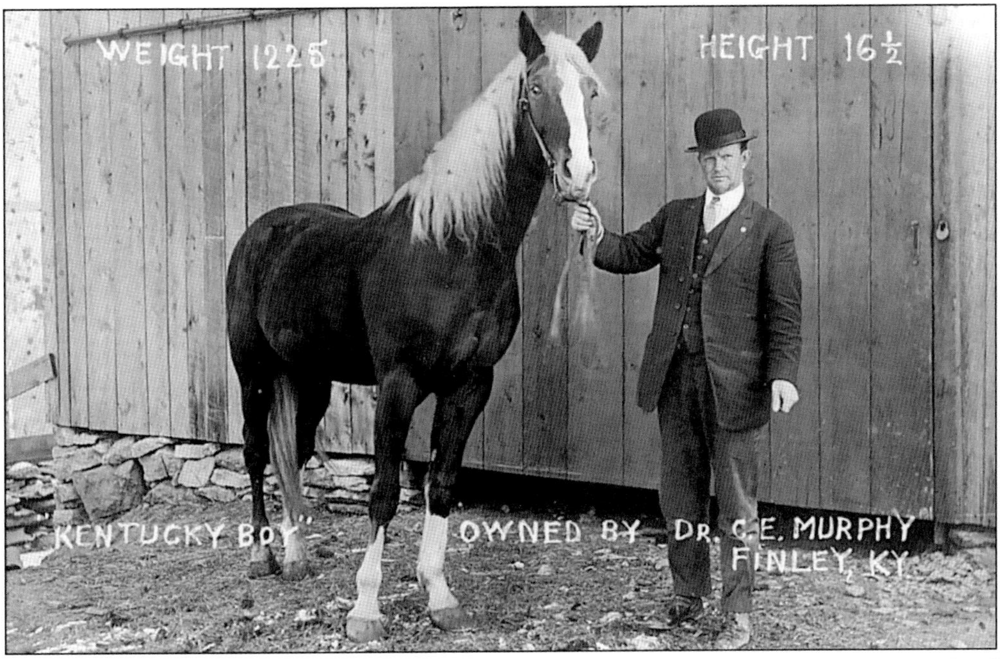

Dr. C.E. Murphy and Kentucky Boy, c. 1914. Dr. C.E. Murphy (1881–1953) was a dedicated and respected country doctor who was known for his honesty and humanitarian traits. He resided in Finley but his office was located at Saloma, also known as Pinchem, in Taylor County. Throughout much of his life, Dr. Murphy owned many of the area's finest horses. During the early 1900s, it was common to see one of his prized animals pulling him in his muddy buggy or carrying him and his big saddlebags to visit patients in Taylor, Marion, and Green Counties. When automobiles became practical, he bought a Model T Ford roadster with tire chains for winter use.

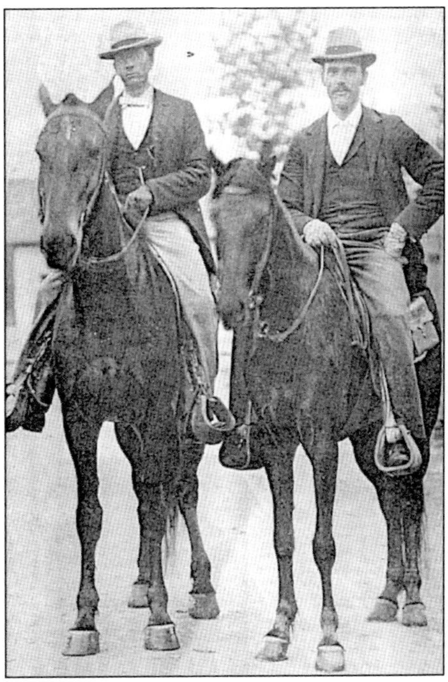

Doctors on Horseback, c. 1900. Dr. C.V. Hiestand (left) began his practice in Merrimac before opening an office in Cambellsville in 1918. Born in 1871, he lived to be 90 years old and was a medical doctor for 65 years. Dr. Hiestand delivered over 6,000 babies and was the oldest practicing physician in Kentucky at the time of his death in 1962. He was a city councilman, school board member, mayor of Campbellsville, and chairman of the Democratic Executive Committee. Dr. Hiestand was named Kentucky's "General Practitioner of the Year" in 1953 and was awarded the Governor's Medallion in 1959. His favorite horse in the early years was "Sorrel" who sometimes would travel as many as 50 miles a day. Dr. George Pruitt of Mannsville (right) was a well-respected doctor who only practiced a few years before his untimely death.

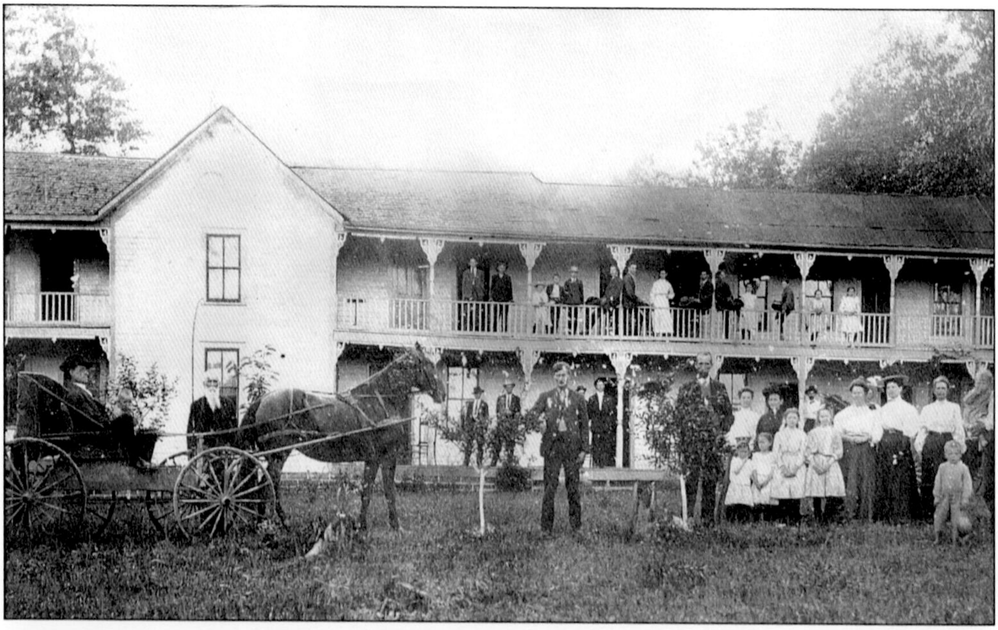

Lorain Wells, c. 1910. Located in the Shiloh area, this two-story hotel was a popular health resort with accommodations for 42 people. The water from the nearby well was advertised as containing 13 to 18 different minerals, which were believed to restore health to the sick that visited there. G.D. Smith and Jim Morrison were early operators of this hotel. Thomas Hardeman Caldwell (with white beard) is shown standing behind the buggy. His son Alfred V. Caldwell, the tall man behind the tree, and wife, Julia, the lady in the center of the group, later assumed the ownership of this resort.

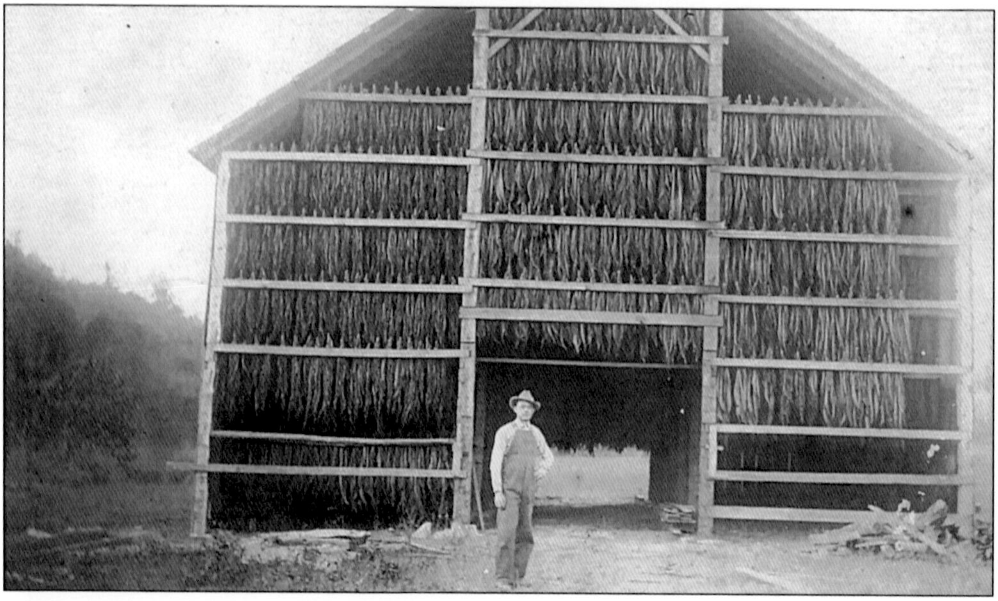

A Barn Full of Burley, c. 1914. Although he hadn't finished construction of the front side of his new barn, Sanford "Sam" Minor has already housed most of his tobacco crop. A model farmer, Minor used agricultural management and conservation methods that were well known throughout the northeast section of Taylor County. Minor's farm was located on Dutton Creek in the Mannsville area.

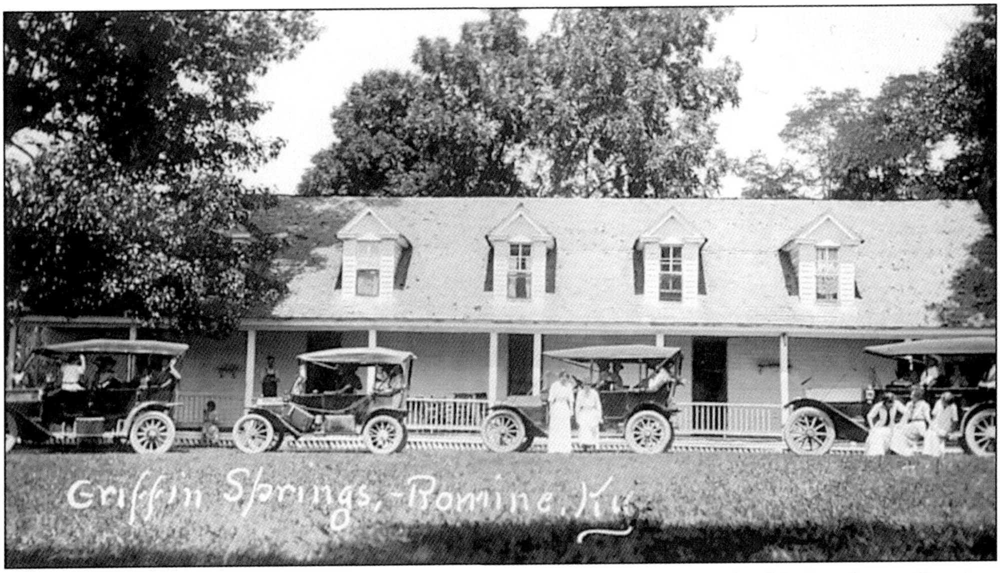

Griffin Springs at Romine, c. 1915. This resort center, located on Columbia Road near Romine, was known for the healing power of its sulphur water. The fine accommodations and recreational activities, such as tennis, croquet, swimming, and dancing, helped make this one of the state's leading resort hotels during the 1920s. Tradition has it that the Griffin family, who were the first settlers on this land, began the resort. Later, Robert Lee Faulkner, known as "Colonel," made several additions during his ownership.

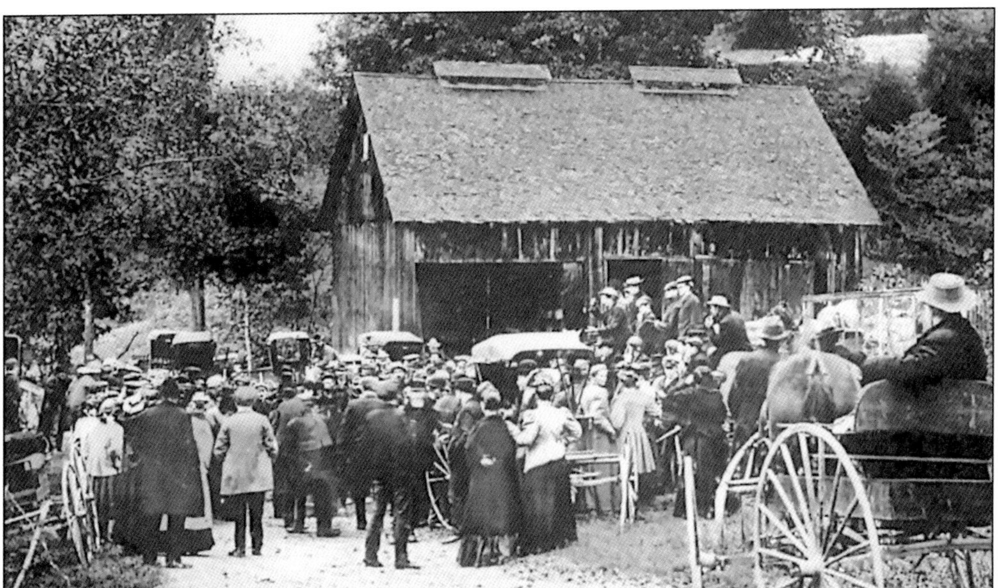

A Country Auction, c. 1911. Hey, well, all right, what'll you give for it? During the early 1900s, the best auctioneers throughout central Kentucky would captivate and amaze both city and county folks alike with their rhythmic, often spellbinding spiel. Whether selling was farm, livestock, machinery, or merely household contents, the auctioneer and his chosen assistants would appear at the site in special attire befitting the occasion. Always wearing the same style hat, they would sometimes "work the crowd" for hours at a time in order to get the highest prices possible for the property owner who hired them.

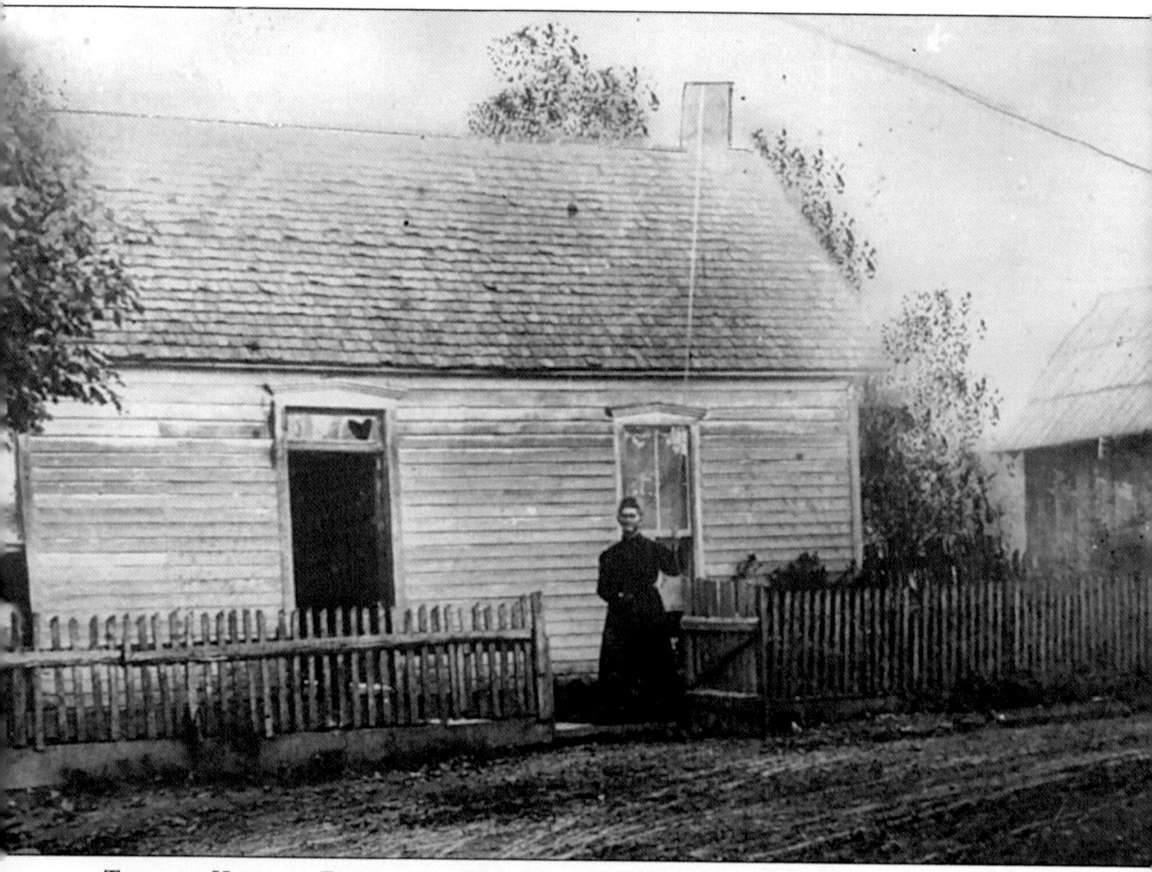

TOLLGATE HOUSE AT ELKHORN, C. 1900. This tollgate house was situated across the road from where the Elkhorn Methodist Church is located today. This privately built road ran from Yuma (also known as Knifley) to White's Ridge. Trudy Murrah holds the rope that raises and lowers the pole. During the early horse and buggy days when there were few roads other than in or near county seat towns, the Kentucky legislature empowered various private companies to sell stock and build roads, then called turnpikes. The payment of dividends and interest necessary to retire the bonds was accomplished by money derived from tolls charged those who traveled the roads. The first roads or turnpikes in Kentucky, built about 1830, were constructed based on a design created by Scottish engineer John Loudon McAdam. Many of the private road companies erected tollhouses every five miles on the macadamized roads, with one or two near the city limits of each town. The job of a tollgate keeper was considered desirable as it provided a good income. Families living in the country were often permitted to pay the tollgate keeper their accumulated tolls at the end of each month.

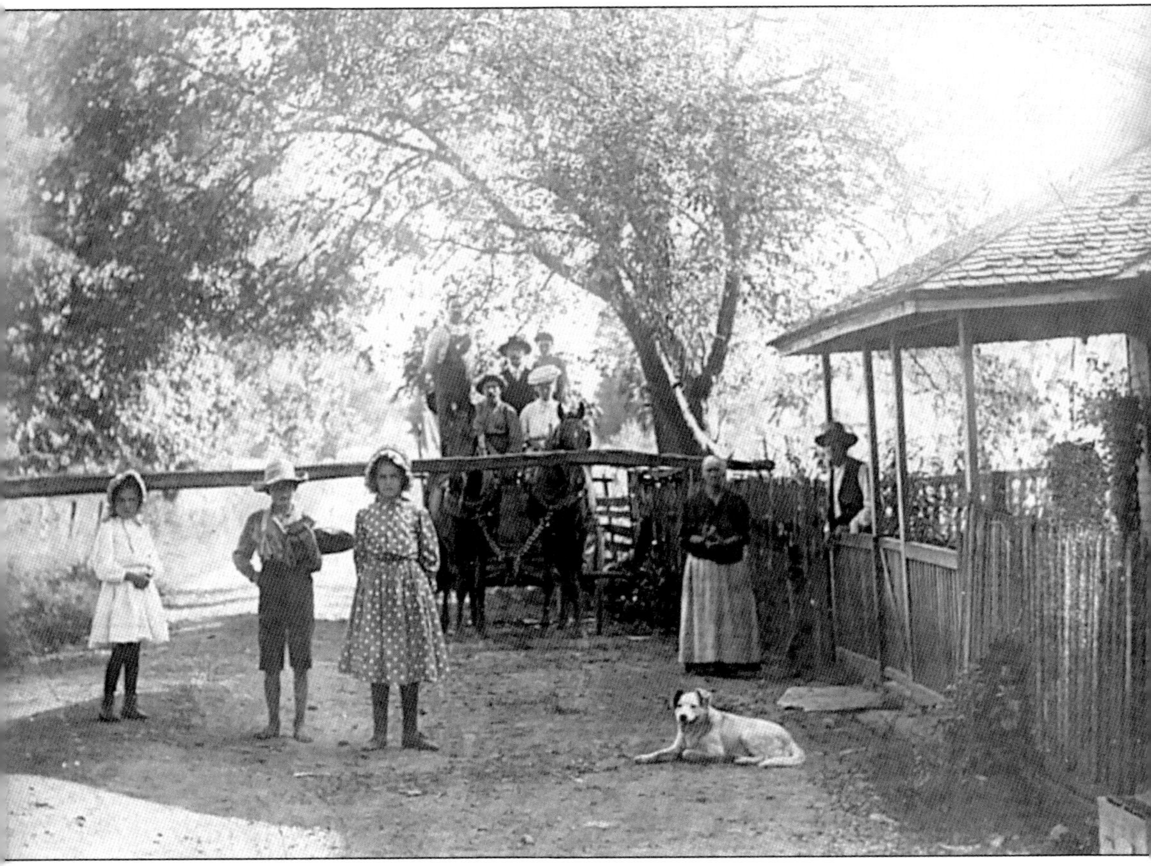

TOLLGATE HOUSE ON CAMPBELLSVILLE AND LEBANON PIKE, 1906. This tollgate house was situated either across the road from where Taylor County Elementary School is located today or across from Pleasant Hill Baptist Church. In the case of a privately owned tollhouse, tolls were charged to keep roads in repair and were assessed in proportion to the perceived damage caused to the road bed. Most privately owned and company-owned turnpikes/roads in Kentucky existed until about 1900 when counties bought them and opened the roads to free and unrestricted travel. This tollgate house was one of the last to operate in Kentucky. In 1906, the owners charged a standard fare of 15¢ for passage. In the late 1800s, customary rates at tollgate houses across Kentucky were as follows: man on horseback, 5¢; horse and buggy, 10¢; two-horse carriage, 20¢; stage-coach and six passengers, 55¢; each hog or sheep, 3¢; and mules or cattle, 4¢ each.

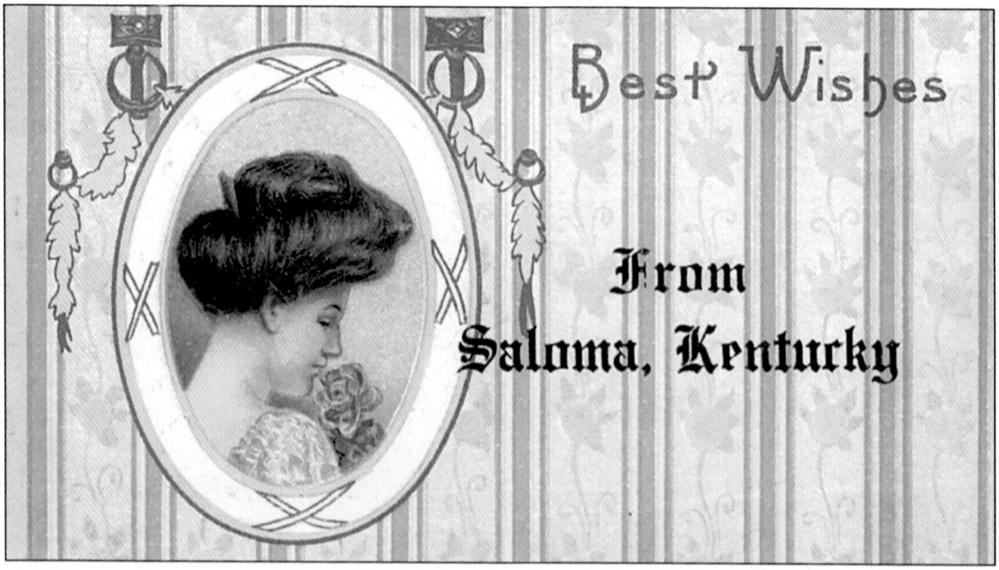

Greetings from Saloma, 1909. During the golden age of postcards (1905–1915), generic images such as this one were sold in stores throughout Kentucky. Postcards depicting photographs and artists' conceptions of lovely ladies and romantically involved couples were designed to promote and highlight rural communities and towns. Frequently, pre-printed poetic messages would be added to the front of the postcard such as the following: "If I should write you what I think, T'would use up all my pen and ink, So I'll just send this card to say, I'll write to you another day." Published in 1909, this postcard was mailed from the small Taylor County town of Saloma in 1912.

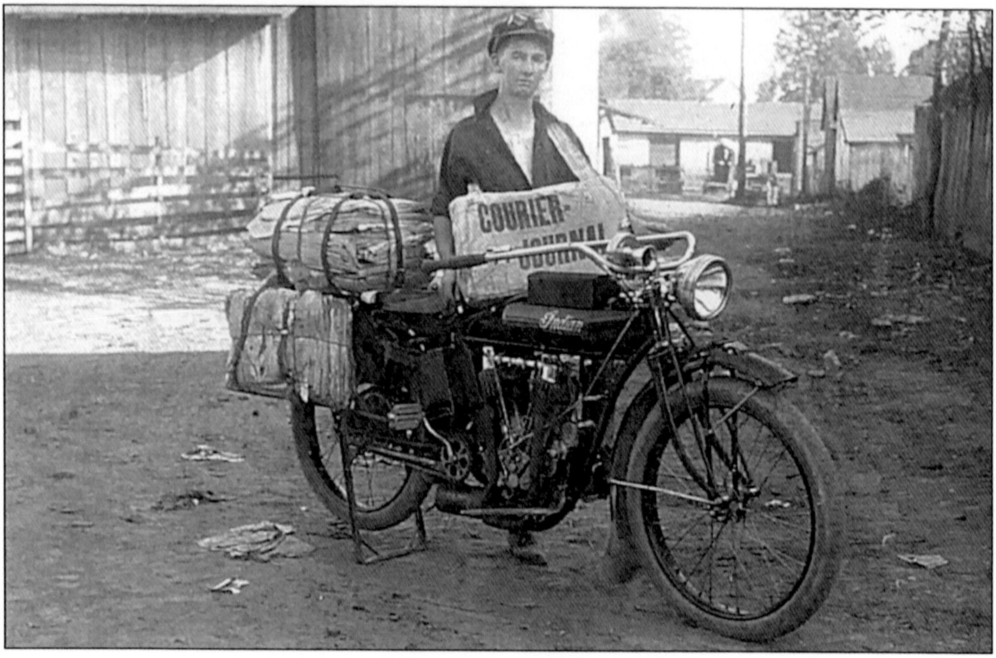

Delivering the *Courier Journal*, c. 1910. This real photo postcard shows Paul Sanders, as a young man, when he delivered *Courier Journal* newspapers from his motorcycle. This picture was made in the alley behind a business later known as Parks-Belk Department Store in Campbellsville.

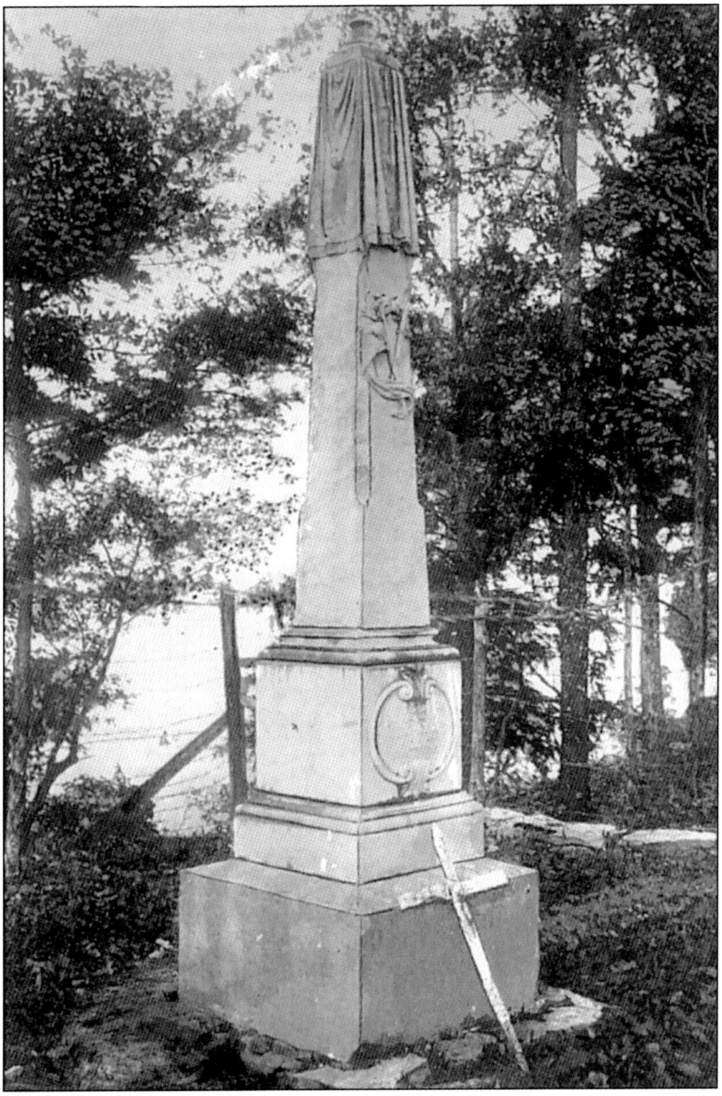

CONFEDERATE MONUMENT, GREEN RIVER BATTLEFIELD, TEBBS BEND, TAYLOR COUNTY, *c.* 1910. The effort to build one of the first Civil War monuments was led by former soldier R.S. Kemper and others from Columbia. John D. Fogle of Lebanon donated an iron fence enclosure for the cemetery of the Confederate dead where the monument would stand. An announcement in a Lebanon newspaper indicated that it was to be erected in 1872 and made of Scotch granite by the Joyce Company of Louisville at a cost of $500. It recalled the Battle of Green River Bridge on July 4, 1863, when part of 2,500 troops, led by Gen. John Hunt Morgan, clashed with 200 men of the 25th Michigan (volunteer) Infantry and 8th Michigan, under the command of Col. Orlando Moore (USA). This horseshoe loop of the river formed a natural defense with felled trees and hastily built defenses. Morgan shelled the defenses and sent a request for surrender. Colonel Moore replied, "Present my compliments to Gen. Morgan and say to him that, this being the fourth of July, I cannot entertain the proposition to surrender." Morgan lost 36 men killed and 45 wounded in eight charges during the three-and-a-half-hour battle. The Union loss was 6 killed and 24 wounded. Morgan went down river and crossed at another ford. He later sent a letter to Moore saying, "that for his gallant defense of Tebbs Bend, he promoted him to be a Major General of the Yankee Army."

ACKNOWLEDGMENTS

We have chosen for this book only the rarest, most historic and, simply stated, the best postcards from the many available images—most previously unpublished—to tell the story of these five counties' rich past. Many of the images are from author Carl Howell's extensive collection of pre-1930 Kentucky postcards and others are from the Hart County Historical Society's collection. A few others have been loaned to us from some of the individuals listed below.

Postcards, information, and/or services have also been furnished by the following to whom we extend our gratitude: (from Adair County) Randy Flowers and Yvonne Kolbenschlag; (from Barren County) Kaye Harbison, Gordon Smith, and Sam Terry; (from Green County) Mickey Cowherd, Edgar L. Cox, Frances H. Cox, Janet Marcum, Emily Martin, and Ruth Perkins; (from Hart County) Mary Willia Branstetter, June Burks, Tom Chaney, Barbara Hood, Jerry Matera, Delores Tapp, and Lucille Waters; (from Taylor County) Samuel Harrison, Tom Hiestand, Steve Keith, Aileen McKinley, and David A. Nunery. Non-area residents who have also furnished pictures, information, and/or services to whom we extend our thanks include Teresa Brackett, Byron Crawford, Kaye Lawson Corbett, John L. Dennis, Gary Gardner, David W. Hayes, Franklin Hibbs, Alviene Hines, Ron W. Morgan, Nada O'Bryant, Tommy Turner, Sharon Weis, and Ashley Whelan.

A sincere expression of appreciation is extended to Betty Gorin-Smith, Sam W. Moore II, and Jane Nichols who have assisted us in answering history-related questions and in locating images from 1900 to 1930 of their respective home counties. Their encouragement and mutual desire to assist us in promoting the early 20th-century history of this five-county area have greatly benefited our endeavors.

In addition to personal interviews conducted with area residents, much of the research material from which information was obtained for this book was found in libraries in these five counties, the Southern Kentucky Cultural Center in Glasgow, and in the Hart County Historical Society museum in Munfordville.

We also extend our profound gratitude to Janice Donan, whose computer expertise and services allowed us to meet our publisher's deadline. Her thoughts and suggestions as to various matters related to the text were always constructive and beneficial.